Consequences of Compassion

Consequences of Compassion

An Interpretation and Defense of Buddhist Ethics

CHARLES GOODMAN

OXFORD
UNIVERSITY PRESS

OXFORD
UNIVERSITY PRESS

Oxford University Press is a department of the University of Oxford.
It furthers the University's objective of excellence in research, scholarship,
and education by publishing worldwide.

Oxford   New York
Auckland   Cape Town   Dar es Salaam   Hong Kong   Karachi
Kuala Lumpur   Madrid   Melbourne   Mexico City   Nairobi
New Delhi   Shanghai   Taipei   Toronto

With offices in
Argentina   Austria   Brazil   Chile   Czech Republic   France   Greece
Guatemala   Hungary   Italy   Japan   Poland   Portugal   Singapore
South Korea   Switzerland   Thailand   Turkey   Ukraine   Vietnam

Oxford is a registered trade mark of Oxford University Press
in the UK and certain other countries.

Published in the United States of America by
Oxford University Press
198 Madison Avenue, New York, NY 10016

Library of Congress Cataloging-in-Publication Data
Goodman, Charles, 1975–
Consequences of compassion : an interpretation and
defense of Buddhist ethics / Charles Goodman.
    p. cm.
Includes bibliographical references and index.
ISBN 978-0-19-537519-0 (hardcover); 978-0-19-020532-4 (paperback)
1. Buddhist ethics. I. Title.
BJ1289.G66 2009
294.3'5—dc22   2008026685

To Nick Goodman, Susan Josephson, Allan Gibbard,
Luis O. Gómez, and all those who have taught me even a
syllable of Dharma: Reverential salutations to you all!

Contents

Consequences of Compassion

Introduction

To many Westerners, the most appealing teachings of the Buddhist tradition pertain to ethics. Many people have drawn inspiration from Buddhism's emphasis on compassion, nonviolence, and tolerance, its concern for animals, and its models of virtue and self-cultivation. During the past few decades, there has been great progress in our understanding of Buddhist ethics, and numerous writers have investigated how the different forms of this tradition respond to various particular ethical issues. But to bring the insights of the Buddhist tradition effectively to bear on the concerns of contemporary ethics, we need some kind of grasp on the theoretical structure of Buddhist ethical thought. And there has been some controversy, and much confusion, about which Western ethical theories resemble Buddhist views, and in what respects.

This book is a systematic, philosophical exploration of the nature of Buddhist ethics, drawing on South Asian and Tibetan sources. I consider texts belonging to all three main branches of Buddhism: namely, the Theravāda, Mahāyāna, and Vajrayāna traditions. I do not make major use of texts from China, nor do I devote much attention to other cultures that have been deeply influenced by China, such as Japan, Korea, and Vietnam. In these areas of East Asia, Buddhist ethics was profoundly influenced by the moral and political teachings of Daoism, Confucianism, and other indigenous traditions. The conclusions I reach about South Asian and Tibetan Buddhist ethics may therefore not apply, or may apply only partially and with qualifications, to East Asian forms of the Buddhist tradition.

I intend this book as a contribution to the history of philosophy, and not primarily as a work of philology, religious studies, or intellectual history. I try to deploy and make interpretive use of the concepts and categories of recent discussions in Anglo-American ethics. My main reason for doing so is my belief that Buddhist texts have much to contribute to the conversation of contemporary ethics; but they can only make those contributions if the values and forms of moral reasoning they exhibit can somehow be connected with the way philosophers discuss ethics today.

To make this connection, I have made use of a methodology commonly employed by philosophers who study the history of European thought, but eschewed by intellectual historians: a methodology described by Richard Rorty, partly with tongue in cheek, as "reeducation."[1] Suppose the great thinkers of the Buddhist tradition, such as the historical Buddha himself, or Buddhaghosa, or Asaṅga, or Śāntideva, were somehow to learn about and come to understand the debates in Western philosophy about free will, ethical theory, justice, virtue, the demands of morality or the justifications of punishment. How would they respond to these debates? What positions would they stake out? When would they endorse the views of certain specific Western thinkers, and when would they reject all the options with which the Western tradition is familiar? Sometimes, these questions cannot be answered with confidence, and they can never be answered with certainty. But from the positions Buddhist thinkers do explicitly take in their texts, expressed in Asian languages and in an Asian technical vocabulary, we can often make justified inferences that lead to answers to the kinds of questions to which the exercise of speculative reeducation gives rise. Whenever we can gain any confidence in these answers, we have also gained a deeper understanding of Buddhist thought than we could acquire by merely restating the categories of the texts themselves. And when these answers are philosophically interesting, they might even help Western thinkers to make progress on issues that have puzzled our philosophical tradition for millennia.

Since I approach Buddhist texts in the spirit of the history of philosophy, I hope that ethicists trained in the analytic tradition will be able to benefit from reading this book. For their benefit, I have included, in chapter 1, a brief discussion of the main doctrines of the Buddhist religion. To understand the background of the ethical theories I discuss in the rest of the book, readers need to be at least somewhat familiar with these doctrines. But I also hope that some of my readers will be specialists in Asian thought, culture, and religion, and so will already be familiar with the Buddhist worldview. These readers should feel free to skip chapter 1.

Since the basic strategy of the book involves comparisons between Buddhist and Western ethical views, I will advance a number of claims that cannot be understood without some knowledge of the various ethical theories that Western philosophers have proposed. Chapter 2 attempts to describe the main common features, and the most important varieties, of consequentialism, deontology, and virtue ethics, the three major families of Western ethical theories. Philosophers trained in analytic ethics will already be familiar with the material in chapter 2; I encourage them to proceed to the later chapters.

I have used the methodology of reeducation extensively in illuminating relations between Buddhist concepts and Western ethical theories. If we draw on recent Western ethical theories in interpreting Buddhism, we can gain a unified perspective on the whole range of Buddhist ethical thought. The ethical positions of the different forms of South Asian and Tibetan Buddhism are not unified in the sense that they all embody the same theory. Rather, they have the same fundamental basis: every version of Buddhist ethics I will consider takes the welfare of sentient beings to be, in one way or another, the only source of moral norms. We could state a version of this claim by saying that Buddhist ethics is based on compassion—since some would define compassion simply as a motivation to promote the welfare of others.[2] On this interpretation, the fundamental basis of the various forms of Buddhist ethics is the same as that of the welfarist members of the family of ethical theories that analytic philosophers call "consequentialism."

Very few readers will be surprised at the assertion that Buddhist ethics is based on compassion. But in exploring the implications of this assertion, we must keep in mind that Buddhists apply the word "compassion" (Skt. *karuṇā*,) to forms of thought and feeling quite different from what ordinary people are capable of, even in their best moments. For example, the *Holy Teaching of Vimalakīrti* (*Vimalakīrti-nirdeśa-sūtra*) offers an account of the kind of compassion that should be developed by a bodhisattva, a practitioner of Mahāyāna Buddhism who vows not to pass into Nirvana, but to remain in the cycle of birth and death in order to liberate all the other beings who are trapped there. The text distinguishes between "sentimental compassion," which "exhausts the bodhisattva" and therefore must be transcended, and "great compassion," which does not lead to exhaustion, but which "does not conceive of any life in living beings."[3] The latter sounds like a strange sort of compassion, but it is not hard to see why it is needed. Professional therapists, doctors, social workers, and other caregivers in the contemporary West often undergo a kind of burnout, leading to cynicism and emotional numbness, after a few years of facing the pervasive suffering of those they try to help.[4] A bodhisattva, meanwhile, is supposed to work tirelessly for the welfare of others, not just in this life but in future lives as well. Whatever qualities might make such a way of life possible, those qualities must go well beyond the emotion that is normally referred to as "compassion."

In several other Indian Buddhist texts, we can find a distinct, threefold classification of types of compassion. Edward Conze explains this classification as follows: "at first the Bodhisattva is compassionate to living beings; then he realizes that these do not exist, and directs his compassion on the impersonal events which fill the world; finally, the compassion operates within one vast field of Emptiness."[5] This is a difficult teaching, and not all scholars would give the same interpretation of what is meant by the classification. But the account I will offer of the nature of the different forms of Buddhist ethics fits quite nicely into the framework it provides.

Compassion toward living beings, the lowest of the three types of compassion practiced in Buddhism, is a feeling or emotion that generates a motivation to promote the welfare of others, but constrains that motivation with considerations depending for their validity on the distinction between different persons. Its ethical expression is a form of rule-consequentialism. As I explain in chapter 3, this kind of compassion is found in Theravāda ethics. It manifests itself also in the system of Asaṅga, whose view is more sophisticated, and in some ways more plausible, than the Theravāda position. As I will show, though, the structure of Asaṅga's view is complex and difficult to understand. The views of Asaṅga, along with the more general ethical teachings of the Mahāyāna, are discussed in chapter 4.

The second form of compassion, which is directed toward impersonal events (Skt. *dharmas*) is based on the realization, fundamental to Buddhist metaphysics, that the boundaries between the lives of sentient beings are conventional, and do not reflect any really existing unity of an individual life, or separateness of distinct lives. Since this form of compassion has transcended the constraints that would result from believing in the separateness of persons, it gives rise to a form of act-consequentialism. This kind of compassion is expressed in the ethical system of Śāntideva, and also appears in articulations of Tantric ethics. These forms of Buddhist ethics are discussed in chapters 5 and 6.

The third form of compassion depends on a realization of emptiness. Those who have it do not believe any ethical theory at all; indeed, they are not committed to any theory about anything. Spontaneously, and without any need for deliberation or practical reasoning, they behave as if they were act-consequentialists. Buddhist texts claim that this form of compassion is expressed in the minds of enlightened beings: Buddhas, Tantric *siddhas*, and other advanced bodhisattvas. In the words of Candragomin,

> The sun's great rays shine everywhere, traveling like a
>   horse-drawn chariot.
> The ground supports the world without calculating the burden—
> Such is the nature of persons of great capacity, who lack any
>   self-interest;
> They are consumed with whatever brings happiness and benefit
>   to the world.[6]

The heart of Mahāyāna Buddhism is the faith that such persons exist, and the determination to emulate their inconceivable wisdom and altruistic deeds. I discuss what such beings would be like, and the ethical implications of their possible existence, in chapter 6.

As we can see from Candragomin's verse, Buddhist ethics can be extremely demanding. It tells us to aspire to emulate beings whose personal projects are utterly eclipsed by their determination to benefit all beings. Some Western forms of consequentialism have similar all-consuming demands, and many philosophers have seen these demands as very implausible. In chapter 7, I explore Buddhist responses to the problems caused by the demanding nature of their ethical views.

A central issue in ethics is the nature and status of moral responsibility. To what extent can agents legitimately be held responsible for their own actions, given that they are part of the causal order of the universe? Buddhist views about causation and the self turn out, in ways that may be surprising, to support characteristically Buddhist normative commitments to compassion, nonviolence, and forgiveness. These issues are examined in chapter 8.

Much of this book is devoted to interpreting Buddhist views, largely in Western terms, so as to facilitate dialogue between people of different cultures and traditions. But I also seek to participate in such dialogue by defending the soundness of Buddhist ethical claims. Much of chapters 6, 7, and 8 is intended to contribute to this project. In chapter 10, I consider a number of objections, both interpretive and substantive, to the views I put forward. I argue that, despite these objections, my accounts of Buddhist views are both faithful to the spirit of the texts on which I draw and defensible contributions to contemporary discussions about ethics. Chapter 11 considers the views of Kant, who developed a sophisticated and enormously influential ethical theory that differs from Buddhist ethics on many points. His views have been further developed and strengthened by insightful contemporary interpreters. Yet I argue that the Buddhist tradition has the resources to respond to the challenge posed by Kant, and to resist the most powerful arguments for his deontological account of ethics.

I also discuss Buddhist-inspired responses to important questions in applied ethics, but here I have been selective. Numerous earlier works, and especially Peter Harvey's excellent *Introduction to Buddhist Ethics*,[7] have examined in detail the views of the Buddhist tradition about such issues as abortion, animal rights, the environment and euthanasia. Rather than consider these questions, which are now increasingly well understood, I have focused my attention on just one area of applied ethics: the justification of punishment, which has never before received sufficient treatment in discussions of Buddhist ethics. Chapter 9 considers this issue at a theoretical level, and then makes some suggestions for sane and compassionate reform of the American criminal justice system. In the conclusion, I try to indicate some unanswered questions facing the field of Buddhist ethics, and make some preliminary remarks about how Buddhist philosophers might begin to address those questions.

This book could not have been written without the invaluable help, advice, and support of numerous other people. Thanks are in order to P. J. Ivanhoe, David Velleman, Louis Loeb, Glen Shadbolt, John Taber, Gareth Sparham, Allan Gibbard, Edwin Curley, and Baylor Johnson for valuable comments about the article that was the basis of chapter 8. I have received a great deal of help from my colleagues Steven Scalet, Lisa Tessman, and especially Christopher Knapp, conversations with whom were crucial in the development of the indirect consequentialist interpretations that figure in chapters 3 and 4. Christopher also suggested several points that made it into chapter 10, and offered helpful comments on chapter 11. Robert Gressis gave me detailed comments on several chapters that led to important improvements in clarity of expression. Both Christopher and Robert offered substantive criticisms that led to significant revisions of chapter 6. Nicolas Goodman and Susan Josephson read the entire manuscript and provided numerous helpful comments. I am especially grateful to Jay Garfield for his powerful philosophical criticisms of many parts of the book, which have required me to think carefully about how to defend some of my most important claims. The writing of certain portions of this book, including Chapter 11, was supported in part by a Franklin Research Grant from the American Philosophical Society. An anonymous reviewer also offered extensive and detailed suggestions and criticisms; working out how to respond has made this a better book. And I am forever grateful for the loving support and assistance of my wife throughout the entire writing process.

I

Fundamental Buddhist Teachings

Buddhism was founded by Siddhattha Gotama, who, according to tradition, lived from 563 to 483 BCE. Though often referred to simply as Buddha, he is more accurately described as the historical Buddha. "Buddha," a title, means "awake" in the ancient Indian languages Sanskrit and Pali. Thus Siddhattha Gotama was the awakened one, the one who woke up from the dream of delusion and saw the world as it really is. He is called the historical Buddha because, according to the tradition, there have been many other Buddhas before him, and there will be more in the future.

The view of existence presented by Buddhism must at first seem quite grim. Your life may now seem pleasant and secure. But soon, you will grow old, become sick, suffer, and die. Then, you will be reborn, possibly in a much less pleasant place in the universe. Where you are born will depend on your actions, either in this life or in previous lives; kind, benevolent, and generous actions will produce a favorable rebirth, whereas greedy, cruel, and harmful actions will simply augment your suffering. But wherever you are reborn, your next life will not last forever either; inevitably, you will grow old again, become sick, suffer, and die. You and all other sentient beings are bound to a vast cosmic wheel of misery that ceaselessly grinds and tears your flesh.

You cannot turn to an omnipotent God for deliverance from this cyclic existence (Skt. saṃsāra). Buddhist teachers, including the historical Buddha himself, have consistently denied the existence of a creator God. In fact, there was no creation. Though the historical

Buddha refused to pronounce on the age of the universe, mature Buddhist philosophical systems hold that cyclic existence is beginningless: the world has always existed. Though there is no God, there are gods, beings of great power and knowledge who dwell in blissful heavens. But they cannot help you escape cyclic existence; in fact, they are transmigrators just like you. Their current pleasure has been created by the force of their previous positive actions; when their good karma runs out, they will die and be reborn somewhere else in the universe. In the Buddhist scriptures, the gods worship the Buddha, and not vice versa.

Buddhas are worthy of reverence because each of them discovers a way out of cyclic existence, a way they then teach to others. Those aspiring to follow this way must cease the negative actions that are causes of future suffering. By practicing calming meditation, they can douse the fires of craving and quiet the chatter of distractions. By studying and reflecting on Buddhist philosophy, they can eliminate the false beliefs that are obstacles to liberation. By attaining advanced states of concentration, they can allow their minds to see things as they really are. To realize the true nature of reality is to attain enlightenment, and thereby to escape bondage to the cycle of death and rebirth.

Because he can teach us how to accomplish all this, the Buddha is described as a refuge from the dangers of cyclic existence. His teachings, known as the Dharma (Skt.; Pali Dhamma) are a second refuge. The third refuge for Buddhists is the Saṅgha, the community of monks, nuns, laymen, and laywomen who follow the Buddha's teachings. The ceremony of "taking refuge" in these Three Jewels, as they are called, is one of the most important Buddhist rituals, and practicing this ritual is, for most of the tradition, part of what defines a person as a Buddhist.

Not all Buddhists would agree on the details of the qualities of Buddhas, but these are typically conceived in fairly ambitious terms. Ancient Buddhist texts describe the historical Buddha as having the power to perform miracles, although these texts also represent him as holding that miracles are not very important or spiritually helpful when compared to the authentic teaching. Buddhas are free from all craving, suffering, and psychological problems. They are also represented as being, in some sense, omniscient. In view of his lofty status, a Buddha can be referred to by numerous additional titles, such as Sugata (Well-Gone) and Tathāgata (He Who has Come in That Way, or perhaps, He Who Has Gone in That Way).

Other Indian traditions, such as Hinduism and Jainism, agree with Buddhism in maintaining that there is a cycle of death and rebirth, and that correct insight coupled with the transcendence of karma will allow us to escape it. In its Indian context, what is most distinctive about Buddhism is the doctrine of no self (Skt. *anātman*; Pali *anattā*). This doctrine, which is also perhaps the most philosophically interesting view in all of Buddhist thought, involves rejecting the real, ultimate existence of people, animals, chairs, rocks, trees, and indeed all composite entities. From the point of view of this doctrine, composition, the relation between a thing and its parts, is not a feature of the world as it really is, independently of how minds conceive it. Thus, composite things do not exist from the perspective of ultimate truth (Skt. *paramārthasatya*). However, discourse about composite things clearly does feature in important human social practices, and these practices are useful for many purposes. For this reason, we can say that composite things do exist from the perspective of conventional truth (Skt. *saṃvṛtisatya*). There are subtle differences between the forms of this doctrine held by different Buddhist philosophical schools, but I have tried to state a version of it that would be acceptable to all of them.[1]

If people do not really exist, then is anything real at all? Many Buddhist texts would say that what in fact exists are *dharmas*: fleeting entities that are constantly appearing and disappearing in accordance with causal laws. These entities are all that is real about the human personality. They can be sorted according to various systems of categories, perhaps the most important of which is the list of the Five Aggregates: Form (Skt. *rūpa*), Sensations (*vedanā*), Conceptions (*saṃjñā*), Conditioning (*saṃskāra*), and Consciousness (*vijñāna*). To a first approximation, Form refers to the matter of which the human body is made. More precisely, Form consists of tiny, momentary material entities analogous to what Western analytic metaphysicians call "tropes."[2] Sensations are the painful, pleasurable, or neutral feelings accompanying many of our experiences. Conceptions are the categories of thought that we use to organize, classify, and identify the things we perceive or think about. Conditioning includes what English speakers would call habits and emotions: various dispositions we have developed that affect the way we perceive and respond to the world. Finally, Consciousness is the awareness we have, through our senses, of such entities as colors, sounds, and tastes.[3] The structure of the Five Aggregates draws its boundaries somewhat differently from any Western system of classification; but once we understand the meaning of the terms, it is neither completely unfamiliar nor without plausibility.

But if Buddhists are prepared to claim that there is no self, how can they continue to maintain their belief in reincarnation? What is it, after all, that is reborn? This question is addressed in an important early Buddhist text, *Milinda's Questions* (*Milinda-pañha*), a dialogue between Nāgasena, a Buddhist monk, and Milinda, a Greek-speaking king of Bactria (modern Afghanistan and northern Pakistan). Nāgasena's main strategy in dealing with this problem is to argue that it is not strictly accurate to describe reincarnation as an event in which one transmigrates (Pali *saṅkamati*). There is no substance that moves from one life to another. Rather, one is in some sense reconstituted (Pali *paṭisandahati*). Naturally, Milinda asks for clarification of this point:

> "How is it, Venerable Nāgasena, that one does not transmigrate, yet one is reconstituted [in a future life]. Give me an example."
>
> "O Great King, it is exactly like the case of a person who would light a lamp [with the flame] from another lamp. Is it that the flame has migrated from the first to the second lamp, O Great King?"
>
> "Certainly not, Venerable."
>
> "It is exactly the same, O Great King, when one does not transmigrate, yet one is reconstituted [in a future life]."
>
> "Give me another example."
>
> "Do you remember, O Great King, when you, as a young boy, memorized verses from your poetry teacher?"
>
> "Of course I do, Venerable."
>
> "Well then, Great King, was it the case that those verses migrated from your teacher [to you]?"
>
> "No, that was not the case, Venerable."
>
> "It is exactly the same, O Great King, when one does not transmigrate, yet one is reconstituted [in a future life.]"[4]

These two similes give us a great deal of information about how Nāgasena conceives of the process of reincarnation, and how he understands the continuity of a human life. The first simile tells us that we should think of reincarnation not as the movement of a substance, but as the continuation of a process. There is no thing called "the fire" that moves from one lamp to another. Instead, a process of burning that is going on in the first lamp causally produces another process of burning that occurs in the second lamp. These causal links loosely unify the two processes into one; though they have no real, ultimate unity, the causal structure makes it appropriate for us, in certain contexts, to describe them as one continuing flame.

The example of the poetry teacher also points us in the direction of causation as the unifying factor, but it also tells us that what passes from one life to the next is fundamentally information. Karmic information travels from life to life, and it plays a causal role; what happens to me today can be causally explained by the actions of beings in the past, in a manner that makes it appropriate to describe me now as a continuation of the life-stories of those past beings. According to the Buddhist tradition, memories also pass between lives, but these memories are kept in a locked box. Ordinary people cannot open the box; only advanced meditators can access memories of their past lives.

If we put these similes together, we can invent a science fiction story that helps us understand how reincarnation is supposed to be compatible with the absence of any self. Imagine that a mining company is operating a number of robots on a faraway planet. These robots are running artificially intelligent computer programs that are able to modify their own structure so as to cope better with the environment. After the robots have been operating for several years, the company decides that these programs are worth more to it than the robot bodies they are running on. Company employees build a warehouse full of deactivated robots. They configure the robots in the field so that whenever one of them detects that its body is about to be destroyed, it sends a radio signal back to the warehouse that contains the source code of its computer program. The source code is then downloaded into one of the deactivated robots, which then trundles out of the warehouse and resumes mining. It seems clear that in this case, the artificial intelligence programs can, in some sense, survive the death of their bodies, even though no one would suppose that they have souls. According to Buddhism, we are relevantly similar to these programs. The causal continuity of our aggregates gives our lives a kind of loose unity, enough to make it appropriate to say, at the level of conventional truth, that I am the same person now that I was ten years ago. The same kind of loose unity, embracing all four nonphysical aggregates, links my present life to many past and future lives. Thus, according to Buddhists, it is just as true to say that I will be reincarnated as to say that I will live another hour.

If, as Buddhists believe, our karma will lead us to be reborn again and again, then those who do not understand the truth in this present lifetime will get additional chances to realize it later. If you fail the test, you can take it again. There is thus no necessity to resort to violence to force others to accept the truth. Perhaps for this reason, Buddhism is a tolerant religion; in India, the land of its birth, it never produced institutions designed to compel monks to follow doctrinal orthodoxy. In the absence of an Inquisition to coerce uniformity, dozens of religious sects and philosophical schools emerged to offer their own interpretations of the Buddhist tradition. Many of these have died out, but enough have survived to give today's Buddhism an immense diversity. Though they differ greatly, the surviving forms of the tradition can all be grouped in three broad categories.

Of these, the Theravāda, or Teaching of the Elders, is the dominant form of Buddhism in contemporary Sri Lanka, Thailand, and Burma. The Buddhists who have survived savage communist persecutions in Laos and Cambodia belong also to the Theravāda tradition. The Mahāyāna, or Great Way, has the greatest number of followers and predominates in Japan, Korea, and Taiwan. Mahāyāna worship also persists, despite great obstacles, in Vietnam and mainland China. The Vajrayāna, or "Diamond Way," is practiced in Tibet, Nepal, Bhutan, and Mongolia.

The highest spiritual aspiration of most Theravāda practitioners is to become a Saint (Skt. Arhat; Pali Arahant). A Saint is any person, man or woman, who has eliminated the negative emotions and afflictive ignorance that prevent liberation. The lifetime in which a person attains Sainthood is that person's last lifetime. After the death of the body, the person passes into Nirvana (Pāli *Nibbāna*).

What exactly is Nirvana? In trying to understand this concept, we might be tempted to claim that it is a permanent state of happiness, basing this interpretation on a number of scriptural passages that use the term "happy" to describe Nirvana.[5] But almost all Buddhist philosophers, especially those in the Theravāda, would reject this account; on their view, a mental state such as happiness is necessarily impermanent. They would regard the scriptural passages about happiness as referring to cessation with remainder: that is, to the condition of someone, a Buddha or Saint, who has had a meditative experience of final liberation. The life of such a person is characterized by stable, unshakable, boundless happiness. In the Theravāda, such a person is destined, at death, to pass into cessation without remainder.

There is some disagreement among Buddhists about how to describe cessation without remainder. Some would claim that cessation without remainder is an ineffable state, not able to be characterized by human concepts, a state beyond all problems and suffering, outside of the cycle of existence. They might refer to the discourse *To Vacchagotta on Fire* (*Aggivacchagotta-sutta*), in which the Buddha seems to say that one cannot characterize the state that he himself, or another who has attained liberation, will be in after death in terms of existence or nonexistence, and that any expression of the form "he reappears" or "he does not reappear" simply does not apply to one who has reached Nirvana.[6]

But there is another possible interpretation of the discourse *To Vacchagotta on Fire*. In it, the Buddha compares passing into Nirvana with a fire that goes out; this simile gives the scripture its title. On the basis of this analogy, one could argue that Nirvana just is the cessation of the causal series of mental and physical events that we conventionally call the existence of a person. On this interpretation, there are two reasons why Nirvana would not be described simply as nonexistence. First, such a description would evoke fear in the unenlightened, motivating them to avoid the Buddhist path. Second, describing Nirvana as nonexistence could be misunderstood to imply that it represents the annihilation of an existing person. In fact, there is no person in the first place who can be annihilated. This interpretation of the goal of Buddhism derives its appeal from a sense of the horrifying nature of the suffering of cyclic existence. To those who become Saints, this interpretation promises one single life of boundless happiness, followed by the complete cessation of all conscious existence.

Sainthood has been an appealing spiritual ideal to many; but it can also seem a bit selfish. Having discovered the cure for greed, hatred, and delusion, the Saint departs into Nirvana, leaving everybody else stranded in cyclic existence. It would surely seem more compassionate to stick around and help out.

This reflection supplies the most important ethical motivation for the Mahāyāna branch of Buddhism. All serious Mahāyānists, and a small minority of Theravādins, choose to follow a path far more demanding than that of the Saints: the path that leads to Buddhahood. Someone who is striving to become a Buddha is called a bodhisattva (Pali *bodhisatta*). In the Mahāyāna, a bodhisattva takes a vow to remain in cyclic existence for the duration, to benefit all beings. As Śāntideva writes: "as long as space abides and as long as the world abides, so long may I abide, destroying the sufferings of the world."[7] In the mature Mahāyāna, even after the bodhisattva finally attains Buddhahood, he or she will continue to manifest in cyclic existence, in order to help all others reach Buddhahood as well.

Mahāyāna texts often refer to those who aspire to be, or have actually become, Saints as Disciples (Skt. Śrāvakas). In addition to the paths of the Disciples and bodhisattvas, the Indian and Tibetan texts recognize a third path: that of the Solitary Realizers (Skt. Pratyeka-buddha). According to traditional Buddhist beliefs, the Buddhist religion as it presently exists will not last forever. Eventually, the religion will degenerate, and the teachings will gradually be lost. Finally, Buddhism will be completely forgotten. After a long time, another Buddha will appear in the world, rediscover the Dharma, and revive Buddhism. During the time when Buddhism is unknown, it will not be possible to become a Disciple or a bodhisattva. But, during this period, it will be possible for a few individuals to realize the truths of Buddhism privately, for themselves; but these Solitary Realizers will be unable or unwilling to communicate these truths to others.

The requirement that practitioners should aspire to become Buddhas is not the only teaching that separates the Mahāyāna, in its mature forms, from other types of Buddhism. Numerous Mahāyāna scriptures advance a profound and difficult teaching known as emptiness (Skt. *śūnyatā*). Both in Asia and in the West, there has been endless scholarly controversy about the correct interpretation of emptiness. The Spiritual Practice School (Skt. *Yogācāra*) of Mahāyāna Buddhist philosophy advances a doctrine of idealism, and interprets emptiness as the absence of any duality between subject and object.[8] However, their doctrines are less important for my ethical inquiries than those of the Middle Way School (Skt. Madhyamaka). The followers of the Middle Way School, known as Mādhyamikas, regarded emptiness as a generalization of the insight expressed in the doctrine of no self. Just as for virtually all Buddhists the self is empty of any objective, real existence independent of the construct- ing activity of concepts, for the Middle Way School, nothing at all—not even the simple, momentary entities that form the early Buddhist ontology—has this kind of objective, real existence. To realize this is to be liberated from attach- ment to theories about reality, all of which obstruct one's ability to see things as they really are. As Luis Gómez has written, "the Mādhyamika seeks to restore the psychological concept of radical detachment to the center of the Buddhist path by interpreting the negation of self as the basis for the radical negation of anything graspable, of any hold for the mind."[9]

It seems quite obvious that a mystical doctrine of this kind poses an im- minent threat to ethics. If all theories are false, and indeed are obstacles to spir- itual progress, then what about ethical theories? And if we abandon our beliefs about ethics, will that turn us into monsters? The Indian Buddhist tradition is well aware of the dangers, but Mādhyamikas insist that only misinterpreta- tions of emptiness pose a real threat to ethics. Genuinely realizing emptiness will not only set us free from our suffering but also make us morally perfect. The exact relation between emptiness and ethics, then, is a crucial issue for Mahāyāna Buddhists, and I consider it at length in chapter 6.

Along with emptiness and the bodhisattva path, several important Indian Mahāyāna texts also teach what is referred to as the doctrine of original en- lightenment. This doctrine, which was enormously influential both in China and in Tibet, states that every sentient being has within itself the actual, fully realized state of Buddhahood. However, one's inner Buddha does not openly appear, because it is covered with and obscured by adventitious afflictions. This teaching can be illustrated with a number of analogies: one's inner Buddha is like a golden statue covered in filthy rags, or a bar of gold hidden in a pile of ordure.[10] But it is already fully present; one does not have to create it or shape it in any way. All one has to do is remove the afflictions that obscure it, and it will shine forth in its glory. Theravādins, meanwhile, would disagree. From their point of view, the most that can be said is that all beings have the potential for enlightenment. If they choose to follow the Buddhist path, enlightenment will eventually develop in them, and along with it, compassion for all other beings who are still mired in suffering.

The doctrine of original enlightenment is also emphasized in the Vajrayāna, the third major form of the Buddhist tradition, where it is central to the theoretical basis for many spiritual practices, such as the meditative system known as the Great Perfection (Tib. rDzogs chen). In fact, the philosophical underpinnings of the Vajrayāna are quite similar to those of the Mahāyāna, so that the Vajrayāna is often seen as one form of the Mahāyāna. In particular, Vajrayāna teachers accept the teaching of emptiness, the bodhisattva vow, and the aspiration to remain in cyclic existence to benefit all beings.

The differences that justify regarding the Vajrayāna as a separate form of Buddhism are at the level of practice. The sacred texts of the Vajrayāna, the Tantras, were composed in India in the latter half of the first millennium CE. These texts are full of metaphors and coded language; many of them are still not well understood by Western scholars. The practice of the Tantras, which involves elaborate rituals and complex visualizations, is intended to lead to the same goal as other Mahāyāna practices: the attainment of Buddhahood for the benefit of all beings. But the Tantric path is described as being both faster and more dangerous than the way of non-Tantric Mahāyāna. In most forms of Buddhism, the sexual and violent impulses present in the human psyche are obstacles in the way of spiritual progress, and should be pacified and cleared away through meditation. Tantric practice attempts to manipulate and transform these extremely strong psychological forces in order to use them as power sources for the rapid attainment of enlightenment. By destroying all inhibitions and psychological blocks, and transforming all selfish impulses into pure, clear energy, Vajrayāna practitioners seek to reveal the inner wisdom and compassion that are already present within.

The idea that great compassion is present in everyone, at least potentially, is fundamental to all major forms of Buddhism. However, Buddhists also make it clear that as things currently stand, compassion is far from being the only important factor motivating human action. Unfortunately, most sentient beings, including most ordinary people, are motivated far more powerfully by the afflictions (Skt. kleśa; Pali kilesa). Though some texts contain lists of many afflictions, it is clear from numerous Buddhist sources that the three most important are rāga, dveṣa, and moha, often translated as greed, hatred, and delusion. Although these English words are, in my view, the closest equivalents to the corresponding Sanskrit terms, none of them is a fully satisfactory translation. Rāga is not limited to what we would call greed, but includes a wide variety of desires and emotions that pull us toward sensible objects and cause us to form attachments to these objects. Dveṣa, in this context, refers to the whole range of aversions and negative attitudes that lead us to reject and avoid not only people but sensible objects. Meanwhile, moha includes not only false beliefs but also ignorance and various kinds of confusion.

The complex relationship between these afflictions forms the basis for many aspects of Buddhist ethics. Of the three, delusion is the most fundamental, and the source of the other two; but many texts teach us that in its active manifestation, hatred is by far the most serious and damaging. Spiritual ignorance (*avidyā*), a concept closely related to delusion, is considered the root cause of all of cyclic existence. Its importance is expressed in its role as the first of the twelve links of the chain of dependent origination (*pratītyasamutpāda*). Dependent origination, which goes back to the beginnings of Buddhist thought, is an analysis of the causal process that keeps cyclic existence going. According to this analysis, by creating the conditions for karma-forming actions, ignorance makes possible the whole miserable process of death and rebirth. To attain enlightenment and cut the root of cyclic existence, one must eradicate delusion; by doing so, one prevents the future arising of both hatred and greed.

Delusion is in many ways the most important of the three main afflictions. Of the other two, hatred is more dangerous than greed, because of its power to create negative karma and produce future suffering. In the Theravāda, hatred is regarded as somewhat worse than greed; but in the Mahāyāna, it is seen as vastly worse. The great Mahāyāna author Śāntideva emphasizes the destructiveness of hatred in these emphatic verses:

1. The worship of the Sugatas, generosity, and good conduct performed throughout thousands of aeons—hatred destroys it all.
2. There is no evil equal to hatred, and no spiritual practice equal to forbearance. Therefore one should develop forbearance by various means, with great effort.
3. One's mind finds no peace, neither enjoys pleasure or delight, nor goes to sleep, nor feels secure while the dart of hatred is stuck in the heart.
4. Those whom one honors with wealth and respect, and also one's dependents, even they long to destroy the master who is disfigured by hatred.
5. Even friends shrink from him. He gives, but is not honored. In short, there is no sense in which someone prone to anger is well off.[11]

The negative effects of hatred apply to all beings, but according to Mahāyāna texts, bodhisattvas have especially strong reasons to avoid hatred. The heart of the bodhisattva path is the development of great compassion, and hatred is directly antithetical to this compassion. The *Definitive Vinaya*, a section of the *Great Heap of Jewels Sūtra*, contains an especially strongly worded statement that hatred is worse than greed: "if a follower of the Mahāyāna breaks precepts out of desire, I say he is not a transgressor; but if he breaks precepts out of hatred, it is a grave offense, a gross fault, a serious degenerate act, which causes tremendous hindrances to the Buddha-Dharma."[12]

For the most part, hatred leads to the worst karmic consequences of all the three afflictions. For example, the *Words of My Perfect Teacher*, a Tibetan text describing the stages of the Buddhist path, tells us:

> Committing any one of the ten harmful acts while motivated by
> hatred brings about birth in the hells. Committing one of them out
> of desire leads to birth as a preta, and out of ignorance to birth as an
> animal. Once reborn in these lower realms, we have to undergo the
> sufferings particular to them.[13]

Since the hells are far, far worse than either the animal realm or the worlds of hungry ghosts (Skt. *pretas*), hatred has worse karmic consequences than either greed or delusion. But delusion remains more fundamental, because of its role in the causation of all the other afflictions.

Normally, according to Buddhist teachings, actions motivated by hatred are more serious than those motivated by delusion. Buddhist thinkers agree with common sense that if someone is ignorant of important facts about her action, so that its negative consequences are largely the result of accident or bad luck, her action is not as morally odious as a corresponding action carried out by someone who knows what she is doing. But the reverse can sometimes be true: delusion is sometimes worse than hatred.[14] The cases where this occurs are cases in which the agent has false views about the moral status of the action. According to Buddhists, an action that is objectively wrong, in which the agent knows the descriptive circumstances but falsely believes that this very action is morally praiseworthy, produces more negative karma than a similar action whose agent knows that it is wrong. Though it may initially be surprising, this view is consistent with many people's intuitions, at least in cases involving serious wrongdoing. A member of the Gestapo or the Spanish Inquisition who wholeheartedly believes in the mission of his institution is even more of a moral monster than a lone killer who is capable of feeling remorse for his actions.

The upshot of this complicated teaching is that many Mahāyāna texts focus most of their attention on trying to eradicate delusion, which is both the original source of the other afflictions and, sometimes, the cause of the very worst actions. They warn against hatred in extremely strong terms, emphasizing that it is far more karmically damaging than greed. Sometimes they express this relationship in terms so strong that they seem to suggest that bodhisattvas hardly need to worry about greed at all. After quoting passages of this kind, Śāntideva adds a useful corrective: he notes that when those who are obsessed by greed do not get what they want, they often become angry and harm others.[15] So the greatest disadvantage of greed, from a Mahāyāna point of view, pertains not to its own character but to its tendency to produce hatred. Still, this tendency must not be ignored.

Sometimes, thinking of our own failings as if they were obstacles set in our path by a living opponent can help us arouse a greater motivation to overcome them. Perhaps this is why so many Buddhist texts contain references to a figure known as Māra, who hinders and obstructs the path to enlightenment. Often, Māra is presented as a malevolent supernatural being who tempts practitioners to stray from the path—though different Buddhist traditions might disagree about just how literally to interpret such passages. Elsewhere, Indian Buddhist texts use the figure of Māra as a personification of the Five Aggregates, or of the three main afflictions, or of death itself.

It should be clear from the preceding discussion of the karmic effects of the afflictions that if there really is such a thing as the Law of Karma, then almost anything we can know about karma will be relevant to ethics. Several writers have argued for an extremely close relationship between the karmic status of an action and the evaluation of that action in Buddhist ethics.[16] Such a relationship might be expressed in a principle like the following:

> (K) Of the available actions, always do the one that would be most karmi-
> cally positive for you.

This principle superficially might seem compelling as one of the dictates of Buddhist ethics. It may, indeed, be a correct principle of Theravāda ethics, if we restrict its scope so that it does not apply to Saints. Theravādin Saints are said to be "beyond merit and wrongdoing" (*puñña-pāpa-pahīna*).[17] There has been some controversy about how to interpret this expression, but the most plausible account is that it means that Saints, who will have no future lives, no longer accumulate good or bad karma.[18] None of the actions of Saints, who are motivated by unattached compassion, will project either happiness or suffering into future lives. Therefore, principle K doesn't apply to them.

When applied to persons other than Saints, Theravāda ethics does not recognize clear counterexamples to principle K. But when we consider the Mahāyāna, such counterexamples frequently occur. I will consider several such cases in later chapters; for now, one will suffice. Edward Conze reports a conversation he had over lunch with a Buddhist lama from Mongolia. Conze had attempted to arrange a vegetarian lunch; on learning that the lama was willing to eat meat, he pointed out that meat-eating violates the *Vinaya* vows the lama had taken. In response, the lama observed that in the nomadic nation of Mongolia, meat is often the only food available. But these circumstances do not change the negative karmic status of meat-eating. The lama told Conze that he recognized the possibility that he might be reborn in hell due to his choices.

But in view of the moral importance of his mission to bring the teachings of Buddhism to the people of Mongolia, he was willing to take the risk of negative consequences to himself.[19]

This example is sufficient to show that the desire to keep one's karmic hands clean can be in tension with great compassion. In cases where the two conflict, Mahāyāna Buddhists give priority to acting in accordance with compassion. No doubt, most people would agree that if the lama was right about the benefits the Mongolians would derive from learning about Buddhism, he made the morally correct choice. I conclude that Mahāyāna Buddhists reject principle K. For them, at least, although karma is a very important part of the descriptive background against which we should make our moral choices, it does not dictate those choices. I discuss this issue further in later chapters.

Depending on their own beliefs, different readers of this chapter may find some Buddhist teachings compelling, others interesting but unproven, others questionable, and still others implausible or even downright antiquated. Nevertheless, we must understand these teachings, since they form the background for the ethical concepts and arguments that are the main topic of this work. During most of the chapters that follow, I will simply be assuming the truth of whichever of these doctrines is relevant at the time. Of the Buddhist ethical views I will consider, it is for the reader to decide which ones can draw additional strength from the nonnormative assertions with which they are associated; which ones must now be discarded as irrelevant, since some of their assumptions are false; and which ones can stand on their own, independently of the truth or falsity of other aspects of the Buddhist worldview.

2

Main Features of Some Western Ethical Theories

During the past three decades, Western scholars have begun to study Buddhist ethics in a serious way. This development may soon make possible a fruitful dialogue between Buddhist and Western traditions of ethical reflection, in which each tradition might be enriched by the ideas of the other. However, such dialogue will be very difficult unless we Westerners can find some way of understanding, in our terms, what kind of ethical theory Buddhism might involve. But before we can analyze the similarities between Buddhist and Western ethics, we must have a firm grasp on the differences among the Western ethical theories that we are taking as possible models. This chapter will present the three most important classes of ethical theories that have been proposed by Western philosophers: consequentialism, deontology, and virtue ethics. I will begin by explaining the general features of each, starting with consequentialism. I will then offer some remarks on a difficult issue that will be of particular importance in the next few chapters. Given that both virtue ethics and consequentialism have many versions, some of which seem to come quite close to each other, can we identify any characteristics that separate consequentialism in general from virtue ethics in general? Once this issue has been clarified, I will be able to examine, in future chapters, which of these theories are the best analogues of the various forms of Buddhist ethics.

Consequentialism is a broad and diverse family of ethical theories. One way to explain what they all have in common is to say that consequentialist views define the *right* in terms of the *good*. The simplest way to produce such a definition is to say that of all the actions available to an agent in any given situation, the right action is the one that produces the best consequences. Any theory that defines the right in this way is a version of act-consequentialism.

Another way to characterize consequentialism in general begins by saying that consequentialists believe that there are certain things that are both objectively and intrinsically good. In this context, when I recognize that something—say, the happiness of my neighbor, or of my dog—is objectively good, I understand that its goodness does not depend on the fact that I happen to have a desire for it. Even if I don't like my neighbor, so that at present I don't want him to be happy, morality nevertheless requires me to take his happiness into consideration in making decisions. Moreover, to regard something as intrinsically good is to see it as good in itself, and not merely as a means to achieve something else. Thus, it can sometimes be good to have a shovel available; but virtually no one would see a shovel as good in itself. It is good only insofar as one can use it to accomplish some valuable purpose. We can say that the shovel is merely instrumentally good. But my neighbor's happiness is good in itself; its goodness does not have to depend on its being a means to anything else. Now, consequentialists believe that the appropriate response to objective, intrinsic goodness is to promote it. If my neighbor's happiness is indeed objectively and intrinsically good, then it follows that I should perform actions that will enhance my neighbor's happiness, and avoid actions that will destroy his happiness.

Of course, my neighbor is not the only person in the world, and his happiness is not the only good I must consider in making decisions. The consequentialist theories that I want to put forward as models of Buddhist ethics are universalist: they evaluate consequences by taking into account the lives of all sentient beings over the entire future history of the universe. I will be ignoring those consequentialist theories that are not welfarist. Nonwelfarist theories assign intrinsic value to states of affairs that have nothing to do with the goodness of the lives of sentient beings. I shall take it as given that the beauty of rock formations and the balance of ecosystems, for example, are not the sorts of matters with which Buddhist ethical thinkers were primarily concerned—except insofar as these matters have effects on sentient beings. So I will focus on consequentialist theories that explain the good in terms of the welfare of all sentient beings, and then define the right in terms of that good. Some philosophers define "utilitarianism" broadly, to mean welfarist, universalist consequentialism. Their definition implies that all the consequentialist theories I consider could be described as versions of utilitarianism.

Universalist consequentialists see selfishness, racism, religious prejudice, chauvinist nationalism, and many other serious moral deficiencies as manifestations of one underlying problem: the tendency to partiality. Humans are strongly disposed to divide the world into "us" and "them," to seek to promote the welfare and advance the interests of "us," and to regard "them" as untrustworthy, not worthy of moral concern, and potentially dangerous. Any attitude of this form shows a lack of appreciation for the truth that the flourishing of anyone is a good, and that the wretchedness of anyone is a tragedy. By closing their eyes to the value and importance of each life, even those in other groups, those who embrace partiality fail to see the fundamental equality of all conscious life. For universalist consequentialists, the perspective from which ethical statements are justified contains no partiality, and is characterized instead by an equal concern for the welfare of all.

The idea of an ethical view based on promoting the welfare of all sentient beings makes a good first impression with many students. Their second thoughts, however, can be less favorable; in a wide range of circumstances, consequentialism can at least seem to have quite counterintuitive implications. Consider a case we may call the Inhospitable Hospital.[1] Doctors in a hospital are concerned that many people are dying whose lives could be saved if more organs were available for transplantation. Conventional methods of obtaining these organs all fail to eliminate the shortage. Finally, one doctor devises a way to reduce these needless deaths. He identifies people who have come into the hospital for minor injuries and illnesses, and who have a range of healthy organs. Pretending to give them medicine for their complaints, he puts them under anesthesia and then carves them up for spare parts, removing all their usable organs for transplantation into the various patients who need them. For each of these unsuspecting victims the doctor kills, he can save the lives of between five and ten transplant recipients.

Are this doctor's actions morally acceptable? It may appear that consequentialists are committed to saying that they are. Virtually all consequentialists hold views about the good that imply that saving the lives of many ordinary, typical people is a good outcome. In virtue of the structure of their theory, consequentialists are not interested in the question of how these results are achieved, but only in the results themselves. Should they regard this doctor, who saves many lives for each person he kills, as a moral exemplar?

No, they should not, if all the consequences of his actions are taken into account. The doctor is unlikely to be able to keep all of his operations secret. Once local people realize that people who enter the hospital with cuts and bruises have a tendency to die there, they will stop coming to the hospital. As a result, the Inhospitable Hospital will lose its ability to serve the community. Public health conditions in the region will decline. Moreover, the fact that relatively healthy patients are no longer coming to the hospital will make it impossible for the doctor to continue to obtain organs for transplantation. Eventually, the hospital will probably have to close. Thus the overall, long-term consequences of the doctor's decisions will be bad, and consequentialists are therefore in a position to condemn them.

This strategy for avoiding a seemingly problematic conclusion is not available to the consequentialist in a related case, known as the Wilderness Medical Outpost. In this case, a doctor operates a small medical clinic that serves a vast, thinly populated region of northern Alaska. One day, a young man staggers into the clinic yard, leading a dogsled on which are piled the bodies of five severely wounded people. Before collapsing from exhaustion, this man explains to the doctor that he and his friends were out on a trek in the wilderness when they suffered a grave accident. One of his friends has suffered severe damage to both his kidneys; another is going into liver failure; still another has suffered major lung damage; and so on. The doctor realizes that if he carves up the one uninjured man for spare parts, he can save all of his friends. No other course of action could save any of the injured people from inevitable death. What should the doctor do?

In this case, no one but the doctor himself will ever know what he did. If he saves the five, he can tell them, on their recovery, that their friend was injured while bringing them in, and that he alone did not survive. It seems that it would be difficult for an act-consequentialist to avoid the conclusion that carving the healthy man up is the morally correct choice in this case.

There are other, even more emotionally compelling cases in which act-consequentialism seems to have problematic implications. In the Lynch Mob, for example, the protagonist is the sheriff of a small town in the southern United States during the 1920s. A white woman claims she was raped by a black man. The police bring in a suspect; but during the day, evidence accumulates that shows he is innocent. In the evening of that day, a mob of white men gathers around the town jail. They demand that the sheriff release the suspect into their custody, fully intending to kill him. The men threaten that if the sheriff does not hand the suspect over to them, they will go on a rampage through the poorer areas of the town, killing all the black people they come across. It is impossible to persuade the mob to change its mind, and the sheriff does not have enough loyal deputies to stop the mob by force. What should the sheriff do?

In this case, the consequences of not handing over the suspect are clearly far worse than those of handing him over: more people will be killed, race relations will be more embittered, and so on. Here, the possibility that the sheriff's actions will be widely known is not an argument for refusing the mob's demands; in fact, if he releases the suspect, and then later everyone becomes convinced that the suspect was innocent, this may have the good effect of undermining the local people's racist prejudices. It seems hard for an act-consequentialist to avoid endorsing the conclusion that the sheriff should release the suspect to the lynch mob. But many people have the intuition that this decision would be morally wrong.

Let's consider one more story that suggests implications of act-consequentialism that many would find difficult to accept: namely, Bernard Williams' important example of George the Chemist.[2] George, a recent Ph.D. in chemistry, needs a job in order to support his wife and children, but is having great difficulty finding one. One of George's friends, an older chemist, offers him a well-paid position developing chemical and biological weapons. George protests that he is morally opposed to these weapons. His friend then informs him that there is another candidate for the position, a brilliant young chemist with an intense and disturbing enthusiasm for all weapons of mass destruction. If George refuses the job, it will go to this malevolent genius, who will develop far more devastating weapons than George ever could.

From a consequentialist point of view, George should, of course, accept the job. His family will benefit; and all the inhabitants of other nations who are not killed by the superior chemical weapons that would have been developed by George's rival will have George to thank for their lives, even if they never find this out. To some people, it seems clear that George has a moral obligation to accept the job—unless, that is, he can find another option that would have even better consequences. But, as Williams points out, the case places demands on George that go well beyond what many think of as the legitimate demands of morality:

> The point is that he is identified with his actions as flowing from projects and attitudes which in some cases he takes seriously at the deepest level, as what his life is about. . . . It is absurd to demand of such a man, when the sums come in from the utility network which the projects of others have in part determined, that he should just step aside from his own project and decision and acknowledge the decision which utilitarian calculation requires. It is to alienate him in a real sense from his actions and the source of his action in his own convictions . . . but this is to neglect the extent to which his actions and his decisions have to be seen as the actions and decisions which flow from the projects and attitudes with which he is most closely identified. It is thus, in the most literal sense, an attack on his integrity.[3]

George, with his deep personal opposition to chemical and biological warfare, is being asked to spend his days designing weapons for this kind of warfare. Many philosophers who have reflected on this case refuse to believe that morality could require him to lead a life that is in such grotesque opposition to his deepest convictions. Moreover, given that George's beliefs about the immorality of chemical and biological weapons are morally justified, it seems paradoxical that morality could tell him to live in a way that is in such conflict with these beliefs. Could the true account of morality really work this way?

Suppose we are unwilling to accept the implications of act-consequentialism in cases such as the Wilderness Medical Outpost, the Lynch Mob, and George the Chemist. We may nevertheless still regard it as an important insight that the source of moral norms is the objective value of the welfare of all sentient beings. It is possible to preserve this view about the source of morality while giving a different answer to some of these problematic cases by adopting a different method of deriving the right from the good. Such a move results in an indirect form of consequentialism.

So, for example, one might say that the way to determine what to do involves first ascertaining the set of rules that, if everyone followed them, would produce the best overall consequences. Since these rules, if they were obeyed, would achieve the maximum welfare of all, they are the true principles of morality. We might argue, then, that the criterion for determining the rightness of actions should appeal to these rules, and therefore should depend only indirectly on consequences. If we adopt this suggestion, we become rule-consequentialists.

Consider, then, the rule that says that one should never, under any circumstances, manufacture chemical weapons. Given the terribly damaging effects of chemical weapons, it seems that the rule that forbids them, if universally followed, would have better consequences than one permitting their use. If George is a rule-consequentialist, then he may be off the hook: he can probably consider himself obligated *not* to take the horrifying job he has been offered. Similarly, the case of the Inhospitable Hospital shows that a general policy of carving up healthy patients for spare parts would probably not, if universally followed by doctors, lead to better consequences; it might well cause the majority of relatively healthy people to avoid hospitals, thus producing a catastrophe. Given, then, that a general rule forbidding harvesting organs from healthy people would produce better consequences, the doctor in the Wilderness Medical Outpost can follow this latter rule, thereby adopting what many people would consider the more morally defensible course.

It seems that rule-consequentialism can generate answers to certain problematic cases that are more acceptable, at least to some people, than those implied by act-consequentialism. But when we put these answers forward, a serious objection may arise. If we allow the rules to become more complicated, we may not get the same answers. Consider the rule "Carve up healthy people to save others, but only when others will never find out; where there is a risk of others learning what you have done, do not harvest organs from healthy people." If this rule were universally followed, it could lead to even better consequences than the rule that forbids carving up healthy people under all circumstances. This problem has led some philosophers to worry that rule-consequentialism is not really different from act-consequentialism, because once we make the rules sufficiently complicated, the two versions will always give the same answers.

Moreover, there is a difficulty involved in trying to use rule-consequentialism to arrive at the conclusion that one should refuse to hand over the suspect in the case of the Lynch Mob. Suppose we assume that everyone followed the same, highly beneficial set of moral rules. What should those rules say about how to respond to the demands of a lynch mob? Well, since lynch mobs consist of people who are, for the moment at least, disregarding their moral obligations, the rules don't need to say anything about how to respond to these demands. In a world of perfect compliance with morality, there are no lynch mobs that need to be dealt with.

We may, therefore, be concerned that the version of rule-consequentialism we are considering gives us insufficient guidance about the real world—or that its guidance can be highly, perhaps excessively, idealistic. We may further notice, for example, that in a world where everyone followed their moral obligations, there would be no wars or crime; therefore, armies, police, and courts would not be necessary, and rules about self-defense, either individual or collective, would not be needed. But even if a rule that said "Never use violence against any other person" would produce very good consequences if adopted by everyone, the consequences of its being adopted by some people—say, the citizens of democracies—and not adopted by certain other people—say, the military forces of tyrannical governments—might be considerably less desirable.

Rule-consequentialism can be modified to deal with situations of imperfect compliance. We might say, for example, that we are seeking that set of rules that would produce the best consequences if *most people* followed them. This formulation will allow us to write rules for dealing with crime, war, insanity, and other deviations from moral principles by some people. Moreover, we might notice that some rules are easier to follow than others. If I accept a set of rules that I find difficult to follow, either because they are very demanding or because they are hard for me to understand, then since I may not succeed in living up to this set of rules, the result in practice may be less good than if I adopt some other set of rules I find easier to follow, even if the first set of rules would produce better results if I actually managed to follow them perfectly. We might, therefore, further modify rule-consequentialism to say that each person should follow the set of rules that would produce the best consequences if *most* people *attempted* to follow them, rather than the set that would produce the best consequences if *everyone successfully* followed them. It should be clear that there will be more than one way to develop a theory of this kind; moreover, since the word "most" is inevitably vague, it will be difficult to state such a theory in a completely precise way.

Notice that versions of rule-consequentialism based on imperfect compliance will be able to handle the objection considered above, that rule-consequentialism will always give the same answers as act-consequentialism when we allow the rules to become complicated. Once we are explicitly considering the fact that people might fail to follow the rules, we can give reasons for keeping the rules simple. Complicated rules are more difficult to understand; people may make more mistakes in trying to follow them. Moreover, if the rules are complicated, people might find more loopholes, more ways to make it seem to themselves that they were following the rules while really just seeking their own self-interest. If, for these reasons, the rules are kept simple, then rule-consequentialism will be a genuine alternative to act-consequentialism.

Since consequentialists seek to promote the good, and since welfarist consequentialists think of the good as consisting in the welfare of sentient beings, it is evident that it will be important for them to specify what they think the welfare, or well-being, of sentient beings actually involves. The most important theory of well-being for the history of ethics has been hedonism, which is the thesis that a being's welfare depends only on how much happiness or suffering it experiences. The conjunction of hedonism with universalist act-consequentialism is called "classical utilitarianism." Thus, in any situation of moral choice, classical utilitarianism tells us to choose that action which will produce the greatest total excess of happiness over suffering.

When we try to formulate hedonism, we must confront a difficult issue about terminology. Is there a difference between happiness and pleasure? Moreover, is there a difference between suffering and pain? The number of possible answers to these questions is sufficiently large to create an endless amount of confusion. For some, happiness and pleasure are the same; likewise, suffering and pain are the same. On this view, hedonism could be stated in terms of either pair of concepts. Other philosophers use "happiness" as a synonym for "welfare" or "well-being." If the word is defined in this way, then the hedonist position, which is very controversial, can be fully expressed in the statement that happiness is pleasure and the absence of pain. Others, regarding pleasure and pain as transitory, momentary phenomena, might define "happiness" as the presence of significant amounts of pleasure, combined with relatively small amounts of pain, over a long period of time or an entire life. In this case, hedonism is concerned both with pleasure and with happiness: pleasure will be theoretically the more fundamental concept, but happiness will be the more important long-term goal.

Another way of distinguishing between pleasure and happiness would be to define "happiness" in terms of something other than experiences. For example, as we will see later in this chapter, Aristotle uses the Greek word *eudaimonia*, often translated into English as "happiness," to refer to virtuous activity during a complete life. If happiness is defined in some such way, then hedonists will deny that it has intrinsic significance. Hedonism, as a theory of well-being, is committed to the claim that all that matters in life is the subjective qualities of your consciousness. Objective, external phenomena have nothing to do with how well your life goes. If this is the distinction between pleasure and happiness, then it is pleasure that hedonists regard as intrinsically valuable.

Still another possible way of distinguishing between these concepts, and one that is very relevant to the topic of this book, considers pleasure and pain to be specific physiological sensations, whereas happiness and suffering are mental attitudes of acceptance and rejection. Thus, Buddhists might claim that Saints and Buddhas continue to experience pain, in the sense of a physiological response to illness or bodily damage; however, this physiological response doesn't *bother* them, since they don't take it personally. If this thesis is true, these individuals would have some pain, but no suffering. When the terms are defined in this way, hedonists should formulate their thesis in terms of happiness and suffering: what matters is not the sensations you are experiencing, but your attitude toward your situation. The good life is the one that primarily involves experiences of accepting the situation at hand, with contentment and perhaps with joy; but a life that is dominated by experiences of rejection, discontent, frustration, and unsatisfied craving is a bad life.

Given all of these possible definitions, there is no perfect choice of words. However, I have observed that in contemporary colloquial American English, the word "pleasure" is used less frequently and in a more restricted set of contexts than was the case in nineteenth-century Britain, the home of the great defenders of classical utilitarianism. Many young people in America who might be tempted to affirm "Life is all about having fun" regard the statement "The goal of life is to maximize pleasure" as expressing a sordid and even somewhat disgusting thought. From now on, therefore, I will define hedonism using the word "happiness" and its counterpart, "suffering." Readers should understand "happiness" in terms of the discussion in the last paragraph: as a mental state of accepting and rejoicing in the present situation. Moreover, I will assume that the Pali word *sukkha*, the Sanskrit word *sukha*, and the Tibetan word *bde ba* are all best translated into English as "happiness." Most scholars have adopted these translations, and it seems to me that the concept expressed by these

Buddhist words has a range of meanings that is not dissimilar to the meanings of "happiness" just examined.

With these terminological issues out of the way, we can consider the substantive question of whether hedonism is a satisfactory theory of well-being. Although hedonism has had some defenders, many people have found it hard to swallow. Is it really true that being happy is the only thing that can make your life go better for you? Many philosophers have thought that it is good to know the truth, to be in love, and to appreciate objects of beauty, for example, and that the goodness of these states does not wholly depend on the happiness they produce. For example, imagine someone whose life is full of happy feelings, but whose happiness depends on a series of false beliefs. Suppose his wife secretly hates him; his colleagues at work secretly despise him; his successes, from which he derives great satisfaction, are his own delusions; and so on. Even if he is happy, does he have the best kind of life?

A consequentialist can accommodate these concerns by switching from hedonism to some other theory of welfare or interest. One option would be the preference-satisfaction theory, on which your life goes well if you get what you want. One difficulty with this view is that people sometimes want things that we might judge to be unimportant, superficial, disgusting, or depraved. If they get what they want, do their lives really become better? Another difficulty is that sometimes, after people get what they think they want, they feel disappointed and unsatisfied. If you wanted something for a long time, and then got it, but getting it didn't make you happy, have you achieved genuine well-being?

The other important option is the objective list theory. On this view, there is a list of features of your life that are intrinsically good or intrinsically bad. The more of the good features your life has, the better your life goes; the more bad features it has, the worse it goes. All the things we regard as having genuine, nonderivative significance for well-being can go on the list.

The objective list theory is flexible enough to handle whatever intuitions we might have. Its main difficulty is theoretical. In putting forward such a theory, we would need to explain what it is about the things on the list that makes them all good. What do all these features have in common, so that it makes sense to consider all of them to be good things? If we cannot answer this question, then the suspicion might arise that our allegedly "objective" list is actually a collection of unjustifiable prejudices, perhaps created by our early education or societal conditioning, not reflecting any rationally defensible view.

All of these theories of well-being, then, have some advantages, but are also open to important objections. Because of the central place of well-being in consequentialist theories, the question of its nature continues to receive considerable attention. But there are other ways of understanding ethics that take a very different approach. In particular, deontological moral theories do not define the right in terms of the good.

From the perspective of deontological ethics, there are some moral rules which we are not allowed to violate, even if breaking them would produce better consequences than keeping them. These rules themselves are not justified in virtue of the consequences of following them, but in some other way. Deontology thus requires a criterion of rightness that does not derive from the idea of promoting the good.

One way to motivate a deontological view is to observe that ordinary moral thought makes distinctions that consequentialist theories do not, and cannot, make. To understand one such distinction, we can examine two cases, both involving what philosophers jokingly call "the ethics of public transportation."

First, consider the Basic Trolley. A trolley is rolling down a track. Some distance ahead of where the trolley now is, the track branches into two separate lines. If the trolley continues in its current direction, it will go down the line to the left. Tied to the tracks of this line are five people; if the trolley heads down their line, they will all be fatally crushed under its wheels. You are standing some distance away, too far to untie any of these people. However, you do have at your disposal a lever you can pull. If you pull the lever, the trolley will instead go down the line to the right. Tied to the tracks of this line is a single person; if the trolley heads down her line, she and she alone will die. What should you do? The majority of people, when confronted with this case, choose to pull the lever.

But now, consider a second case, the Trolley and Bridge. Here also, a trolley is rolling toward five people who are tied to a track. However, in this case there are no separate branches, and you have no lever. Instead, you are standing on a bridge, above the track and ahead of the trolley's present position. Standing next to you on the bridge is an obese man. If you push him off the bridge, he will fall onto the track. When the trolley reaches the bridge, it will strike him and stop. In this case, he and he alone will die. This man is the only available object heavy enough to stop the trolley. In particular, since you are small and slender, if you jump off the bridge onto the tracks, the trolley will simply roll over you and go on to kill the five people. If you do not push the fat man, the five people will certainly die. What should you do? In my experience, when confronted with this case, most people say that it would be wrong to push the man. This includes many people who believe that it would be permissible to pull the lever in the Basic Trolley.

Many people are led by their intuitions to treat these two cases as importantly different. What is the difference between them? From the point of view of consequentialism, they are the same: in each case, you can sacrifice the life of one person to save the lives of five. The distinction between direct and indirect forms of consequentialism does not seem relevant here.[4] So the consequentialist theories we have been discussing are structurally unable to distinguish between these cases. Deontologists, however, can focus on the nature of your relation to the single person who, in each case, might die as a result of your actions. In the Trolley and Bridge, you use the death of the man as a means to achieve the goal of saving the five. In the Basic Trolley, by contrast, the one person is not being used as a means; she merely dies as an expected result of you pulling the lever. One way to see that the person in the Basic Trolley is not being used as a means is to notice that if she were not there, and if the track to the right were empty of people, pulling the lever would still work as a way of saving the lives of the five. On the other hand, in the Trolley and Bridge, if the obese man were not on the bridge with you, you would be unable to save the five. In the Trolley and Bridge, then, you use the large man, without his consent, as a means to achieve the goal of saving the five; whereas in the Basic Trolley, even if you pull the lever, no one is used as a means.

Considerations of this kind have no role in most forms of consequentialism. But they are central to the ethical views of Immanuel Kant. Kant is considered one of the greatest philosophers in the entire Western tradition; he is certainly by far the most important advocate of deontological ethics. For Kant, the fundamental principle of morality can be expressed in several different versions, one of which is the formula of humanity: "So act that you treat humanity, whether in your own person or that of another, never solely as a means, but always also at the same time as an end." To treat people solely as means is to use them to advance your goals in ways that they do not, or perhaps cannot, consent to. On Kant's view, using someone as a mere means in this way is always wrong, no matter what the circumstances may be. It is important to note that, in this formula, "humanity" is a technical term. Allen Wood explains the term this way:

> Put most generally, humanity is the capacity to set ends through reason. . . . It enables us not only to set ends but to compare the ends we set and organize them into a system. . . . Hence humanity also involves the capacity to form the idea of our happiness or well-being as a whole.[5]

So far as we know, humans are the only creatures on Earth who possess these capacities; but if there are space aliens who are rational beings, they would also have humanity in Kant's sense, and would, in his ethical system, have the same status as human beings.

Kant describes humanity as the end in itself, as the only thing that has absolute worth. Thus, in his system, humanity has a kind of objective value that is able to override any considerations deriving from what anyone happens to desire. But the consequences of ascribing objective value to humanity in Kant's system are not the same as those that a consequentialist would draw from such a claim. A consequentialist who believed that humanity had objective value would try to promote it, perhaps by attempting to maximize the number of rational beings in the world. For Kant, though, the right response to objective value is not to *promote* it, but to *respect* it. Morality requires us to express, through our actions, an attitude of respect toward humanity that precludes treating others as mere means by using them without their consent. Humanity commands this kind of respect through its absolute worth.

Kant's view can also be expressed as a claim about *rights*. In virtue of their humanity, people are said to possess rights that can never permissibly be violated. Kant's system, then, can serve as a theoretical basis for the discourse of human rights that has become such an important part of international law, political theory, and social activism.

For Kant, we may never violate the formula of humanity, no matter how severe the consequences of following it would be. Thus Kant notoriously claims that if a murderer comes to my door and asks the whereabouts of my friend, intending to find him and kill him, it would be wrong for me to answer with a lie. Kant can thus be classified as a "hard-line" or "absolute" deontologist: he thinks that there is a moral principle, the formula of humanity, that always overrides consequentialist considerations. Hard-line deontology is vividly expressed in the slogan *Fiat iustitia, ruat coelum*: "Let justice be done, even if the skies fall."

We can test our intuitions about hard-line deontology by considering a case in which the falling of the sky becomes an apt metaphor. Imagine that giant alien spaceships suddenly appear above many of the world's cities, including Washington, D.C. The leader of the aliens sends the American president this message: "We laugh at your feeble military technology. If you fail to comply with our demands, we will incinerate all your cities and kill three billion people." The president, naturally, asks what these demands are. The alien leader replies, "There is a man named Joe who lives in a small town in Kansas. He has a particularly interesting genetic structure. We wish to perform a series of extremely painful, and ultimately fatal, medical experiments on Joe. Hand him over, and we promise to go away."

To make the case work as intended, let's stipulate that these aliens are psychologically rather different from humans, and that both Joe and the president know this. In particular, due to their psychology, the following statements are true of them. If Joe is handed over, they will keep their promise, leave the Solar System, and not return for a hundred years or more. If Joe is not handed over, they will carry out their threat and murder half of the human race, but they will not seize Joe by force. After incinerating all major human cities, they will depart for their home planet, leaving Joe behind, and, again, not return for a hundred years or more.

Joe knows these facts, and he does not wish to be tortured to death by space aliens. Moreover, he also knows that, since he lives in a small town, he will survive the incineration of the cities. He refuses to go with the aliens. What should the president do?

Kant's view seems to imply that since Joe refuses to consent, if the president orders the army to seize him by force and hand him over to the aliens, the president will be using Joe as a mere means to save the lives of half of humanity. Since using people as mere means is never permissible, doing so in this case would be wrong.

Of the people with whom I have discussed this case, very few agree with Kant's position. Most people believe that the president should hand Joe over, even without his consent, to save the cities from destruction. This response is incompatible with hard-line deontology, but it is not incompatible with deontology in general. Robert Nozick, who rejects consequentialism and places strong emphasis on the concept of human rights, nevertheless concedes that these human rights can be overridden whenever not doing so would result in "catastrophic moral horror." In this respect, at least, Nozick could therefore be considered a moderate deontologist. Unlike consequentialists, moderate deontologists hold that there are moral rules whose force is not derived from considerations about consequences, such that in many cases we should obey these rules even when doing so would have worse consequences than violating them. On the other hand, in extreme cases, moderate deontologists maintain that very severe negative consequences can have enough weight to override rules that would otherwise be binding.

Moderate deontologists could say, then, that in the case of the aliens and Joe from Kansas, saving the lives of three billion people could justify violating one person's right to life; at the same time, they could maintain that in the Wilderness Medical Outpost, saving the lives of five people is not sufficient to justify violating one person's right to life. The next question to ask is fairly obvious. Where do we draw the line between three billion and five? Could it possibly be that we are permitted to use a person as a means to save eighty-seven others, but forbidden to use him as a means to save eighty-six? A principle that draws a line in this way would be unacceptable to almost anyone; but it seems to follow that the concept of "catastrophic moral horror" is vague, and that this vagueness cannot be eliminated.

Vagueness by itself might not constitute a decisive objection to moderate deontology, especially since that view seems closer to our intuitions than the hard-line version. But the issues about vagueness point to what may be a more fundamental problem. Kant's version of deontology has a very appealing elegance and theoretical simplicity. Because of this simplicity, Kant is able to offer deep theoretical arguments for the claim that morality is rationally required, so that being immoral necessarily involves being irrational. Though many philosophers have criticized these arguments, some others have found them convincing.[6] It seems unlikely, however, that deep arguments of this kind could be offered in favor of a moderate view that involves a complex and imprecise compromise between consequentialist considerations and deontological rules. The moderate deontologist may thus find it much more difficult to respond to a moral skeptic who questions whether we ever have any reason to allow moral rules to override our own self-interest.

Both consequentialism and deontology attempt to provide a system of moral principles that can settle, in every case, whether a given action is right or wrong. However, the various versions of these theories all seem to encounter cases in which the principles they advocate lead to strange and disturbing results. We might continue to refine these theories so as to remove the counterintuitive consequences. Alternately, we might attempt to undermine the intuitions that clash with our preferred theory, showing that our refusal to endorse its consequences arises from prejudice, youthful indoctrination, irrational psychological processes, or some other untrustworthy source. And there are still other ways for consequentialists and deontologists to deal with problem cases. Yet over the past few decades, some ethicists have become more and more dissatisfied with such strategies. These ethicists have concluded that the attempt to formulate general principles that can tell us what to do in all cases is a failure. But they do not wish to abandon the enterprise of rational reflection on morality. Instead, they have turned to the ancient tradition of virtue ethics, and to its most important exemplar, the ancient Greek philosopher Aristotle.

For Aristotle, although there are straightforward moral questions that anyone can assess correctly, only those who are themselves virtuous can know what to do in difficult cases. The knowledge of what to do in problematic situations where different moral considerations pull in different directions must derive from a kind of practical wisdom, and cannot be reduced to a general rule. Possession of practical wisdom necessarily involves having various particular virtuous qualities. Those who lack these qualities may often act wrongly, but nevertheless believe that they are doing the right thing. For example, people with a serious drinking problem may believe that they just know how to have fun; they may see moderate drinkers as boring, stuck-up prudes with dull lives. Those whose judgment is distorted in this way can attain accurate knowledge of the best way to live only through an arduous training in virtue.

At the most general level, each of the ethical views I have been considering accepts a certain conception of objective value and recommends a certain kind of response to that value.[7] Thus, consequentialism tells us to promote objective value, and deontology tells us to respect it. We could characterize virtue ethics in a similar way. This tradition conceives of objective value as the virtue, or perfection, of the human character. And it recommends that we respond to objective value by embodying it. Since perfection is objectively valuable, each of us should strive to attain it.

Aristotle offers a very clear answer to the question of why we should make the strenuous effort necessary to become truly virtuous. His answer takes the form of a view called eudaimonism. According to this view, there is an extremely close connection between the morally praiseworthy status of an agent's actions and character traits and that agent's *eudaimonia*, a term commonly translated as "flourishing" or "happiness." *Eudaimonia*, which is the good for human beings, is claimed to be "activity of the soul in accord with virtue . . . in a complete life."[8] Even though "happiness" has many advantages as a translation of this term, it is important to keep in mind that Aristotle is not referring to a mere mental state, but to a form of activity realized in one's entire life. Thus his conception of happiness is quite different from the hedonist views held, for example, by classical utilitarians.

For Aristotle, happiness is the highest level of well-being that humans can attain, and it consists of activity in accord with virtue. Without virtue, then, it is impossible for us to attain that which is good for us. Therefore, if we want to live in what is genuinely the best possible way, we must strive to embody the virtues. Self-interest, on this view, is not in conflict with our moral obligations, but, when correctly understood, actually supports them.

Even if we succeed in becoming virtuous, our happiness is not guaranteed. For Aristotle, virtue alone cannot bring about *eudaimonia*:

> Nonetheless, happiness evidently also needs external goods to be
> added, as we said, since we cannot, or cannot easily, do fine actions if
> we lack the resources. For, first of all, in many actions we use friends,
> wealth, and political power just as we use instruments. Further,
> deprivation of certain [externals]—for instance, good birth, good
> children, beauty—mars our blessedness.[9]

One might think that since a lack of external goods interferes with our happiness, we might face difficult tradeoffs in which particular wrong actions, though impairing our virtue, would improve our external situation so much as to make us better off. But Aristotle denies this possibility in the *Politics*, where he asserts that "he who violates the law can never recover by any success, however great, what he has already lost in departing from virtue."[10] If it is never the case that doing the wrong thing will benefit the agent, it seems to follow that doing the right thing will always be the best way to promote the agent's welfare—even if unfavorable circumstances make it impossible for the agent to achieve complete happiness.

The kind of circumstances we need in order to attain happiness, and the content of the various virtues that, when expressed in action, help to constitute happiness, depend on facts about human nature. Aristotle's claims about ethics are often special cases of his general views on metaphysics and philosophical biology. For Aristotle, each substance has a particular function. For this substance to have and exercise virtue is for it to perform its function well; if it is able to do so, it is a good thing of its kind. If the function of a bread-knife is to cut bread, then the virtues of a bread-knife are those qualities that allow it to cut bread well, and a good bread-knife will be one that has these virtues. Moreover, the function of any thing defines its essence. Anything that cannot cut bread, and therefore cannot perform the function of a bread-knife, is not a bread-knife. If some change causes a bread-knife to lose its ability to perform its function, then that change destroys the knife.

On Aristotle's view, the function of the human soul is to live; its virtues are those qualities that enable it to live well. Without these qualities, one cannot live well; living well is flourishing or happiness, *eudaimonia*. The details of what is involved in living well depend on the human essence. This essence, in turn, includes the functioning of the three aspects of the human soul: the vegetative soul, which consists of our capacities for digestion and growth; the animal soul, which involves capacities of perception and locomotion; and the rational soul, which can form beliefs and decide what to do. Since the last of these is what is distinctive about human life, it plays the central role in defining the function of humans, and therefore in determining the nature of the good life.

All of these assertions must be understood in the context of Aristotle's social conception of the self. According to Aristotle, my flourishing does not depend solely on what happens to me; there will be a small group of people, including my relatives and close friends, whom I care about and whose welfare directly contributes to my own. If I am to be happy, they, too, must possess virtue and enjoy external goods.

The issue of the relation in Aristotle's thought between my flourishing and that of people outside this small group is a delicate one, on which the texts give us less guidance than we would like. A. C. Bradley goes so far as to write that "Aristotle never explicitly raises the question, so obvious to us, in what relation a man's happiness stands to the realization of the same end in others, and whether it is possible for one to be attained without the other, and, therefore, to be preferred or sacrificed to the other."[11] But in addition to his views about friends and family, summarized in the preceding paragraph, Aristotle does say that "the good of a city is apparently a greater and more complete good to acquire and preserve. For while it is satisfactory to acquire and preserve the good even for an individual, it is finer and more divine to acquire and preserve it for a people and for cities."[12] It can be very morally important for me, on Aristotle's view, to promote the welfare of the political community to which I belong. My obligations to those outside that community, for Aristotle, are more tenuous, and seem frequently to approach nonexistence.[13]

Of course, modern virtue ethicists are not compelled to follow Aristotle's views on this matter. But they point to what some have seen as a significant difficulty for the tradition of virtue ethics: that this way of thinking about morality makes it more difficult for those within a given society to offer a fundamental critique of that society's values. When John Stuart Mill denounced slavery and racial prejudice and campaigned for equal rights and freedoms for women, and when Kant opposed monarchy, criticized imperialism, and defended universal human rights, they were able to argue that their own societies fell seriously short of the general moral principles in which they believed. But what if there are no such general moral principles, and the ultimate court of appeal is the judgments of the virtuous? In that case, practices endorsed by those whom a society sees as virtuous must be morally unobjectionable. However, even societies that inflict needless suffering on many of their members, and that assign people to higher and lower degrees of wealth and status for no rational reason, contain people who meet their own prevailing standards of virtue and who fully endorse the justice and propriety of the system. If such a society contains an exceptional individual whose shining qualities command the respect of all even as he criticizes his society's deficiencies—someone like the Mahātma Gandhi, for example—then the problem can be overcome. If no such person is available, then it will be difficult for those living in that society who accept the form of moral reasoning I am calling virtue ethics to explain why anything needs to change.

Another difficulty facing advocates of virtue ethics is the necessity of explaining what it is about virtues that makes them virtues. Works in the tradition of virtue ethics commonly offer lists of those traits of character that they accept as virtuous. But simply providing such a list is surely not sufficient; readers are owed some sort of justification for why these qualities, and not others, are the genuine virtues. In his *Nicomachean Ethics*, Aristotle notoriously makes no attempt to provide such a justification; he simply appeals to common sense, drawing on the virtues generally accepted in his social environment. But since the relevant social environment consists solely of upper-class Athenian men, a consensus prevailing in that environment does not seem like sufficient justification for an ethical view. In general, once we are aware of the great differences among the world's cultures, it would be indefensible ethnocentrism simply to accept our own society's conception of virtue without argument. Since virtue is one of the fundamental concepts of their view, virtue ethicists cannot reasonably be expected to define this word in more basic terms; but they can be asked to provide an explanation of what it is about the qualities on their list that makes those qualities, and only those, the virtues.

My purpose in introducing these three different families of ethical theories is to provide the materials for a better understanding of Buddhist thought. As it happens, few writers have been inclined to claim that Buddhism has much affinity for deontological views. The main interpretive hypotheses in the field so far claim either that Buddhist ethicists accept some form of consequentialism or that they advocate a version of virtue ethics. To decide between these hypotheses, we will need to have a clear understanding of how consequentialism, in general, differs from virtue ethics, in general.

However, as many writers in the field agree, the concept of "virtue ethics" is slippery; it is not easy to make clear distinctions between virtue ethics and other forms of ethical thought. One such distinction is especially difficult to draw. Consider a universalist consequentialist view based on an objective list theory, such that the list of intrinsic goods includes certain character traits. Thus, one of the things a follower of this theory will try to do is to create good states of character. This is the view Thomas Hurka has called "perfectionist consequentialism";[14] if the word "utilitarianism" is understood broadly, as explained earlier, this view could also be referred to as "perfectionist utilitarianism." It is a relative of, but is not identical to, the position P. J. Ivanhoe has named "character consequentialism."[15] Despite these differences, the term "character consequentialism" seems to me to summarize quite well the nature of the view I want to consider, so this is the term I shall use.

Now, of course, a follower of virtue ethics takes as her central ethical goal the cultivation of good states of character. So what is the real difference between virtue ethics and character consequentialism? Indeed, if Buddhist ethics has strong similarities to each of these two positions, how will we ever tell which position it more closely resembles?

Analytic ethicists have been thinking about these positions for some time, and they have discovered certain differences between these ethical perspectives. Of course, we need to keep in mind that there are several different forms of virtue ethics, and that different advocates of virtue ethics articulate their positions in quite different ways. Since Buddhist ethics is often compared to the views of Aristotle in particular, I will offer some remarks on the ways Aristotle's specific form of virtue ethics differs from any view that could be called consequentialist. But we can also make some claims of more general application: it turns out to be possible to identify fundamental differences between virtue ethics and any universalist form of consequentialism.

As I have shown, Aristotle defends the view called eudaimonism, which postulates a very close connection between virtuous actions and the agent's own well-being. Universalist consequentialists hold a very different view. According to consequentialists, one of my actions can be right even though it is harmful to my flourishing, so long as its consequences are sufficiently beneficial to others, including others who are in no important way related to me. Moreover, to a consequentialist, the value of generous acts derives from the benefits they confer on all those involved: the contributions to the welfare of both the giver and the recipient matter, and matter equally, in deciding the value of the action. These are important differences between Aristotle's virtue ethics and all forms of consequentialism. Aristotle holds eudaimonism, whereas consequentialists would reject it. And consequentialists justify actions with reference to the welfare of all sentient beings, whereas this form of justification is not found in Aristotle.

There is room for debate about the extent to which these remarks about Aristotle can apply generally to all forms of virtue ethics. Modern virtue ethicists have plenty of room to reject Aristotle's ethnocentrism and his apparent lack of concern for the citizens of other political communities. Moreover, one can modify eudaimonism, or add qualifications to it, and still remain in the general sphere of virtue ethics. However, a commitment to something in the neighborhood of eudaimonism still forms part of what is distinctive about virtue ethics, and supplies much of the appeal of that form of ethical reflection: if my cultivation of virtue will lead to my flourishing, that goes a long way to answering the question of why I should be moral. Moreover, contemporary virtue ethicists, like Aristotle, tend to be very wary of appeals to such grand cosmic concepts as the aggregate welfare of all sentient beings; they either banish such appeals from ethics entirely or assign them a peripheral and subordinate role.

Another important difference between these types of views is closely related to the issues just examined. A practitioner of virtue ethics, both in its ancient and in its modern forms, takes her own virtue as her central ethical goal: she is to develop the skills, habits, and attitudes of mind necessary to be the best agent she can be. But a practitioner of character consequentialism will have a very different goal: to bring about as much virtue among all sentient beings as possible. That means that a character consequentialist would be willing to make himself worse in order to make others better, so long as the total amount of virtue in the universe increased.[16] This is another difference between character consequentialism and virtue ethics in general: the issue of whose virtue is to be promoted.

The differences I have just discussed can be summarized in the following way. Each of the versions of virtue ethics of which I am aware is an agent-relative theory; that is, it gives different aims to different agents.[17] Such a view gives each agent the aim of that agent's own flourishing, where the flourishing of each agent involves the flourishing of the small group of people that the agent cares about. But all versions of universalist consequentialism are agent-neutral. They give to all agents : that the lives of all sentient beings go as well as possible. Agent-neutrality is a very powerful assumption, and can have quite striking consequences.

Because consequentialist theories are agent-neutral, they do not allow agents to assign any intrinsic moral significance to the distinction between their own welfare and the welfare of others. Everyone's happiness, and everyone's virtue, must be taken into account equally. The result is that consequentialism, at least in certain versions, can be extremely demanding: it can often call for acts of heroic self-sacrifice to benefit others. Moreover, because of its agent-neutrality, consequentialism could often require an agent to neglect the people she cares about most in order to benefit people she may never even have met. For example, Peter Singer argues that a genuinely moral agent living in a rich country under modern conditions should definitely give a very substantial portion of her income to alleviate the suffering of famine victims. According to Singer, her obligations may even extend beyond this, to require that she give almost all of her resources to famine relief, until the point at which her material situation, and that of her family, is almost as bad as that of the victims themselves.[18]

Virtue ethicists, by contrast, reject such extreme demands. Defenders of virtue ethics try to delimit a sort of personal moral space in which each individual can legitimately promote his own welfare and the welfare of those he cares about, without reference to what might be good for the world as a whole. Though virtue ethicists agree that benevolence is sometimes morally required, they would place common-sense limits on this requirement, and argue that other moral considerations, such as family obligations, can often override its demands.[19]

Some consequentialists, especially those who are not act-consequentialists, have also defended ethical theories that are not as demanding as Singer's view.[20] They have offered a number of arguments for their less demanding consequentialist views, pointing out, for example, that I am better informed about my own needs and the needs of those close to me than I am about the interests of people who live very far away and have no connection to me. So even though the distinction between self and other can have no intrinsic moral significance, these consequentialists argue that this distinction can have substantial instrumental significance. We may conclude that if we find a thinker presenting an ethical position that is extremely demanding, that is evidence that we are dealing with a form of consequentialism; but if a view is not extremely demanding, it could fall into either of these two categories of ethical theories, or perhaps some other.

Act-consequentialism may call on us to do more than sacrifice ourselves: it may ask us to sacrifice others. A commonly noted feature of the act-consequentialist view is that it can require us to do things that would seem, prima facie, to be wrong, when the consequences of not doing them would be sufficiently terrible. An ideal act-consequentialist agent would have to lie, break promises, or even kill innocent people when doing so would be of benefit to many sentient beings. By contrast, virtue ethics does not necessarily have this feature. Virtue ethicists may be in a position to side with our natural revulsion against performing certain terrible actions, even when these actions are necessary to avert great evils.

Another difference between virtue ethics and consequentialism has come to light only since the work of Derek Parfit, especially in his book *Reasons and Persons*. Because of its commitment to agent-neutrality, consequentialism regards the divisions between the lives of different individuals as no more significant than differences between different periods of a particular individual's life. Actions that benefit the agent, or the agent's family and friends, at the expense of sentient beings in general are just as irrational as actions that benefit me in the short run but do much greater harm to my long-term interests. These ethical claims could draw support from metaphysical theses that undermine the significance, or even the existence, of the unity of an individual human life, and thereby of fundamental distinctions between persons. Thus, Parfit uses destructive criticisms of the notion of personal identity to undermine egoism and support his own consequentialist views about ethics.[21] Note that there would be no inconsistency involved in combining virtue ethics with a rejection of ultimately real enduring selves. The ethical views of David Hume in many ways anticipated and influenced later formulations of utilitarianism, but his views also contain elements that come much closer to virtue ethics; and Hume famously advanced a bundle theory of personal identity and rejected belief in a real soul or self. But there is no natural way for this kind of metaphysics to provide argumentative support for virtue ethics, in the kind of way that Parfit's reductionist view backs up his consequentialism and Aristotle's philosophical biology grounds his ethical theories. Moreover, insofar as reductionism involves a denial that there is such a thing as the essence of a human being, this metaphysical thesis would undermine any specifically Aristotelian view of ethics. I would argue, then, that a significant difference between perfectionist consequentialism and virtue ethics involves the metaphysical bases that could be used to support each of the theories.

Once we consider the possibility of an objective list theory of well-being, the concept of welfarist consequentialism becomes much more general, and a wide variety of theories are able to be described as forms of that view. In particular, what I have described as perfectionist consequentialism is, in some respects, quite similar to virtue ethics. But introducing objective list theories does not trivialize the whole notion of consequentialism; there are still charac-teristics that are distinctive to, or at least indicative of, consequentialism, such as agent-neutrality, extreme demands, injunctions to promote the welfare of others, and the ability to draw support from critiques of personal identity. Once we turn to the interpretation of Buddhist ethics, these differences can be used as tests. If we want to determine which kind of theory can most appropriately be attributed to some school of Buddhist philosophers, it makes sense to look for passages that respond to the issues I have just raised. In this way, we can determine whether any particular form of Buddhist ethics embodies a form of consequentialism or a version of virtue ethics. We can then try to establish which specific theory within these broad families of views it makes most sense to attribute to the tradition we are examining.

3

Theravāda Ethics as Rule-Consequentialism

The Structure of Theravāda Ethics

In this chapter, I examine a form of Buddhist ethics that has a plausible claim to be a continuation of early Buddhist thought, and therefore to represent the views of the historical Buddha: the ethics of the Theravāda tradition. Although there were once many forms of non-Mahāyāna Buddhism, the Theravāda is the only living form of Buddhism that does not fall within the Mahāyāna tradition, whose ethics I will examine in the next two chapters.

Damien Keown's influential work on this topic has convinced many scholars that Theravāda Buddhist ethical views are not very similar to utilitarianism. Keown holds that these views should be understood through analogies with Aristotelian virtue ethics. However, if we draw on current debates in Western ethics to clarify the range of theories available for comparison, Keown's position becomes less plausible. In fact, the ethical views of the Theravāda and related Buddhist traditions are similar to consequentialism in important respects. Moreover, when we consider the differences between consequentialism and virtue ethics that I discussed in chapter 2, we see that, with respect to many of these issues, Theravāda ethics takes positions that are more reminiscent of certain versions of consequentialism than of virtue ethics. In particular, the Western theory that seems most closely to resemble Theravāda views is not a direct, or act-consequentialism, but an indirect, or rule-consequentialism. After defending these claims, I will investigate what kind of theory of well-being might be found in the Theravāda.

It is actually quite easy to find passages in which early Buddhist thinkers explicitly endorse what sounds like consequentialism. The Pāli Canon, which contains the scriptures of the Theravāda tradition, portrays the historical Buddha as himself offering a clear statement of a consequentialist ethical principle:

> When you reflect, if you know: "This action that I wish to do with my
> body would lead to my own affliction, or to the affliction of others,
> or to the affliction of both; it is an unwholesome bodily action with
> painful consequences, with painful results," then you definitely
> should not do such an action with the body. But when you reflect, if
> you know: "This action that I wish to do with the body would not lead
> to my own affliction, or to the affliction of others, or to the affliction
> of both; it is a wholesome bodily action with pleasant consequences,
> with pleasant results," then you may do such an action with the
> body.[1]

This passage says that actions are to be evaluated in terms of their consequences for both self and others, just as in universalist versions of consequentialism. It refers only to happiness and suffering, suggesting a hedonist consequentialism such as classical utilitarianism; however, later I will look at passages that seem to involve a more complex objective list theory. This statement purports to state a criterion that distinguishes right actions from wrong actions. Since virtue ethicists deny the possibility of offering such a criterion, we see that this statement is powerful evidence in favor of a consequentialist interpretation of early Buddhist ethics.

Though these principles are consequentialist, they are not the same as more recent formulations of utilitarianism. To see the difference, notice that the Buddhist rules of conduct just mentioned say nothing about conflicts: they say nothing about what to do when a particular possible course of action would cause painful consequences for some, but happy consequences for others. It might be possible to seize on this fact as an important difference between modern consequentialist theories and Buddhist ethics, and from a certain point of view it is. But I suggest that the difference comes not from a divergence in the form of the ethical theories, but rather in the theories of value and descriptive premises that give content to those theories.

Western ethical theories differ from each other in the different degrees of significance they assign to conflict in human society. As J. B. Schneewind shows in his important historical survey *The Invention of Autonomy*,[2] early modern thinkers in the natural law tradition saw law and justice as solutions to the problems caused by the "unsocial sociability" of humans, who, though their desires lead them to try to live together, are constantly in conflict over the limited supply of the resources they need for their well-being. By contrast, perfectionist thinkers, who regarded spiritual development as a more important component of human well-being than material resources, tended to downplay the importance of conflict in ethics. Given a fixed pool of wealth, if you have more, I must have less; but an increase in your love for God has no tendency to decrease mine. Utilitarian legal reformers such as Jeremy Bentham, who were much more interested in changing the social arrangements that distribute resources, honors, rewards, and punishments than in developing spiritual or religious values, naturally made conflict between different individuals an important theoretical issue in the development of their views.

Clearly in this respect at least, the concerns of the early Buddhist tradition were much closer to those of the perfectionists than to those of the natural lawyers or the utilitarian reformers. Although Theravāda Buddhists, as I shall show, thought that wealth could make some contribution to human happiness, they thought of moral virtue, religious knowledge, and spiritual progress as more important contributors to how well someone's life goes for her. And these values don't create any conflict between individuals; in fact, the more of such goods some people in society have, the easier it is for others to develop them. Thus, if we interpret the Theravāda as regarding virtue as the primary component of well-being, we can explain the fact that their formulations of consequentialism seem not to address the issue of conflicts of interest. As I will show in chapters 3 and 4, the Mahāyāna went significantly beyond the Theravāda in its understanding of these issues.

Some Mahāyāna thinkers have criticized the Theravāda and other related sects, whose members they refer to as Śrāvakas, followers of the so-called Hīnayāna or "Lesser Vehicle" who strive to become Saints, by claiming that their religious practice and aspiration is purely selfish, and that they are lacking in sympathy and compassion. They engage in meditation and follow moral rules, these writers allege, solely in order to achieve a personal Nirvāṇa that can be of no benefit to anyone else. But as numerous writers have pointed out, this criticism misrepresents non-Mahāyāna traditions. For instance, in the *Cūḷagosiṅga Sutta* of the *Majjhima Nikāya*, the Buddha describes three of his students who have attained Sainthood—Anuruddha, Nandiya, and Kimbila— in the following terms: "See, Dīgha, how those three clansmen are practicing for the welfare and happiness of the many, out of compassion for the world, for the good, welfare and happiness of gods and humans."[3] The formula we find in this passage is repeated at several places in the Pāli Canon.[4] The inner peace and freedom from suffering of the Saint's life benefits him, of course, but the Saint's teaching, inspiration, and example can benefit others. Moreover, the benefit to others derived from a Saint's religious life is a central part of the justification of that form of life.

Central to the spiritual practice of the Theravāda is the cultivation of four qualities known as the Four Divine Abidings (brahma-vihāra); these are loving-kindness (metta), compassion (karuṇā), sympathetic joy (pamudita), and equanimity (upekkhā). Love is defined as a wish for others to be happy. Compassion is a wish for others to be free from suffering. Sympathetic joy is rejoicing in the happiness of others. Equanimity, which might also be referred to as impartiality, extends these emotions to all beings equally, without discriminating between relatives and strangers, or between friends and enemies.

What is particularly interesting about this list is that embedded within it are the materials to articulate a form of consequentialism: in particular, classical utilitarianism. Love will motivate us to promote the happiness of others, and compassion to remove their suffering. Once we extend these motivations to all beings, and thereby attain impartiality, we have arrived at the fundamental principle of utilitarianism. Of course, the Four Divine Abidings do not exhaust Theravāda ethics; perhaps there is more to this form of ethics than utilitarianism. But the basic idea of utilitarianism certainly seems to be present.

Indeed, the form of compassion advocated in Theravāda ethics has a feature which we will come to see as part of the core of Mahāyāna ethics, and as a crucial mark of a consequentialist outlook: the connection between the doctrine of no self and the universal character of compassion. An experiential realization of the truth of no self can eliminate our belief in the significance of the distinction between self and other, and thereby eradicate our selfishness; in the process, this realization will also remove our attachment to false views that interfere with compassion. If I define my identity through radical Serb nationalism, and I then perceive another person as a Croat, I will become unresponsive to that person's suffering. I am unable to see it clearly, and my natural motivation to remove it is obscured.[5] But if I see the absurdity of taking Serb nationalism, or any other such view, to express the ultimate truth, and if I no longer allow lies to get in the way of seeing situations as they are, then just in virtue of seeing the suffering of the other person, I will be motivated to relieve it. Seeing beyond the illusion of self allows our natural compassion to shine forth.

Winston King reports that this connection is indeed made by modern Theravādins: "the goal is that of the spontaneous exercise of a compassion that cannot, or does not, distinguish between one's own suffering and another's; false distinctions between one 'self' and another 'self' are to be wiped out."[6] Putting this kind of compassion into practice would obviously require a level of concern for others much greater than what people usually display. In many situations, this impartial compassion would not require self-sacrifice: sometimes, of the options open to me, the one that would produce the greatest overall sum of benefits would give some or all of those benefits to me. But in other cases, I could bring great benefits to others by making myself slightly worse off; in such cases, the kind of compassion Theravādins endorse would require me to benefit others rather than myself. Certainly, in deciding what to do, most people do not assign as much importance to the welfare of others as to their own. But if King is correct, those who attain the goal of Theravāda Buddhist practice will embody a compassion that involves this kind of impartiality.

It is not true, then, to say that the Saints who represent the normative ideal of Theravāda Buddhism are lacking in compassion. The great Tibetan Buddhist philosopher Tsong kha pa, while avoiding this false criticism, offers a fairer account of how, on his view, non- Mahāyāna practitioners fall short of the bodhisattva ideal he urges his readers to adopt:

> Although *śrāvakas* and *pratyekabuddhas* have the immeasurable love
> and compassion whereby they think, "If only beings could have
> happiness and be free from suffering," these non-Mahāyāna followers
> do not think, "I will take on the responsibility to remove the suffering
> and provide the happiness of all living beings." Therefore you must
> develop wholehearted resolve that surpasses all other courageous
> thoughts.[7]

Since the Saints do not remain in cyclic existence but depart into Nirvāṇa while others are still suffering, they evidently do not accept that they should act so as to actually achieve the benefit and welfare of all beings.

And yet there are Theravāda texts that seem to uphold very altruistic ideals. Far from being selfish, many statements of early Buddhist ethics are characterized by an extremely demanding view of how we should treat others, both in feeling and in action. The *Metta Sutta* expresses this view as follows: "Even as a mother protects with her life her child, her only child / So with a boundless heart should one cherish all living beings." This view attains a kind of stark nobility and horrifying beauty in a text called the *Mahāsattva Jātaka*. Each story in the Jātaka genre recounts the activities of a Bodhisattva (Pāli: Bodhisatta) one of the historical Buddha's previous incarnations before his enlightenment. In this text, the Bodhisattva encounters a hungry tigress who is so weak and emaciated that she cannot hunt and thereby feed her offspring. Moved by compassion for her, the Bodhisattva feeds himself to the tigress. It is clear that the ethic of total, self-sacrificing love expressed in these two texts is quite dissimilar to the everyday morality of most people in any human society.

Though this ethical perspective may be foreign to common-sense moral thought, it is quite similar to the very demanding character of universalist consequentialism. Recall Peter Singer's argument that we may be morally required to give away most of our resources to save famine victims from their plight. Many non-consequentialist ethicists have regarded Singer's advocacy of sacrificial giving as too extreme. He demands, they think, more than it is reasonable to expect from people. But even Singer does not ask as much of us, in the name of morality, as the *Mahāsattva Jātaka* does. Under some circumstances, I may be confronted with the option to sacrifice my own life to preserve some good that has, in the grand scheme of things, even greater importance. In that situation, consequentialism implies that I am morally obligated to make this sacrifice. No other Western ethical theory—not Kantian deontology, and certainly not Aristotelian virtue ethics—would endorse this kind of conclusion. Only consequentialism shares both the noble altruism and the frightening extremism of Buddhist ethics.

To balance this striking similarity, there is an important difference between the conceptual framework of Buddhist ethics and that of Western consequentialism. Buddhists would not say that the Bodhisattva has a moral obligation to give up his life; they would not say this because, so far as I can tell, they do not have any concept that closely corresponds to the Western philosophical concept of moral obligation. Pāli texts often talk about what we *should* do, expressing their recommendations in the form of gerundives[8] or optatives.[9] But they seem not to have a way of talking about what we are *obligated* or *morally required* to do.

How are Buddhists able to do without such a fundamental moral concept? Do they never regard anyone as required to follow a rule? Certainly they do— they see people as required to obey the moral rules that they have explicitly and voluntarily promised to obey. These are such rules as the Five Precepts for laypeople and the Pātimokkha vows for monks. Someone who has not promised to follow these rules is not required to follow them. On the other hand, life without the rules is still subject to the Law of Karma, and the grim consequences of performing the actions that would be forbidden by the rules can give people prudential reasons to choose to accept the rules as binding on them. To have voluntarily taken on a certain set of action-guiding rules, and to have those states of character that allow one reliably to follow this set of rules, is the condition that Pāli Buddhist texts call *sīla*. Once we have this understanding of the nature of *sīla*, we can see why the most common translation of this word, "ethics," and the less common alternative translations, such as "propriety," are at the same time appealing and inaccurate. We have no English word for *sīla*.[10]

Am I wrong, then, to describe Buddhist ethics as "demanding," since on a Buddhist view, ethics makes no demands of those who choose to ignore it?

I reply that the Buddhist conception of what one *should* do goes well beyond what most people think morality could ask of them. Many people believe that when they pursue their own interests and those of their families without harming others in any egregious manner, they are doing what they should do, even if they do not "cherish all living beings" in any sense, much less to the degree that leads a mother to sacrifice her life for her children.

Another objection would be that if we define consequentialism as a view about our moral obligations, then any theory that doesn't talk about moral obligation can't be consequentialist. But I think this objection takes too narrow a view of what could count as a consequentialist theory. Any theory that defines what we should do by appealing to consequences, either directly or indirectly, can be considered a version of consequentialism.

Some readers may object further that the *Mahāsattva Jātaka* should not, in fact, be interpreted in a consequentialist way, since the act of self-sacrifice it describes is so extreme that consequentialism would not, in fact, endorse it. Consequentialist writers such as Singer emphasize that the ideal moral agent should keep herself alive in order to continue to benefit others. It seems that the benefit gained by saving the life of the tigress, though significant, is far less than the sum of benefits the Bodhisattva could produce by spending the rest of his life engaging in generous and altruistic acts, even if no one of these acts was by itself as spectacular as feeding himself to the tiger. It seems that the ideal of generosity in the *Mahāsattva Jātaka* is too extreme even for consequentialists.

The thought that the conception of generosity in this and other Jātakas is too extreme occurred to ancient Indians just as it occurs to us. Reiko Ohnuma has analyzed the protests by various characters in the stories against the spectacular self-sacrifices of the bodhisattvas, as well as qualms that writers of Buddhist philosophy had about the ethics of these texts.[11] The characters who advise the Bodhisattva not to give up his body include ministers, commoners, wives, and local deities; Ohnuma refers to them as "opposers." In his view, these opposers, who are "internal" because their objections are presented in the texts themselves, highlight the tension between the abstract and universal character of Buddhist ethics and the nature of other moral systems prevalent in Indian society: "each group of opposers represents some kind of limited social, familial, political, or religious interest against which the absolute ethical value of *dāna* must be shown to take priority."[12] This account squares well with our interpretation of the fundamental character of Buddhist ethics. However, for our purposes, the external opposition is more interesting than the internal.

By the "external opposition" Ohnuma means Buddhist philosophical texts that regard the gift of the body as too extreme, as a manifestation of emotional tendencies that don't embody a fully satisfactory realization of the Buddhist ideal. As these thinkers saw the matter, the literal act of sacrificing the body does not embody the essence of the perfection of generosity. Rather,

> it is purity of intention above all that truly characterizes the gift of the body as an ideal form of gift. Though the gift of the body is defined in terms of the object given (the body), the gift of this particular object is understood to be intimately associated with a particular intention (wholly pure and motivated only by generosity and compassion). In a sense, it is the extremity of the gift that serves to prove its ideal nature, since it is assumed that only someone whose generosity is ideal would engage in such an extreme act of giving.[13]

Thus, readers of the Jātaka texts are not supposed to go out and feed themselves to tigers. Instead, they should try to cultivate their compassion. Buddhist philosophers, in other words, express "opposition to the overzealous Buddhist practitioner who would foolishly try to imitate a literal gift of the body instead of imitating the nonattachment and spirit of self-sacrifice that underlie the bodhisattva's deed."[14] The qualities of nonattachment and self-sacrifice are essential to being able to bring about the best consequences for all beings.

Thus, it would make sense for consequentialists to tell stories such as the *Mahāsattva Jātaka* in order to provide examples of the kind of pure intention that those who wish to be good should cultivate. And even if the actions of the characters in the texts do not, in the short run, bring about the greatest benefit to all beings, we must remember that each of these characters is a bodhisattva, a spiritual practitioner engaged in a path of training that is understood to extend over many lives and to eventually result in Buddhahood, a state that produces vast benefits to all sentient beings. Once they have reached the appropriate stage of this path, by giving up their bodies and lives, bodhisattvas can generate a level of generosity and renunciation that will vitally contribute to their future spiritual development. Without developing these qualities, they would not be able to attain Buddhahood, and the great benefits to the world of their attaining that realization would be lost. It follows that the bodhisattva's self-sacrifice cannot helpfully be described as supererogatory, or above and beyond the call of duty; such sacrifices are a necessary part of the path that the bodhisattva has chosen to walk. It also follows that such spectacular acts of self-sacrifice really are productive of the best consequences in the sufficiently long run.

This discussion of compassion and self-sacrifice in the scriptures of the Theravāda casts doubt on Keown's view that early Buddhist ethics is a close relative of Aristotelian virtue ethics. Recall that according to Aristotelian virtue ethics, there is a very close connection between right action and the happiness and well-being of the agent. The flourishing of the agent himself is central to Aristotle's account of ethics; and while this flourishing does depend, in part, on the welfare of a small group of other people, it does not involve that of other, unrelated sentient beings. Now there is a strong similarity between this Aristotelian interpretation and the crude conception of early Buddhist ethics found in some Mahāyāna texts: that the Śrāvakas practice compassion and moral restraint toward others, but solely in order to achieve Nirvāṇa for themselves. Ironically, then, to adopt Keown's Aristotelian interpretation of Theravāda ethics is to accept the claim that the Saints are selfish, a false accusation that we have refuted. Now, there are other versions of virtue ethics than Aristotle's, and some of them could certainly embrace the kind of universal compassion Buddhism advocates. So these considerations do not rule out the general thesis that the Theravāda endorses a form of virtue ethics. But if we focus on the specific comparison with the Aristotelian version of virtue ethics, then with respect to the question of whether the ultimate justification of action refers to the agent's welfare or the welfare of all sentient beings, early Buddhism sides with consequentialism against Aristotle.

The passages I have quoted suggest that there is, at least, a strong consequentialist strand in the ethical thought of the Pāli Canon. But this account of the Canon's ethical teachings might seem in tension with some of the advice that these texts actually give. The *suttas* focus on personal self-cultivation, the elimination of greed, hatred, and delusion, and the development of good mental states. These favored activities seem to be less directly related to advancing the welfare of the world than, say, feeding the hungry, caring for the sick, and reforming society to promote the welfare of its inhabitants. Why would early Buddhists, if they were indeed consequentialists, promote self-cultivation rather than social action? This seeming discrepancy makes much more sense when we consider two background descriptive premises that are basic to Buddhism, premises expressed well by the *Dhammapada*:

> Your worst enemy cannot harm you
> As much as your own thoughts, unguarded.
> But once mastered,
> No one can help you as much,
> Not even your father or your mother.[15]
> You are the source
> Of all purity and impurity.
> No one purifies another.[16]

If the main contributor to your well-being is the state of your mind, and if you have relatively little control over anyone's mind but your own, then the way for you to promote the welfare of sentient beings is to cultivate your own mind. Buddhists, of course, don't really hold that no one can have any effect on anyone else; such a view would make the mission of the Buddha useless. Rather, the most a spiritual teacher can do for you is to show you the path to awakening; you yourself have to walk it. But in order to show the path to others, someone must first walk it for herself. Therefore, if you want to be able to make the most important kind of contribution to the well-being of others, by showing them how to purify their minds, you must first work on your own perfection.

As this example suggests, even though consequentialists do not regard the distinction between the agent and other sentient beings as having any intrinsic significance, they can admit that this distinction will sometimes have instrumental importance in decision making. So although consequentialism can require spectacular acts of self-sacrifice in certain special cases, a number of considerations about the information available to agents and the scope of their powers to act will mean, in a large number of instances, that consequentialism will tell them to promote their own well-being. Sometimes, the sentient being whom I can most efficiently benefit is myself.

As an account of the ethical thought in the Pāli Canon, consequentialism does well. It fits harmoniously with at least some of the occasional statements by authoritative texts about the normative basis of the religious life. And, given early Buddhist descriptive premises, it is capable of endorsing the forms of life and action that the texts actually propose. We have also seen that on certain of the tests I have explained, early Buddhist ethics sounds more like consequentialism than like virtue ethics: it is extremely demanding, appeals for justification to the welfare of all beings, and purports to state criteria in words to determine which actions are right and which are wrong.

There are, however, important aspects of the moral outlook of Theravādins that seem to be clearly non-consequentialist. For many Theravādins, the precepts are absolute rules that must not be broken even to prevent terrible consequences. For example, the tradition tells us that Saints, who perfectly exemplify Theravādin moral ideals, would never kill any sentient being, whether person or animal, under any circumstances.[17]

This sort of attitude toward the precepts has persisted into modern times. Thus Winston King reports the belief of some modern Burmese Buddhists that it would entail negative karma to kill a poisonous snake that is about to bite a small child. The reasoning behind this assessment is parallel to Kant's justification for a similar ethical absolutism:

> However, a strict Buddhist may well say that killing the snake is
> certainly a sin, while it is not so certain in fact that the child would

have been killed or would not have been saved by other means. Hence my supposedly good deed is of dubious ethical worth.[18]

King's report does not make quite as many distinctions as we might like. His Burmese informants may have believed that the action in question would be justified, all things considered, even if it did entail some negative karma for the actor. But the most straightforward way to read his account represents his informants as believing that killing the snake would be wrong, and therefore as holding a very inflexible attitude toward the precepts. Perhaps, then, we should consider an interpretation of Theravāda ethics as a form of deontology, perhaps related to the views of Immanuel Kant.

In considering this possibility, we must immediately be struck with a number of important differences between Kant's thought and the Theravāda position. Theravādins would emphatically reject the transcendental self whose existence Kant sees as a necessary postulate of the practical life. As I show in chapter 8, they would also deny the existence of free will, which for Kant is essential to the very possibility of a moral law. And the concept of practical reason that is so central to Kant's view of ethics is difficult to locate in Theravāda texts, and may be entirely absent. This is not to say that Theravādins never think about what to do; but their account of the causation of action gives a much larger role to feeling and perception than to cognitive activity, which on their view actually *follows*, rather than precedes, the formation of intentions.[19]

There is a further significant difference between the Theravāda and the views of Kant. Kant defends a principle, which he derives from Rousseau, that all normal human beings are equally well equipped to know what to do.[20] But Buddhist writers, in both the Theravāda and the Mahāyāna traditions, deny this, affirming instead that in order to know the best action in many difficult situations, one needs a level of wisdom that is well beyond the ordinary. The Mahāyāna writer Āryaśūra put the Buddhist position this way:

> Ethical discipline does not become pure
> Unless wisdom's light dispels the darkness.
> Ethical discipline without wisdom usually
> Becomes sullied by afflictions through faulty understanding.[21]

While placing Buddhism at a substantial remove from Kant, this view also constitutes a significant and little-noticed similarity between Buddhist ethics and the thought of Aristotle.

A further difference results from the fact that, as I explained in chapter 2, Kant derives all of our obligations to other people from the objective value of their humanity: in other words, the capacity that they have as rational beings to choose, through practical deliberation, to pursue certain ends. For Kant, only those beings that possess this capacity have unconditional, absolute worth. Any beings that do not manifest humanity are, as we might say, simply out of luck. Their moral status is vastly inferior to that of all rational beings. Either we have no obligations at all toward them or our obligations toward them are somehow indirectly derived from what we owe to other rational beings. This stance is not just an objectionable view Kant happens to have; it flows from the structure of his theory. The Theravāda position, which involves taking such a strong stand against killing *any* sentient being, must evidently derive the force of this rule from some source other than the considerations to which Kant appeals.

These differences are not trivial; they show that Theravādins could not accept fundamental features of Kant's theory. Of course, there are forms of deontology that do not involve affirming all of Kant's views. Perhaps the Theravāda could usefully be compared with some non-Kantian version of deontology.

Perhaps the most important difficulty facing any deontological interpretation is that Theravāda texts group together, and treat in a parallel fashion, actions that are wrong because they harm others and actions that are regarded as wrong for other reasons. Consider, for instance, the well-known list of the Ten Good Paths of Action (Pāli: *dasa-kusala-kamma-patha*):[22]

1. Abstention from taking life
2. Abstention from taking what has not been given
3. Abstention from sexual misconduct
4. Abstention from lying
5. Abstention from slanderous speech
6. Abstention from harsh speech
7. Abstention from idle chitchat
8. Noncovetousness
9. Nonmalevolence
10. Right views

The first, second, fourth, and fifth of these would be requirements of a deontological morality, since not abstaining from these actions would, from a deontologist's point of view, entail violating the rights of others. These requirements plausibly flow from respect for the humanity and integrity of others. On the other hand, my covetousness does not harm anyone; for a deontologist, I may have an imperfect duty of self-cultivation that requires me to try to eliminate my covetousness, but this sort of requirement is bound to be less stringent than those created by others' rights. It is implausible, meanwhile, that others have a right not to be spoken to harshly. And it is hard to imagine a deontologist thinking that there is an obligation not to engage in idle chitchat with others, since this activity is almost always carried on by mutual consent. From just about any deontological point of view, the Ten Good Paths of Action mix together strict moral requirements, general and not very urgent guidelines, and matters that are of no moral concern at all.[23]

On the other hand, if the goal of ethics is to produce good consequences, and if we accept Buddhist descriptive claims about how these consequences are to be achieved, then what all of the Ten Good Paths of Action have in common is that they avoid obstacles that interfere with making the world a better place. Moreover, at least some of these so-called paths of action seem to be virtues that Theravādins are directed to cultivate, rather than actions they are required to perform. So the structure of this very important list seems to point us in the direction of a theory that makes virtue central to its structure in a way deontology usually does not. Consideration of this list, it seems, suggests that a deontological interpretation of Theravāda ethics would have little to recommend it. How are we, then, to reconcile the seemingly deontological character of an inflexible attitude to the precepts with the consequentialist strains in some Theravāda texts?

There is at least one plausible way to tie these disparate strands together into a coherent ethical view. We might ascribe to the Theravāda tradition a theory that is consequentialist at the foundational level, but deontological at the factoral level. We have seen a theory like this in chapter 2: rule-consequentialism, which tells us to make decisions in everyday life by following inflexible rules, but then justifies those rules in terms of the consequences of following them. Such a theory could explain both the insistence on following the rules no matter what and the scriptural statements that those who practice Buddhism are practicing for the benefit of the many.

Rule-consequentialism is not the only possible way to try to reconcile the various different kinds of moral evaluation that seem to be present in the Pāli sources. One could adopt an approach of insouciant pluralism, and maintain that the Buddhist tradition advises us to look at ethical problems from a variety of different points of view, without assigning any form of theoretical or practical priority to any one of them.[24] This insouciant pluralism has the advantage of making it very easy to explain all the data: any form of ethical evaluation that may seem to be present in Buddhist texts can be accommodated with ease. But this interpretation gives up any aspiration to understand Theravāda ethics as having theoretical unity; moreover, in cases where different forms of moral reflection give conflicting answers, it gives us no guidance whatsoever. Before we give up the aspiration to understand Buddhist ethics in a unified way, we should explore whether a rule-consequentialist interpretation can provide us with such an understanding. In order to make such an interpretation specific, though, we must now consider a fundamental issue: whether we can find a coherent conception of welfare in the Theravāda tradition.

Well-Being in Theravāda Ethics

To construct a specific version of consequentialism that might claim to represent the ethical views of the Theravāda tradition, we need to know something about how Theravāda Buddhists conceive of the welfare of sentient beings, so that we can understand what, on their view, makes certain kinds of consequences good.

A passage in the Pāli Canon offers some evidence about the conception of well-being found in early Buddhism. In the *Lakkhaṇa Sutta*, in the course of explaining how the Buddha came to have the bodily "marks of a great man," the text gives us a kind of list of components of well-being:

> Monks, in whatever former life the Tathāgata . . . desired the wel-
> fare of the many, their advantage, comfort, freedom from bondage,
> thinking how they might increase in faith, morality, learning, renun-
> ciation, in Dhamma, in wisdom, in wealth and possessions, in bipeds
> and quadrupeds, in wives and children, in servants, workers, and
> helpers, in relatives, friends and acquaintances.[25]

The wording of the passage clearly implies that the things that the Buddha, in his previous incarnations, sought to increase are components of welfare. These components seem to fall into two classes: forms of worldly prosperity, such as "wealth and possessions," and forms of virtue, such as "faith, morality, learning, renunciation."

Should we interpret the elements of the first category—the various possessions that come with worldly success—as components of well-being in their own right, and thus as intrinsic goods? Or should we regard them as means to something else? In an essay on Buddhist social ethics, the prominent Theravāda monk Phra Rājavaramuni clearly opts for the second claim: "In Buddhist ethics wealth is only a means, not an end."[26] On Rājavaramuni's interpretation of the canonical sources: "No less evil and blameworthy than the unlawful earning of wealth is to accumulate riches and, out of stinginess, not to spend them for the benefit and well-being of oneself, one's dependents, and other people."[27] Thus, the possession of wealth does not in itself help to constitute well-being; the wealth must be spent in an appropriate way if it is to produce any benefit. Rājavaramuni's interpretation is based on such scriptural passages as this one:

> Herein, housefather, with the wealth acquired by energetic striving
> . . . and lawfully gotten, the Ariyan disciple makes himself happy and
> cheerful, he rightly contrives happiness, and makes his mother and
> father, his children and wife, his servants and workmen, his friends
> and comrades cheerful and happy, he rightly contrives happiness.
> This, housefather, is the first opportunity seized by him, turned to
> merit and fittingly made use of.[28]

Thus, the Pāli Canon's view is just what most reflective people in the West would say: wealth can be genuinely beneficial, but only if it is used in such a way as to make oneself and others happy.

According to the *Lakkhaṇa Sutta*, to wish for people's well-being is to wish for them to have both worldly success and virtue. But it seems that wealth and other forms of worldly success are valuable only as means to the happiness of oneself and others. If we combine these teachings in the most natural way, we will get an objective list theory of well-being, which regards well-being as consisting of two main components: worldly happiness and virtue.

One text for which this dichotomous conception of well-being seems very appropriate is the *Bāhitika Sutta*, in which King Pasenadi asks Ānanda a number of questions about Buddhist ethics. One series of such questions goes as follows:

> Now, venerable Ānanda, what kind of bodily behaviour is censured by
>   wise recluses and Brahmins?
> Any bodily behaviour that is unwholesome, great king.
> Now, venerable Ānanda, what kind of bodily behaviour is
>   unwholesome?
> Any bodily behaviour that is blameworthy, great king.
> Now, venerable Ānanda, what kind of bodily behaviour is
>   blameworthy?
> Any bodily behaviour that brings affliction, great king.
> Now, venerable Ānanda, what kind of bodily behaviour brings
>   affliction?
> Any bodily behaviour that has painful results, great king.
> Now, venerable Ānanda, what kind of bodily behaviour has painful
>   results?
> Any bodily behavior, great king, that leads to one's own affliction, or
>   to the affliction of others, or to the affliction of both, and on
>   account of which unwholesome states increase and wholesome
>   states diminish. Such bodily behavior is censured by wise recluses
>   and brahmins, great king.[29]

In this passage, Ānanda uses a number of morally charged terms that relate to the wrongness of an action, most of which involve the consequences of that action. One factor he mentions is the tendency of the action to ripen as suffering (*dukkhavipāko*, translated as "has painful results" in the English translation I am quoting). Closely related to this is the tendency of the action to cause, for oneself, others, or both, "affliction" (not *kilesa*, but *vyābādha*, meaning something like "harm" and having to do with painful feelings). Another factor is that the action causes "wholesome states" (*kusalā dhammā*) to decrease and "unwholesome states" (*akusalā dhammā*) to increase. Put in Westernized language, this factor is the tendency of the action to make someone—normally the agent, but the person is unspecified—less virtuous. He also uses two terms that might be seen as referring to intrinsic features of the action that are independent of consequences: the status of the action as "unwholesome" and as "blameworthy."

One could interpret the *Bāhitika Sutta* as offering a variety of different perspectives from which to judge actions, and not giving us any way of combining those perspectives. Velez de Cea reads the text in this way.[30] But this reading ignores the structure of the series of questions. It is natural to interpret the passage as defining the earlier expressions successively in terms of the later ones: "unwholesome" is defined as "blameworthy," which is defined as "bringing affliction," which is defined as "having painful results." The series of definitions terminates with reference to two aspects of the consequences of the action: its tendency to promote "affliction," that is, painful feelings, and its tendency to cause bad states of character to increase and good ones to diminish. If this final formulation represents the most fundamental account of what makes an action wrong, then the moral theory of the *Bāhitika Sutta* is a consequentialist theory with a two-part objective list theory of well-being.

My account of the Theravāda tradition's theory of well-being implies that wealth is, or at least can be, instrumentally good. Why, then, do many Theravāda texts contain passages that minimize the value and importance of wealth and worldly success, and deplore the "ignoble search" for possessions, status, and power?[31] These passages are easy to explain if we notice that although wealth and other forms of worldly success genuinely are instrumentally good, the craving for them is intrinsically bad, since it is a form of vice; attachment to them, and the anxious desire to preserve them, are also vicious. Moreover, the pursuit of wealth can draw one's attention and energies away from meditation and the cultivation of virtue, which can make an even greater contribution to one's well-being. The texts that deprecate the pursuit of wealth tend to be addressed to monks, for whom the desire for worldly pleasures is a temptation that distracts them from the path. We see here a manifestation of the important fact that in

Buddhism, there are two different kinds of life, the lay life and the monastic life, each with its own kinds of goods. The monastic life may be higher and better, but the lay life allows people to attain things that are genuinely and authentically good. As the *Dhammapada* tells us, the people who are to be pitied are those who lead neither of these two kinds of good life:

> Those who do not find their way to a higher life,
> Or who fail to earn wealth during their youth,
> Look back with regret in their old age,
> Like large old wading birds beside a dried pond.
> Having attained neither the higher life of the seeker,
> Nor having acquired wealth and power in their youth,
> They lie like spent arrows that have missed their mark,
> Bewailing their misspent past.[32]

On my interpretation of the Pāli Canon, wealth and the other external trappings of conventional success are instrumentally valuable, and the pleasures and happiness that can result from them are intrinsically valuable. These claims can be challenged in at least two additional ways. First, there are passages in the early Buddhist scriptures that seem to say that sensual pleasures are bad for you and should be avoided. Second, it might be possible to claim that the actions that result in happiness and worldly prosperity are not good for that reason but are good only because, and to the extent that, they lead in the direction of Nirvāṇa.

The first challenge draws on the kind of criticism of sensual pleasures that is made with great vividness in the *Māgandiya Sutta*:

> So, too, Māgandiya, in the past sensual pleasures were painful to touch, hot, and scorching; in the future sensual pleasures will be painful to touch, hot, and scorching; and now at present sensual pleasures are painful to touch, hot, and scorching. But these beings who are not free from lust for sensual pleasures, who are devoured by craving for sensual pleasures, who burn with fever for sensual pleasures, have faculties that are impaired; thus, though sensual pleasures are actually painful to touch, they acquire a mistaken perception of them as pleasant.
>
> Suppose, Māgandiya, there was a leper with sores and blisters on his limbs, being devoured by worms, scratching the scabs off the openings of his wounds with his nails, cauterising his body over a burning charcoal pit; the more he scratches the scabs and cauterises his body, the fouler, more evil-smelling and more infected the

openings of his wounds would become, yet he would find a certain measure of satisfaction and enjoyment in scratching the openings of his wounds. So too, Māgandiya, beings who are not free from lust for sensual pleasures, who are devoured by craving for sensual pleasures, who burn with fever for sensual pleasures, still indulge in sensual pleasures; the more such beings indulge in sensual pleasures, the more their craving for sensual pleasures increases and the more they are burned by their fever for sensual pleasures, yet they find a certain measure of satisfaction and enjoyment in dependence on the five cords of sensual pleasure.[33]

Is this passage telling us that the enjoyment of sensual pleasures is entirely an illusion, and that there is nothing at all good about these pleasures? That does not seem like the best reading of the text. An ancient commentary, the *Majjhima Nikāya Ṭīkā*, "says that sensual pleasures are painful because they arouse the painful defilements and because they yield painful fruits in the future."[34] This interpretation is quite consistent with the simile of the leper who obtains a small amount of satisfaction and enjoyment for the present at the cost of aggravating his illness. And it does not imply that sensual pleasures are intrinsically bad; in fact, they have a small amount of positive intrinsic value. However, indulging in them is typically associated with, and strengthens, states of craving and attachment that lead to much greater suffering in the future. So it would be better, on the whole, to give them up, if one is capable of doing so.

Suppose we reject this interpretation, and claim that sensual pleasures have no genuine intrinsic value. Then it would follow that there is nothing good about the kind of high status that leads to such pleasures; in particular, there would be nothing good about being reborn in the heavens, since the only good thing about the heavens is the pleasures one can enjoy there. But then it would be difficult to account for such passages as this one, from the discourse on *Fools and Wise Men* (*Bālapaṇḍita Sutta*):

A wise man who has given himself over to good conduct of body, speech, and mind, on the dissolution of the body, after death, reappears in a happy destination, even in heaven. Were it rightly speaking to be said of anything: "That is utterly wished for, utterly desired, utterly agreeable," it is of heaven that, rightly speaking, this should be said, so much so that it is hard to find a simile for the happiness of heaven. . . .

Bhikkhus, suppose a gambler at the very first lucky throw won a great fortune, yet a lucky throw such as that is negligible; it is a far more lucky throw when a wise man who conducts himself well in body, speech, and mind, on the dissolution of the body, after death, reappears in a happy destination, even in the heavenly world. This is the complete perfection of the wise man's grade.[35]

Can we really read this passage and maintain that being born in heaven does not benefit this wise man? Why is his destination "lucky" if it is not a good place to go?

If we reflect carefully on the passages in the Canon that praise rebirth in the heavens, we will find ourselves in a position to answer the second challenge I mentioned earlier. Scholars such as Damien Keown have claimed that in Buddhism, "Nirvāṇa is the good."[36] Now, if we take a claim like this seriously, it follows that virtuous actions that lead to happiness are not valuable because they lead to happiness, but *only* because the happy states they produce are also states in which one can make progress toward Nirvāṇa.

For the most part, it is true that the happier one's situation is, the better our opportunities for spiritual practice will be. But there is an important exception: the heavens. Early Buddhist texts consistently tell us that going to heaven is, in one important way, inferior to being born as a human Buddhist: life in the heavens does not usually bring one closer to Nirvāṇa. In the heavens, one's good karma is gradually lost by being transformed into happiness, instead of creating the conditions for spiritual progress. The gods who inhabit the heavens cannot attain enlightenment in their present lifetime; they are too contented with their situation to do the difficult practices needed to see the truth. Only humans, constantly pricked by the spur of suffering, can find the motivation to follow the steep path up to the mountain peak of enlightenment. Yet still, the discourse on *Fools and Wise Men* certainly seems to be telling us that being born in heaven is a very desirable piece of good fortune. And Damien Keown himself states that "a heavenly rebirth is often cited as one of the benefits of a moral life."[37]

In such passages as the simile of the leper from the *Māgandiya Sutta*, the Buddha is encouraging his audience of monks to abandon both the pursuit of sensual pleasures and any attachment to them. On the basis of this simile alone, we might think that the Buddha would never endorse the quest for sensual pleasures, including heavenly pleasures, to anyone or in any context. Yet when speaking to those who do not seem capable of abandoning attachment to the world or of understanding the Buddha's profound teachings, the Buddha often gives advice about how to be reborn in heaven; one example is the *Tevijja Sutta*, in which the Buddha advises the young Brahmin Vāseṭṭha about how to be reborn in the world of Brahmā.[38] On my interpretation of the Buddha's teachings, the sensual pleasures of human life have bad consequences for two

reasons: because when we indulge in them, attachment to them is strengthened, and because we are strongly tempted to commit actions that harm others
in order to get these pleasures. One reason why rebirth in the heavens is so
fortunate is that in the heavens, it is easy to obtain sensual pleasures without
having to harm others to get them. Another reason is that we can be just as attached to the scanty and fleeting pleasures of the human and animal realms as
to the long-lasting and intense pleasures of the heavens; if it is inevitable in the
short term that we are going to be attached to something, since we are not now
ready to abandon attachment, it is better for us, in the morally relevant sense, to
experience and be attached to the pleasures of heaven. But the value of rebirth
in heaven, while real and important, pales in comparison with enlightenment,
which brings the end of all sorrow. In short: if life in heaven is not an effective
means to spiritual progress, and if the pleasures of heaven are not intrinsically
good, then it makes no sense for the Buddha to praise the heavens or give
others advice about how to get there. But he does both of these things; so the
pleasures of heaven must be intrinsically good.

This evidence casts serious doubt on Keown's claim that Nirvāṇa is the
good. But let us evaluate this claim on its own merits, to see what kind of moral
theory we would get if we understand Theravāda ethics through it. A consequentialist theory could be built around the view that Nirvāṇa is the good. Its
egoistic version would hold that I should do whatever will allow me to achieve
Nirvāṇa in the shortest possible time. Its universalist version would hold that
I should do whatever will allow as many beings as possible to achieve Nirvāṇa in
the shortest possible time. But this kind of consequentialism would be very difficult to motivate. How is the world made better if a Saint passes into Nirvāṇa?
After all, Nirvāṇa, insofar as it can be said to exist at all, is permanent and
unchanging. It cannot be made better or worse in any way; its contribution to
the value of the universe is constant. Besides, since there is no self, there is no
substantial entity that could pass into Nirvāṇa. The process of making the transition to Nirvāṇa, if we can even speak in any such terms, is literally inconceivable: it is beyond our conceptual resources to understand or describe it.

Moreover, there is textual evidence that directly conflicts with the claim that
Buddhists think of Nirvāṇa as the good. A passage from the *Aṅguttara Nikāya*
says that Nirvāṇa is "neither black nor white,"[39] meaning that it is neither good
nor bad. This statement seems hard to square with the idea that Nirvāṇa is *the
good*. We can try to make sense of it in terms of the interpretations of Nirvāṇa
we considered in chapter 1. For some Buddhists, at least, Nirvāṇa so radically
transcends our conceptual resources that we are unable even to describe it as
good. Still less can it usefully be described as the good. Others would interpret
Nirvāṇa as the simple cessation of the series of conditioned phenomena; this

account of Nirvāṇa as the absence of any continued rebirth would clearly imply that it is, in itself, neither good nor bad.

One way out of the difficulty would be to argue that for the Theravāda, ethics is consequentialist and regards happiness and virtue as intrinsically good, but that ethics as such must, at some point, be transcended. Sometimes Winston King writes as if he accepted the idea that Nirvāṇa is beyond anything we would exactly want to call ethics: "In one sense we can scarcely say that there is a nibbanic *ethic*. There is a nibbanic quality of life, and a nibbanic experience, and the hope of final attainment of full Nibbana. But just because of its transcendent position and quality it can scarcely be put in ethical terms."[40]

This sort of claim raises a number of questions. Does going beyond ethics make you an immoral monster? Can we say that you *should* transcend ethics? Once you have transcended the ethical state of being, can you ask yourself whether you should return to that state? Does the Saint or Buddha transcend ethics only after entering Nirvāṇa at the death of the body, or does the transcendence occur earlier?

Damien Keown has argued at length that in the Theravāda tradition, Saints do not, during their last lifetimes, transcend ethics in any important or threatening sense.[41] Instead, what Saints transcend is any tendency to create merit (*puñña*) and wrongdoing (*pāpa*), karma that would ripen as happiness and suffering in future lives. Saints don't have future lives, and this is precisely because they have overcome the greed and hatred that are necessary conditions for the psychological processes that project future lives. But they do not transcend the rules of Buddhist ethics; in fact, they have internalized these rules so completely that they are incapable of knowingly breaking them. Keown's arguments are convincing; they show that the idea of some kind of transcendence of ethics is not developed in the Theravāda tradition. (However, we find this idea flourishing in the Mahāyāna; it is the main topic of chapter 6.)

What, then, is the role of Nirvāṇa in Theravāda Buddhist ethics? We could try to characterize it in the following way. Cessation with remainder is a life of pure happiness, unblemished by any suffering; if happiness is intrinsically good, then this sort of existence is the best one there could be. Cessation without remainder is the permanent elimination of suffering in a particular series. This means that the terrible cycle of craving and misery has been stopped in one of its manifestations—a morally important achievement, if a negative one. For Theravāda Buddhists, a permanent state of happiness is not attainable. So even though cessation without remainder is not in and of itself either good or bad, we can see how Theravādins could maintain that Nirvāṇa is the best possible thing that could happen to someone. Any other attainment or success merely temporarily improves the situation, which will eventually degenerate again; Nirvāṇa permanently solves all problems in that series by the simple expedient of making it stop. (We will return in later chapters to consider how Nirvāṇa is understood in Mahāyāna Buddhism.)

This understanding of the role of Nirvāṇa may help us to understand the important distinction in early Buddhist ethics between mental states that are *puñña*, or meritorious, and those that are *kusala*, a term we might translate as "skillful," "good," "wholesome" or "virtuous."[42] Meritorious actions are those that are the cause of temporary happiness in future lives. Mental states and actions are referred to as skillful primarily because they cause one to advance along the path to Nirvāṇa, the final end of suffering.[43]

What exactly is the logical relationship between these terms? When we consider the Theravādin tradition as a whole, we find that the texts use these two words in such a variety of ways as to confuse the clear distinction between those actions that make our stay in cyclic existence more pleasant and those that liberate us from cyclic existence. Consider the following passage from Buddhaghosa's commentary to the Dīghanikāya:

> There *kusala* is two-fold, as that which conduces to the round of
> births and that which opposes the round of births . . . the end result
> of *puñña*, which is conducive to the round of births is the might and
> glory of a universal monarch in the world of men, and that of *kusala*
> which opposes the round of births is the attainment of *nibbāna* which
> is the fruit of the path.[44]

Since states of temporary happiness can easily become objects of attachment, it is very possible for meritorious actions to bind one even more tightly to cyclic existence. Therefore, meritorious actions may not lead us any closer to Nirvāṇa. On the other hand, since it is better to be happy than miserable, the Buddha often recommended to those at lower levels of spiritual development that they perform meritorious actions and thereby gain access to higher and less painful regions of cyclic existence. But it would be even more beneficial to cultivate states and perform actions that lead in the direction of the final end of pain and suffering. It would be helpful to be able to use the term *kusala* to refer to the latter states and actions as opposed to those that are meritorious, but unfortunately, as we can see from the passage just quoted, actions that are meritorious are often also referred to as *kusala*, even if they don't lead to Nirvāṇa. There don't seem to be cases of *puñña* actions that the Theravāda tradition clearly labels as *akusala*. Indeed, one Theravāda text, the *Mahāniddesa*, logically rules this possibility out by saying "*Apuñña* means all *akusala*."[45] Here a- is a Pāli privative, so *apuñña* is the opposite of *puñña*, and *akusala* is the opposite of *kusala*.

Martin Adam has proposed a very interesting theory of the *kusala/puñña* distinction that accommodates most of the evidence. On his view, the actions of ordinary people are "teleologically *puñña*," in that they are intended to produce temporary happiness, but also "instrumentally *kusala*," in that they also function to bring the agents closer to Nirvāna. By contrast, the virtuous actions of disciples in higher training are "teleologically *kusala*" because they are intended to produce progress toward Nirvāna, and "instrumentally *puñña*" because in the process, they create the conditions for happy and fortunate future existence leading up to the achievement of Nirvāna.[46] But although Adam's account has much to be said for it, we should note that it can't handle the Buddhaghosa passage just quoted, because it makes no room for actions that are intended to produce temporary happiness, and that actually do so, but that have no tendency to bring the agent any closer to Nirvāna. Buddhaghosa seems to think there are such actions, and later forms of Buddhism, such as the Tibetan tradition, clearly agree with him.[47]

It may not be possible to have a fully satisfying account of the distinction between *puñña* and *kusala*. But we can have a clear understanding of the dichotomy between actions that are meritorious but don't lead to Nirvāna and actions that bring us closer to Nirvāna. It is in terms of this dichotomy that we should understand the twofold distinction in the texts between temporal welfare (*ditthadhammikattha*) and spiritual welfare (*samparāyikattha*).[48] And however it is interpreted, it's hard to see how the existence of the distinction between the meritorious and the skillful could threaten the consequentialist interpretation of Buddhist ethics; insofar as we understand it clearly at all, this distinction seems to fit fairly comfortably within the consequentialist framework.[49]

I have tried to argue for an interpretation of Theravāda ethics as a form of rule-consequentialism, with a theory of well-being that counts both happiness and virtue as intrinsically good. So far as I know, no other scholar has suggested rule-consequentialism as an account of the Theravāda. But other aspects of my interpretation, such as the general framework of a consequentialist interpretation, have certainly been proposed by previous scholars. P. D. Premasiri, for example, has written: "What we need to bring in defence of moral judgements are facts about the world and ourselves which have a relation to the consequences turning out to be happy (*sukha*) or unhappy (*dukkha*)."[50] An ethical theory that embraced this account of the justification of moral claims would certainly be some variety of consequentialism. In support of his claim, Premasiri is surely right to point out that in reading early Buddhist texts, "one cannot fail to be struck by the importance attached to concepts such as *sukha* (happiness/pleasure/satisfaction), *dukkha* (unhappiness/suffering/pain/unsatisfactoriness), *attha* (profit), *anattha* (loss), *hita* (welfare) and *ahita* (woe) in the sphere of ethics."[51] (As I will show, the importance of these concepts only increases when we turn to Mahāyāna literature.)

The theory of well-being that I propose to attribute to the Buddhist tradition has also been suggested before. In his account of the ethical beliefs current in Burmese Theravāda, Winston King attributes to that tradition a view of well-being similar to the one I have been discussing: "Not only are material benefits the sign and result of virtue, they are inseparable from virtue in the complete good. Purity of character without pleasantness of condition is not completely good in the Buddhist sense; nor of course is pleasantness of condition without purity, completely good either."[52] These statements are not quite as specific as we might like. They leave open the question of whether someone who enjoys sensuous pleasures now, because of past good karma, but is vicious and stores up much bad karma for the future, has a life that is good in any important sense. We might be inclined to say that this person's life must be in some sense good, since the past karma that produced its enjoyments is referred to as good. On the other hand, this kind of life seems to be exactly the target against which Buddhism would direct its most strenuous moral criticism. The exact relative position of the different factors that might make up well-being on a Buddhist view is not easy to ascertain, but it seems clear that both worldly happiness and traits we would consider virtues will have a part to play in determining one's welfare.

Premasiri attributes a similar interpretation of the Buddhist view of well-being to Rhys Davids: "Her opinion is that in the earlier ethics of the Buddhists 'good' meant that which ensures soundness, physical and moral, as well as that which is felicific."[53] The only difference between this view and the interpretation I have proposed is that Rhys Davids's account assigns intrinsic significance to physical health, whereas on my view health is valuable only as a means to happiness and to the cultivation of virtue.[54]

In this book, I will use the term "character consequentialism" to refer to any consequentialist theory that is based on a twofold theory of well-being that assigns intrinsic value both to happiness and to virtue. Any such theory will have important affinities with P. J. Ivanhoe's proposed interpretation of early Confucian ethics. But my account of Theravāda ethics differs from the theory Ivanhoe calls "character consequentialism" in at least two main ways. First, Ivanhoe repeatedly refers to the fact that, according to Mencius and many other Confucian thinkers, the virtuous life is "the way to develop one's Heavenly endowed nature."[55] This claim marks a respect in which Confucian ethics is importantly similar to the views of Aristotle, who also holds that the virtues are the realization of the human essence. But the Theravāda interpretation of the universal Buddhist teaching of no-self would seem to commit Theravādins to rejecting any claims of this kind. For the Theravāda, humans have no essence. At the level of ultimate truth, there are no humans; the word "human" is just a convenient designation for an extremely complex process. Virtue cannot be the realization of human nature because there is no human nature to realize.

The second major difference between what Ivanhoe calls "character consequentialism" and the theory I will use the term to designate concerns the role of particular human relationships in ethics. Ivanhoe's formulation of character consequentialism allows individuals to assign much greater weight to the interests of their own family members, and of others with whom they have special relationships, than to the interests of random strangers.[56] This modification of consequentialism is entirely appropriate in a theory that is intended as an interpretation of the Confucian tradition, which lays great stress on family relationships. But it would be out of place in any interpretation of Buddhist ethics. The beginning of the holy life for a Buddhist monk or nun is the "going forth," the departure from home and family. The historical Buddha himself left a wife and son behind when he departed to seek enlightenment. In interpreting the Buddhist tradition, we should not modify consequentialism to assign special significance to family or other close human relationships. If these differences are kept in mind, however, it seems appropriate to use the term "character consequentialism" to describe Theravāda ethical views.

The evidence we have considered makes possible a nuanced understanding of the complex theoretical structure of Theravāda ethics. Throughout the spiritual path, which leads from the ignorance and confusion of ordinary people all the way to Sainthood and liberation, Theravādin practitioners are expected to follow a largely inflexible set of rules and precepts. Yet Theravāda definitions of compassion and stories of self-sacrifice, along with explicit statements of the basis of ethics, strongly suggest that for them, as for Western consequentialists, the source of morality is the welfare of all sentient beings. We can reconcile these elements of the ethical perspective of Theravāda thinkers if we ascribe to these thinkers a form of rule-consequentialism whose theory of well-being includes both happiness and virtue. This proposal is by no means the only way to understand Theravādin ethical views, but I suggest that it may be the best way. Rather than seeking "superficial and ephemeral" pleasures, as in Keown's characterization of classical utilitarianism,[57] an adherent of this version of consequentialism would follow a set of rules that are designed to advance the compassion, moral qualities, and knowledge of all beings, together with their happiness. This theory is phrased in the terms of contemporary Western ethics; early Buddhists could not have expressed their view in just this way. But if we reconstruct their position in these terms, that position can then be evaluated on its merits. Perhaps this sort of inquiry can help us to see Theravāda ethics as a contribution to a global conversation about ethics, one in which the wisdom of all world cultures can help us find a better way forward.

4

Mahāyāna Ethics before Śāntideva

I have suggested that we might understand Theravāda ethics better if we think of it as a form of rule-consequentialism. Many of the reasons for adopting this kind of interpretation also apply in the case of Mahāyāna ethics; indeed, as we move later in the tradition, the case for a consequentialist interpretation grows stronger, and the ethical positions presented seem slowly to gravitate toward act-consequentialism. Certain features of a full-fledged act-consequentialist view seem not to appear, at least explicitly, until Śāntideva, writing in the seventh century CE, whom I will consider in the next chapter. But the developments in moral thought found in earlier Mahāyāna writers are well worth our attention.

The most ethically significant development that occurs in the Mahāyāna tradition is, of course, that all Mahāyāna practitioners must vow to attain Buddhahood for the benefit of all beings. The goal is no longer Sainthood and individual liberation, as for a large majority of Theravāda and other non- Mahāyāna Buddhists. Instead, Mahāyānists must follow the much longer path to Buddhahood, so as to help bring about the enlightenment of all beings.

Recent careful readings of early Mahāyāna texts have uncovered evidence that this aspiration to attain Buddhahood was virtually the only thing that differentiated the earliest Mahāyānists from other Buddhists in their environment.[1] Chinese travelers from the middle of the first millennium, such as Hsuan-tsang, reported that bodhisattvas and Disciples could be found living together in the same monasteries and following the same disciplinary rules; it now appears that this kind of situation was typical during the early history of the Mahāyāna.[2] The first Mahāyānists also had few, if any, beliefs that other Buddhists would have seen as unorthodox; characteristic Mahāyāna doctrines such as emptiness and the supermundane character of the Buddha, and practices such as devotion to celestial Buddhas and bodhisattvas, appear to be later developments.[3] The only distinguishing characteristic of Mahāyānists that applies to the entire history of their tradition is that, rejecting any intention to attain liberation for themselves alone, they aspire to become Buddhas and free others from suffering.

In keeping with this new spiritual goal, Mahāyāna texts are full of references to the moral importance of benefiting others. Such texts repeatedly tell us that a bodhisattva should be concerned with the welfare of all beings, and should not succumb to selfish concern for her own welfare. This reorientation, in and of itself, brings Mahāyāna ethics significantly closer to the moral concerns of Western universalist consequentialism.

Although the Mahāyāna devotes more attention to cultivating concern for the welfare of others, such concern is also endorsed in the Theravāda. Indeed, in the previous chapter I showed that the ethical perspective of such Theravāda texts as the *Mahāsattva Jātaka* can recommend acts of extreme self-sacrifice for the benefit of others. Numerous Mahāyāna texts are just as demanding; an important source for this aspect of Mahāyāna ethics is the *Sūtra on Upāsaka Precepts*. The practice of generosity advocated in this Sūtra extends to such an extreme that "even if a wise person was in the situation whereby he would live if he ate the last handful of food but would die if he gave it away, he should still give it away."[4] Thus, the bodhisattva is not allowed to make distinctions between his own welfare and the welfare of others, except when these distinctions oppose the natural human tendency and favor others over self. The text seems sometimes to bend over backward in opposition to the selfish tendencies of human nature: "When friends and foes are suffering, he first benefits his foes."[5] By counteracting natural tendencies to partiality, the bodhisattva can move closer to the ideal of impartial great compassion for all beings. This ideal of impartiality finds expression in many passages in the text: "he benefits both foes and friends without discrimination";[6] his goal is "to be compassionate to all regardless of their relationship to oneself";[7] he "sees all foes as dear friends."[8]

These statements are echoed in other Mahāyāna scriptures, such as the *Inquiry of Ugra*. This Sūtra cautions the practitioner not to be biased in favor of his own son: "If for his sake I bring forth excessive affection toward that son of mine while not doing the same toward other beings I will be deviating from the training prescribed by the Buddha."[9] The *Inquiry of Ugra* also tells us that a true Mahāyānist "is even-minded toward those who are his friends and those who are not,"[10] and that "*Bodhi* belongs to the bodhisattva whose mind is impartial, not to the one whose mind is partial."[11]

This repeated emphasis on impartiality is strong evidence that the ethical view of these Sūtras is an agent-neutral theory. Thus, if Mahāyāna ethics is a form of virtue ethics, it would have to be *very* different from all Western versions of virtue ethics, since they all embrace agent-relative perspectives. It seems more reasonable to interpret it in terms of consequentialism, since consequentialist views do accept agent-neutrality. Can we say anything about what form of consequentialism might be in play here? If the bodhisattva is supposed to engage in acts of impartial compassion, such as giving away his last mouthful of food, only when he is confident that doing so will have good consequences on the whole, then we would be dealing with a version of act-consequentialism. But it seems more faithful to the texts to say that these injunctions to impartiality, generosity, and benevolence represent rules that bodhisattvas must follow in all circumstances, as part of their training. If so, then the most plausible interpretation would seem to be some form of rule-utilitarianism.

Of course, by practicing altruism and nonviolence, the bodhisattva can achieve various good things for himself: he cultivates the roots of good, develops knowledge of religious truth, and so on. One might wonder whether the ultimate justification for the bodhisattva's practice is these benefits to himself. In fact, the *Precepts Sūtra* contains what looks like an explicit endorsement of eudaimonism: "to benefit others is to benefit oneself."[12] Moreover, even some of the bodhisattva's most impressively altruistic actions, such as being reborn as an animal or in one of the hells for the benefit of others, may not be as costly as they look: "If this person dwells in the three evil realms, he will not have to suffer as other beings do."[13] Once the bodhisattva attains an advanced stage of enlightenment, but before Buddhahood has been achieved, no degree of damage to the physical body will cause the bodhisattva to suffer at all; so being born in unfavorable circumstances is not really a great sacrifice. As regards our first difference between virtue ethics and consequentialism, the question of whether doing the right thing always benefits the agent, there is some reason to suppose that Mahāyāna ethics would agree with virtue ethics.

We can cast doubt on this interpretation by studying the ritual of the "dedication of merit" (*puṇya-pariṇāmanā*). The *Precepts Sūtra* gives a brief summary of this ritual's purpose: "He always transfers his merits and virtues to others."[14] Through his religious activities, the bodhisattva constantly accumulates merit (*puṇya*). This merit, if he retained it, would cause him to be both happier and more virtuous. But rather than promote his own well-being, or even his own virtue, the bodhisattva gives away this merit in order to make other beings happy and virtuous. If this interpretation of the purpose of the ritual is correct, then Mahāyāna Buddhism both allows actions to be moral that don't promote the well-being of the agent and places the virtue of all beings above the virtue of the individual agent. According to the *Precepts Sūtra*, then, as in character consequentialism, the goal of each agent should be to promote virtue in general, not just the virtue of that agent.

The concept of the dedication of merit, as presented in the last paragraph, may be different from the way this concept functioned when it was first introduced. Jan Nattier has discussed this issue in her analysis of the *Inquiry of Ugra* (*Ugraparipṛcchā*), a very early Mahāyāna scripture. In this text, for a bodhisattva to dedicate merit is for him

> to perform the mental act of transferring his merit from (as it were) one karmic bank account to another, so that it will contribute not to his rebirth in heaven or to other worldly rewards, but to his future attainment of Buddhahood.
>
> It is important to note that the *Ugra* is not recommending the "transfer of merit" in the sense in which that expression is most commonly understood—that is, diverting its benefits from one recipient to another. On the contrary, in the *Ugra* this act of transferral (pariṇāmanā) results not in a change of beneficiary, but in a change in the kind of reward that will accrue to the bodhisattva himself. Other beings will of course benefit from this transformation, but only in the distant future when the bodhisattva has succeeded in becoming a Buddha and is at last in a position to perform the ultimate service of rediscovering the Dharma and teaching it to others.[15]

Clearly, if the dedication of merit is understood along these lines, it will be compatible with a eudaimonist interpretation.

Which of these two senses of the term *pariṇāmanā*—transforming the type of benefit to be obtained from good karma, as in the *Ugra*, or giving it away to others, as in the *Precepts Sūtra*—was more important in Indian Mahāyāna? Important evidence that bears on this question comes from Gregory Schopen's careful work on Buddhist donative inscriptions in India. According to Schopen, a certain formula found in these inscriptions is associated with, and in fact distinctive to, the Mahāyāna.[16] The formula is found in a large number of inscriptions, dating from the fourth century to the twelfth century. It also occurs on the Kuṣān image of Amitābha, the earliest known Mahāyāna inscription from India, datable to the second century CE.[17] Although this formula has many variants, Schopen eventually concluded that its basic form was "Yad atra puṇyaṃ tad bhavatu sarvasatvānām anuttarajñānāvāptaye,"[18] which we might translate as "Whatever merit is here, may that be for the obtaining of supreme wisdom by all sentient beings." Schopen argues that a large majority of the Indian inscriptions that we have reason to identify as Mahāyāna are, in fact, instances of this formula. The formula in question clearly intends the transfer of the merit arising from a gift to beings other than the giver.

We may conclude, then, that the concept of the dedication of merit, understood in the sense of giving merit away to others, played a central role in at least some aspects of actual Mahāyāna Buddhist practice in India. This practice of ritually giving away merit to all sentient beings was already in place in the earliest periods of Indian Mahāyāna for which we have archaeological evidence. In fact, the inscriptional evidence also tells us that non-Mahāyāna Buddhists also practiced the transfer of merit, sometimes to deceased parents or teachers, but often to all sentient beings. The main difference Schopen finds between the inscriptions associated with these two Buddhist traditions is that non-Mahāyānists stated the purpose of their gift of merit through such expressions as *sarvasatvahitasukhārtha*, "for the welfare, happiness, and benefit of all beings."[19] Mahāyānists, on the other hand, specifically dedicated their gifts to a single purpose: the attainment of supreme wisdom, that is, of Buddhahood, by all beings. If giving away merit to others is evidence of a consequentialist ethical orientation, as opposed to an orientation toward virtue ethics, then the votive inscriptions provide such evidence for the Indian Buddhist tradition generally.

Throughout its history in the West, the utilitarian tradition has placed great emphasis on social activism and legal reform. Most Indian Buddhist texts clearly do not share this emphasis. As Jan Nattier points out, a number of Mahāyāna scriptures, including the *Inquiry of Ugra*, recommend a life of meditation in wilderness areas. But

> A key element of life in the wilderness is its isolation: that is, that
> the bodhisattva will be able to avoid all contact with other human
> beings. For those who are used to thinking of the bodhisattva as a
> kind of "social Arhat"—compassionate toward others, concerned for
> the welfare of all beings, and expressing that concern in concrete
> and constructive activities in society—the portrait of the bodhisattva
> presented in the *Ugra* will seem foreign indeed. Yet this portrait
> was clearly widely held, and the expectation that a bodhisattva's
> compassion should be manifest in the world here and now appears
> to have been largely unknown in medieval India. On the contrary,
> the renunciant bodhisattva is commonly exhorted to withdraw from

society to an even greater extent than most of his *śrāvaka* monastic counterparts.[20]

Is this dramatic difference in the nature of the lives recommended by these two traditions evidence that early Mahāyāna ethics was not consequentialist? I think not. Nattier offers an analysis of the *Ugra*'s justification for wilderness living that can be seen as a clear example of consequentialist moral reasoning:

> The isolation of the bodhisattva, in other words, is seen as a tactical investment in his future: the strenuous practices in which he is presently engaged will eventually enable him to benefit all beings when he finally becomes a Buddha and can teach others far more effectively than he could do now.[21]

Moreover, this extreme isolation applies only to those bodhisattvas who have become monks. For those who are still living as householders, the *Ugra*'s advice would be far easier for a Western utilitarian to recognize: "Upon the poor, one should bestow wealth; to the sick one should give medicine. One should be a protector to those who have no protector, a refuge for those who are without a refuge, an asylum for those who have no asylum."[22] Valuable as these activities are, however, Mahāyāna Buddhists have always believed that attaining Buddhahood would be even more helpful and important, so that activities directed toward that goal are more pressing and more praiseworthy.

As I explained in chapter 2, one issue that can be used to distinguish different forms of ethical theory is whether they require agents to perform morally terrifying actions when these are necessary to avoid great catastrophes. As it turns out, a number of Mahāyāna texts argue that sometimes, a bodhisattva ought to perform actions that would otherwise be considered wrong in order to benefit large numbers of sentient beings. Perhaps the most important text of this kind is Asaṅga's "Chapter on Ethics," a part of his larger work *The Bodhisattva Stages (Bodhisattva-bhūmi)*.[23] Several writers have discussed the fact that this text argues for the permissibility of lying, stealing, sexual misconduct, and killing, when these actions are motivated by a compassionate wish to benefit all beings.[24] In this respect, Asaṅga's views are quite different from those found in most non–Mahāyāna Buddhist texts.

Careful examination of Asaṅga's position reveals a very interesting view about when the precepts may be broken. Here is Asaṅga's general account of when a bodhisattva can break the precepts:

> If the bodhisattva sees that some caustic means, some use of severity would be of benefit to sentient beings, and does not employ it in order to guard against unhappiness, he is possessed of fault,

possessed of contradiction; there is fault that is not defiled. If little
benefit would result for the present, and great unhappiness on that
basis, there is no fault.[25]

It is clear that this criterion has a very consequentialist flavor: when the consequences of breaking the rules would be good, violations of the rules are sometimes actually required, and are justified by their consequences. But there is an
ambiguity in this passage. Does Asaṅga mean that the precepts can be broken
if doing so would be of benefit to sentient beings *collectively*, in a sense that allows balancing the welfare of some against the welfare of others, and therefore
permits harming some to benefit others? Or does he mean that the act of breaking the precepts must benefit sentient beings *distributively*, so that every being
affected must benefit, or at least not be harmed?[26]

If we examine the examples Asaṅga offers of permissible precept-breaking,
they turn out all to fit the second, distributive pattern. This fact may be surprising, since Asaṅga includes killing as one example of permissible precept-
breaking. Here is the only example he supplies of permissible killing:

> Accordingly, the bodhisattva may behold a robber or thief engaged
> in committing a great many deeds of immediate retribution, being
> about to murder many hundreds of magnificent living beings—
> auditors, independent buddhas, and bodhisattvas—for the sake of a
> few material goods. Seeing it, he forms this thought in his mind:
> "If I take the life of this sentient being, I myself may be reborn as
> one of the creatures of hell. Better that I be reborn a creature of hell
> than that this living being, having committed a deed of immediate
> retribution, should go straight to hell." With such an attitude the
> bodhisattva ascertains that the thought is virtuous or indeterminate
> and then, feeling constrained, with only a thought of mercy for
> the consequence, he takes the life of that living being. There is no
> fault, but a spread of much merit.[27]

In this case, the being who is killed is actually better off dead, since he was
about to condemn himself to an immensely long (though finite) period of hor-
rible suffering. This would be the karmic retribution for killing a large number
of spiritually advanced people, including both non- Mahāyāna practitioners[28]
and bodhisattvas. By killing him, the bodhisattva rescues the robber from a fate
much worse than mere death.

The same pattern is also seen in Asaṅga's examples of permissible violations of the second precept, which forbids "taking what is not given." The
bodhisattva is allowed to overthrow "violent and pitiless" kings, taking their

power from them without consent, but preventing them from incurring further negative karma through their oppressive rule. If robbers steal property
from religious communities and shrines, the bodhisattva may steal it back,
thus protecting them from the very grave karmic consequences of consum-
ing such stolen items. A bodhisattva may also remove corrupt or incompetent
storekeepers and custodians from office, to prevent them from incurring serious karmic misfortune from their own waste and embezzlement.[29]

Asaṅga never explicitly denies that balancing is permissible. He simply
does not address situations in which some beings must be harmed to benefit
others. But he is enumerating exceptions to the generally valid rules of morality, rules he takes very seriously indeed. It seems plausible to assume that he
intends these to be the only kind of exceptions that are allowed; if he thought
there were more classes of exceptions, he would probably have indicated them.
He also makes it clear that the rules can be violated only for the benefit of others. It is never permissible for a bodhisattva to break the precepts for his own
benefit, even in a small way.

Though Asaṅga does not give us anything like a worked-out view of balancing between individuals, there is one passage where he countenances something like balancing:

> When something of body or speech done to someone else would
> result in pain and unhappiness for a third party, whereas neither
> party would be moved from an unwholesome to a wholesome
> situation, the bodhisattva will reflect upon it and reject that act of
> body-speech on the grounds that it would not comply with the incli-
> nations of the third party. If, on the other hand, he sees that either
> party, or both would be moved from an unwholesome to a whole-
> some situation, the bodhisattva will reflect upon it adopting nothing
> but a thought of mercy, and perform the action.[30]

In this case, the bodhisattva is permitted to inflict suffering on one party in
order to increase the virtue of a second. The permissibility of this form of balancing is easy to explain if we regard Asaṅga as holding that there are two kinds
of value, happiness and virtue, the second being much more important than
the first. I shall argue for this interpretation.

The evidence I have presented would lead us to interpret Asaṅga as a
kind of rule-utilitarian. On the interpretation suggested by these passages, a
Mahāyāna practitioner should normally follow the precepts. These are moral
rules that are justified by appeal to the good consequences of following them;
they are "lived for the benefit and pleasure of all sentient beings."[31] But these

rules may permissibly be broken if, and only if, doing so significantly benefits at least one sentient being other than the agent, and leaves no one worse off than if the rules were followed. The interests of one being cannot normally be sacrificed to benefit another; but it is at least sometimes permissible to inflict pain on one being to achieve the virtue of another.

One might think that the strictness of the conditions Asaṅga imposes on permissible rule-breaking would mean that there would be little difference in practice between his views and a perspective that would never allow breaking the precepts. In fact, though, there are important classes of cases of real contemporary significance in which the conditions could be met. Consider, for example, a case of humanitarian military intervention to stop genocide. Imagine that Western nations had invaded Rwanda to put a stop to the genocide of 1994. This would clearly have been of benefit to the Tutsis and moderate Hutus who were the targets of the massacres. But from a Buddhist perspective, the invasion would also have benefited the militant Hutus who carried out the genocide, since it would have prevented them from accumulating a truly horrifying karmic burden. Thus, it seems clear that Asaṅga's ethical views would permit such an invasion—at least, if it would work, and if it would have no negative unintended consequences comparable in moral significance to the events it would prevent. Since what such an intervention might have prevented was the massacre of as many as eight hundred thousand people, the latter condition would not have been very difficult to meet.

I have tried to offer several kinds of evidence for interpreting certain Mahāyāna texts as holding versions of universalist consequentialism. Assuming that I am right about this issue, what theory of well-being do we find in the Mahāyāna? On my view, it makes sense to attribute to Mahāyāna thinkers a view on which happiness and the absence of suffering, as well as virtues and the absence of vices, are elements on an objective list that defines well-being. Keown has rejected this suggestion, but he does not altogether reject the idea that Mahāyāna ethics might involve some form of consequentialism. In his book *The Nature of Buddhist Ethics*, he tentatively puts forward an alternative proposal, one I find extremely strange: that the Mahāyāna accepts exactly one good, namely, love. This suggestion arises from a comparison between the Mahāyāna and a version of Christianity called situation ethics. According to Joseph Fletcher, an advocate of situation ethics, "Only one thing is intrinsically good; namely, love: nothing else at all."[32] Given the immense emphasis given by Mahāyāna writers to the concept of great compassion, this theory is at least worth discussing. But there is a wide range of evidence that seems in tension with this account.

Asaṅga, for example, makes it clear that, on his view, the goals of Mahāyāna practice include bringing about the pleasure of others:

> To undertake and proceed to train oneself in the essence of ethics endowed with these four qualities, should be understood as "wholesome," because of benefit for oneself, benefit for others, benefit for many people, pleasure for many people, mercy for the world, and welfare, benefit, and pleasure for divine and human beings.[33]

In this passage, it seems clear that pleasure is regarded as one of the genuinely valuable consequences of the bodhisattva's efforts.

Scriptural sources from the Mahāyāna tradition indicate that pleasures, including worldly pleasures, do have some value greater than zero. We read in the *Sūtra of Golden Light*, for instance, that if people expound the *Sūtra*, the benefits will include

> that the whole of Jambudvīpa will become plentiful, happy, and full of many people and men, that the beings in the whole of Jambudvīpa will be blessed, will experience various pleasures, that beings during numerous hundreds of thousands of millions of aeons will experience inconceivable, most exalted blessings, will have meetings with the Lord Buddhas, in future time will be fully enlightened in supreme and perfect enlightenment.[34]

This fairly typical text certainly regards happiness and pleasure as goods. In the *Inquiry of Ugra*, we read that "the householder bodhisattva who lives at home exerts himself in order to make all beings happy."[35] The Sūtra *on Upāsaka Precepts* also affirms the moral importance of happiness; but this text regards happiness as twofold: "Good son, just as there are two kinds of happiness: (1) the happiness of this life and (2) world-transcending happiness, so are the blessings. If the bodhisattva possesses these two kinds of happiness and blessings and also teaches them to sentient beings, he is benefiting himself and others."[36] Thus a person can be benefited not just by becoming more loving, but by becoming happier. And passages that discuss removing the suffering of sentient beings are even more common than those advocating bringing about their happiness. If only love is of intrinsic moral importance, it is hard to understand why Mahāyāna texts see pleasure and happiness, and the absence of pain and suffering, as central goals and as being benefits to beings.

A great deal of the ethical discourse of the Mahāyāna is specifically concerned with happiness and the absence of suffering. Thus an interpretation of Mahāyāna ethics as a form of classical utilitarianism would have something to be said for it, and would certainly be much closer to the truth than any interpretation in terms of either situation ethics or Aristotelian virtue ethics. Indeed, I cannot decisively refute this classical utilitarian interpretation. But I think there is some reason to think that, for Mahāyāna Buddhists, pleasure is not the only intrinsic good.

Mahāyāna writers frequently allude to a number of normatively charged characteristics that human beings can have. Happiness and suffering are just some of these characteristics. The most important good qualities a human can have, from the Mahāyāna point of view, seem to be the "roots of good": nongreed (arāga), nonhatred (adveṣa), and nondelusion (amoha). Though negatively stated, these roots of good include such obvious virtues as generosity, compassion, and insight. Buddhist texts from various schools often classify these qualities as kuśala (Pāli kusala). Two interpretations of the value of the roots of good are possible. One account would be that they are merely of instrumental value. The roots of good cause one to make progress toward Nirvana; they also counteract their opposites, the three main afflictions, which are major causes of suffering. So on this account, the roots of good are valuable only insofar as their presence tends to bring about good consequences. But there is another possible interpretation, one which I shall follow: namely, that the roots of good are good in themselves, that they make an intrinsic contribution to the value of lives in which they occur. This is the understanding of the roots of good that leads to character consequentialism.

When we try to decide between these two accounts, what is at stake? The question is whether the virtues are an intrinsic part of a Buddhist conception of the good life or simply happen to be effective means for bringing about the happiness that is the sole component of the value in our lives.[37] Now, as it happens, there is a thought-experiment that can be very helpful in pulling these two views apart. It appears in one of the world's earliest inquiries into the nature of well-being: Plato's *Gorgias*. In the relevant portion of this dialogue, the sophist Callicles defends hedonism, which he and Socrates express in the form of the thesis that "pleasant and good are the same."[38] Socrates raises a series of objections against hedonism, some of them not very impressive. One of his most important objections, though, is a question: "Tell me now first whether a man who has an itch and scratches it and can scratch to his heart's content, scratch his whole life long, can also live happily."[39] Callicles is prepared to say that such a person would be happy, since he acknowledges that this claim follows from hedonism, but he is understandably reluctant to accept this and other related consequences of his view.

How would Mahāyāna Buddhist thinkers evaluate a life devoted to the pleasure of scratching? In view of their beliefs about reincarnation, they would clearly regard such a life as wasted; given the impermanence of all states of existence, it would be better to devote oneself to spiritual practices that bring good consequences in future lives. But this response does not settle whether the life of scratching is intrinsically or merely instrumentally inferior to the religious life that Buddhist texts recommend. My view is that Mahāyānists would regard a virtuous life of spiritual practice as intrinsically better than a life of uninterrupted delicious scratching, even if it was less pleasant. If I am right about this, then character consequentialism is more in accord with the intentions of Buddhist writers than hedonism would be.

Is there any textual evidence for an interpretation of the Mahāyāna that assigns intrinsic value to the virtues? Consider the passage above from the *Sūtra of Golden Light*, which I introduced to suggest that the Mahāyāna tradition attaches some positive value to pleasure. Here, the experience of pleasure is not by any means the only good to be achieved. And some Mahāyāna writers make an explicit distinction between what is pleasant and what is good. Candragomin, for example, says:

> For others, as for oneself
> What is suffering may be beneficial,
> Do beneficial pleasant things
> But not the pleasant, if unbeneficial.[40]

This text should not be interpreted as showing that pleasure has no significance; rather, we should read it as asserting that actions that bring temporary pleasures may be harmful, overall, in the long run. In the Mahāyāna tradition generally, temporary pleasure is seen as being good, but not very important, while religious and spiritual values are assigned great importance. The *Sūtra of Golden Light* emphasizes the value of virtues, specifically, by comparing them with jewels: "The Buddha's virtues are like the ocean, a mine of numerous jewels."[41] This analogy strikes me as some evidence that this text is implicitly committed to the intrinsic value of virtuous qualities.

Some crucial aspects of the idea of character consequentialism as an interpretation of the Buddhist tradition as a whole have occurred to Peter Harvey. While discussing the issue of gender equality in Buddhism, Harvey writes:

> The bottom line, from a Buddhist perspective, is whether a
> particular idea, attitude or practice conduces to an increase or
> decrease—for both men and women—in such qualities as generosity,
> nonattachment, calm, kindness, compassion, clarity of mind, and
> awareness of, and insight into, the nature of mental and physical
> states. The aim, then, is true human welfare.[42]

This is a fairly accurate description of the method of evaluation that would be used by character consequentialists to settle issues in applied ethics—though

Harvey neglects the genuine importance of worldly happiness. But Harvey does not notice that his method of evaluation is a consequentialist one; indeed, earlier in his book, he rejects utilitarianism as an appropriate interpretation of Buddhist ethics. Given this statement, it is not clear how much room Harvey would have to object to my proposed character consequentialist interpretation.

Damien Keown, meanwhile, is explicitly aware that one might try to make an analogy between Buddhist ethics and character consequentialism. But the analogy strikes him as unhelpful, largely because he doubts the coherence of character consequentialism as an ethical theory. Keown's attempt to refute character consequentialism, it turns out, involves an anecdote that can help clarify further the nature of Mahāyāna ethics. He argues as follows:

> certain choices may corrupt moral character yet have beneficial
> consequences for society. For example, an emperor may choose to
> deceive his people in order to promote social harmony. If he succeeds
> in his aim and takes the knowledge of his lies to the grave, will he
> have done right or wrong by the standards of character consequen-
> tialism? If he is considered to have acted rightly, then character is
> always subordinate to social good and has no intrinsic value. If he is
> considered to have acted wrongly, then consequences have no priority
> in moral judgments, and all reference to "consequentialism" can
> simply be dropped.[43]

This example is valuable largely because we know exactly how Mahāyāna Buddhists would respond to it. It closely parallels the story of King Anala from the *Avatamsaka Sūtra*.[44]

In this story, the aspiring bodhisattva Sudhana is advised by one of his teachers to go and visit King Anala and ask him for instruction. But when Sudhana arrives in the city, he discovers that the king is surrounded by frightening, wrathful demons who are constantly engaged in meting out severe punishments to those who violate the city's laws.

Sudhana reacts with horror to this grotesque violation of Buddhist injunctions to be nonviolent and lenient to criminals. But King Anala reveals to him that both the wrathful guardians and their criminal victims are actually illusions created by Anala's magical powers. As a result of the punishments meted out to these wholly illusory malefactors, the real citizens are terrified into acting rightly. King Anala explains his intentions in this way:

> It is by this method that I encourage people not to involve themselves
> in any of the ten nonvirtues, but to demonstrate the path toward the

ten virtues. I make this effort to end the suffering of the people in my country and establish them in the path to the omniscient state.[45]

By Keown's own test, King Anala, and the texts that repeat his story with approval, must be consequentialist. But there is a further interesting lesson in the story. One of the things he is trying to bring about in deceiving his people is *virtue*. He is prepared to tell lies—thereby, perhaps, impairing his own virtue—in order to bring about a much greater total amount of virtue among the populace, including the virtue of not telling lies. Of course, it may not be entirely clear whether the lies he tells do impair his virtue; they may simply be examples of a kind of extraordinary virtue that is not bound by the moral rules of thumb that apply to most people. Yet this idea—that rules such as "Don't tell lies" are merely rules of thumb, which can be broken when breaking them would have good consequences—may itself be an indication of a consequentialist moral perspective. We have some reason, it seems, to interpret King Anala as a (perhaps tacit) character consequentialist.[46]

The story of King Anala is one of many passages in Mahāyāna scriptures in which enlightened beings use deception to help the spiritually undeveloped make progress on the path. Some of the most famous parables from the *Lotus Sūtra* (Skt. *Saddharmapuṇḍarīka- sūtra*), such as the Prodigal Son, the Burning House, and the Phantom City, involve this kind of deception. Mahāyānists had no choice but to develop this theme: they had to explain why the historical Buddha, whom they thought of as perfect and omniscient, had taught doctrines some of which they rejected, along with a spiritual path, the path to Sainthood, which they considered inferior to their own. Early Mahāyāna teachers adopted the view that the Buddha doesn't necessarily tell people the truth; instead, he tells them whatever will be most beneficial for them to hear at the time. This assertion makes it necessary to draw a distinction between scriptural passages of definitive meaning (Skt. *neyārtha*, Tib. *nges don*) and those of provisional meaning (Skt. *nītārtha*, Tib. *drang don*). Passages that are of provisional meaning are not authoritative, and may even be literally false. They are meant to help a particular interlocutor at a particular time.

This hermeneutical distinction can sometimes take on great importance in philosophical debates among Buddhists. Here, its main significance is that it implies an important divergence between Kantian ethics and Mahāyāna ethics. On a very general level, the willingness of Mahāyānists to make exceptions to moral rules when the stakes are high is obviously in tension with Kant's approach. But it seems to me that the Mahāyānist view about the usefulness of lying to people in order to benefit them would strike Kant as particularly objectionable. He would see this view as evidence of a failure to give proper respect to the dignity of people's rational nature. We can see it as evidence of the distance between the Kantian view and Mahāyāna Buddhist ethics.

I will now discuss one final theoretical argument that could further clarify how Mahāyāna Buddhists understood well-being. First, note that character consequentialism and hedonism have something important in common. Both views of well-being imply that the only intrinsically valuable properties are mental states. Though many Western philosophers have defended this claim, others have questioned it. One well-known case that calls this claim into question is Nozick's example of the Experience Machine. Suppose that a person with a perfectly ordinary, fairly good life is offered the chance to abandon that life and plug himself into the experience machine, a virtual reality environment that uses powerful computers to create the completely convincing illusion of a life of high adventure, great achievement, and intoxicating pleasure. After entering the experience machine, the person will immediately forget his earlier life and will never see through the illusion. Would this person's life go better for him if he chose the experience machine over the real world?

When confronted with this case, many people say that life outside the machine is better, because there one's achievements are real, not imaginary. They would hold that a life that is lived in relation to a real external world is better than a qualitatively identical life that is based on an illusion. They would seem, then, to be taking issue with the claim that only mental states have intrinsic value. What would Mahāyāna Buddhists say about this case?

It appears that they can take at least part of the common intuition on board by noticing that virtually all of the beliefs of the person in the experience machine are false. Though only mental states are valuable, one of the things that can make a belief valuable is the property of being true. Insofar as the people living outside the machine have more true beliefs, their lives go better for them.

Perhaps surprisingly, though, many Mahāyāna Buddhists cannot rest content with this answer. According to the idealist philosophers of the Spiritual Practice School (Yogācāra), ordinary physical objects are just as unreal as the illusions created by the experience machine. To them, being the architect of a physical skyscraper is metaphysically no different from being deceived by the experience machine into thinking that you are; therefore, this difference cannot change your level of well-being. These thinkers are forced to adopt the thesis that only mental states matter, because for them, mental states are the only really existent entities.[47] This conclusion would be relevant, for instance, in interpreting the ethical thought of Asaṅga, who was one of the founders of the Spiritual Practice School.

On the other hand, members of the Middle Way School (Madhyamaka) do not share this idealist metaphysics; for them, mental states are unreal in the same sense and to the same extent as material things. I will discuss the difficult question of the ethical implications of the Middle Way School's teachings in chapter 6. However, we should note the agreement of Indian sources on the claim that the Middle Way School and the Spiritual Practice School hold identical views about ethics. If the Spiritual Practice School necessarily holds that only mental states have intrinsic value, then we may have some reason to attribute the same view to the Middle Way School. Given the textual evidence and theoretical arguments we have considered, I conclude that character consequentialism fits well with the general philosophical outlook of Mahāyāna Buddhism.

5

Śāntideva and After

The System of Śāntideva

It has become a commonplace among scholars that the Buddhist tradition did not produce any systematic ethical theory.[1] There is some truth to this assertion; the Theravāda tradition and such Mahāyāna texts as the "Chapter on Ethics" do not present reasoning about the nature of morality or the rationale for particular ethical norms that rises to the level of generality found in numerous ancient and modern Western treatments of the subject. Of all the productions of the Indian Buddhist tradition, the texts that come closest to a worked-out ethical theory are the two works of Śāntideva: the *Bodhicaryāvatāra*, or *Introduction to the Bodhisattva's Way of Life*, and the *Śikṣā-samuccaya*, or *Compendium of the Trainings*.[2] In many cases, Śāntideva draws on earlier scriptural sources; but in synthesizing them, he creates a system of substantially greater theoretical coherence. The sophistication, generality, and power of Śāntideva's arguments give him a legitimate claim to be the greatest of all Buddhist ethicists.

The heart of Śāntideva's ethical perspective is expressed in this passage from the *Compendium*:

> Through actions of body, speech, and mind, the Bodhisattva sincerely makes a continuous effort to stop all present and future suffering and depression, and to produce present and future happiness and gladness, for all beings. But if he does-not seek the collection of the conditions for this, and does

not strive for what will prevent the obstacles to this, or he does not
cause small suffering and depression to arise as a way of preventing
great suffering and depression, or does not abandon a small benefit
in order to achieve a greater benefit, if he neglects to do these things
even for a moment, he is at fault.[3]

Not one of the major characteristics of classical act-utilitarianism is missing
from this passage. The focus on actions; the central moral importance of happy
and unhappy states of mind; the extension of scope to all beings; the extreme
demands; the absence of any room for personal moral space; the balancing of
costs and benefits; the pursuit of maximization: every one of these crucial features of utilitarianism is present. Notice also that the passage does not say anything about who receives the benefits or burdens that we are to balance against
each other. If we go by this passage alone, we will conclude that Śāntideva is
prepared to allow what Asaṅga will not: the balancing of the interests of some
against the interests of others. But this passage is not all we have to go on; nor
does it exhaust the available evidence for an act-consequentialist reading of
Śāntideva's ethical philosophy.

Śāntideva offers us not only a statement of consequentialism, but a powerful rhetorical exploration of its demanding nobility. Chapter 3 of the *Introduction* is full of poetic expressions of radical altruism and total, self-sacrificing
compassion:

> 8. May I avert the pain of hunger and thirst with showers of food
>   and drink. May I become both drink and food in the intermediate
>   aeons of famine.
> 9. May I be an inexhaustible treasure for impoverished beings. May I
>   wait upon them with various forms of offering.
> 10. See, I give up without regret my bodies, my pleasures, and my good
>   acquired in all three times, to accomplish good for every being.[4]

Clearly, Śāntideva is much more similar to certain act-consequentialist writers
such as Peter Singer, who insist on the supreme moral significance of altruistic
self-sacrifice, than to the advocates of virtue ethics and other versions of consequentialism who want to allow the individual some moral space to act in ways
not dictated by universalist moral considerations. And Śāntideva expects us not
only to be ready to make spectacular self-sacrifices on specific occasions; we
should try to develop our minds to a point at which we can make the welfare of
all beings our full-time occupation, renouncing all frivolous pastimes: "One
should do nothing other than what is either directly or indirectly of benefit to
living beings, and for the benefit of living beings alone one should dedicate

everything to Awakening" (5.101).[5] The ethics of the *Introduction*, like some forms of consequentialism, is extremely demanding—at least in what it says to those who have reached a sufficiently high level of spiritual development.

At this point, it would be fair to raise an issue parallel to one considered in the previous chapter: whether the impressively selfless actions Śāntideva recommends to advanced practitioners should be classified as true self-sacrifices. Once again, we can address this issue through the lens of the dedication of merit; and Śāntideva's discussion of this key practice is much more informative than the brief remarks in the *Precepts Sūtra*. All of the *Introduction*'s chapter 10 is devoted to this topic, and references to it are scattered through the entire text.

There are a few passages in the *Introduction* where the dedication of merit does seem to involve changing its fruition from worldly pleasure or high status into the requisites for progress toward Buddhahood. For example, when Śāntideva says in the passage just quoted (5.101) that "one should dedicate everything to Awakening," Nattier's explanation certainly seems to capture his meaning.

Yet there are other passages in the *Introduction* involving the dedication of merit that clearly cannot be interpreted as involving the understanding of this term that Nattier finds in the *Inquiry of Ugra*. The following verses are found in chapter 10:

> 10.2. Through my merit may all those in any of the directions suffering
> distress in body or mind find oceans of happiness and delight.
> 10.31. By this merit of mine may all beings without exception desist
> from every evil deed and always act skillfully.[6]

Here Śāntideva certainly seems to be wishing that his own merit will be transferred to others, benefiting them. Verse 3.6 also seems to be most naturally interpreted as involving a transfer: "With the good acquired by doing all this as described, may I allay all the suffering of every living being."[7] Could Śāntideva possibly mean that this merit will allow him to become a Buddha, and that once he is a Buddha, he himself will allay this suffering? This does not seem like the most natural interpretation of the passages just quoted; moreover, it does not seem like a possible interpretation of the following: "May they constantly meet with Buddhas and the Buddhas' kin. May they worship the Teacher of the Universe with unending clouds of worship (10.38)."[8] This passage occurs in a context in which Śāntideva is listing the beneficial consequences that he hopes will flow from his dedication of merit. Here the author himself as a future Buddha is evidently not the one conferring benefits; the recipients of his merit will meet with other Buddhas and bodhisattvas, listen to their teachings, and acquire further merit by worshipping them.

Chapter 10 reaches its climax with a verse like a sledgehammer: "Whatever suffering is in store for the world, may it all ripen in me. May the world find happiness through the pure deeds of the Bodhisattvas (10.56)."[9] I do not think the prospects of a eudaimonist interpretation of this verse are very good. Nor can it be read in terms of the dedication of merit as a change in the nature of the fruition from that merit.

At some point after the composition of the *Inquiry of Ugra*, the meaning of *puṇya-pariṇāmanā* changed from a transformation of merit into a transfer of merit. Archaeological evidence strongly suggests that this change had taken hold by the fourth century CE. It was certainly fully in place at the time of the composition of the *Introduction*. This change fits into the general pattern I have been suggesting: a gradual evolution of the Indian Mahāyāna tradition toward act-consequentialism, as the ethical implications of the bodhisattva ideal slowly unfolded.

What Śāntideva offers us, I would argue, is not merely a version of consequentialism, but a well-thought-out and philosophically quite interesting version. One striking measure of the level of his reasoning is the degree to which he anticipates a key development in recent Western ethical theory. As I showed in chapter 2, Derek Parfit has argued that his reductionist views about personal identity can be used to support a consequentialist view of ethics. Though Parfit was unaware of this when he wrote *Reasons and Persons*, Śāntideva had made analogous philosophical moves more than a thousand years earlier. It is now quite well known that in the *Introduction*, Śāntideva offers a justification of his ethical views that appeals to the Ābhidhārmika form of the Buddhist doctrine of no-self.[10] According to this doctrine, which I summarized in chapter 1, what we take to be the fundamental, and fundamentally significant, distinction between ourselves and the rest of the universe is, in fact, an illusion. In reality, there are no such things as souls, selves, or even human bodies. Reality is a vast and complex process, consisting of innumerable tiny, momentary entities called *dharmas*, which a contemporary analytic philosopher would classify as tropes.[11] The process of singling out some of these tropes as constituting "me" and "mine" is profoundly deluded. It leads to attachment, egoism, pride, greed and hatred, and finally to suffering.

Once we recognize the nonexistence of the self, however, egoism, along with all forms of practical reasoning that depend on a distinction between self and other, are exposed as irrational:

> 8.97. If I give them no protection because their suffering does not afflict me, why do I protect my body against future suffering when it does not afflict me?

8.99. If you think it is for the person who has the pain to guard against
it, a pain in the foot is not of the hand, so why is the one protected
by the other?

8.102. Without exception, no sufferings belong to anyone. They must
be warded off simply because they are suffering. Why is any
limitation put on this?[12]

In these verses, Śāntideva rejects the identity of people over time, the unity of a
person at a time, and the real existence of a person who could be the owner of
mental states. These arguments are strikingly similar to those offered by Parfit.
Like Parfit, Śāntideva starts with a denial of people's ordinary views about personal identity, and attempts to use that denial to defend an ethics of self-sacrifice
for the good of all sentient beings.

This form of argument, which we might call Śāntideva's strategy, gives this
part of the *Introduction* more than merely historical interest. If we accept the
doctrine of no self, it will be very difficult to resist the claim that the only ethical
theory that could possibly be viable is some form of universalist consequentialism. What makes that fact important is that there are numerous powerful arguments in favor of the doctrine of no self. Once we understand these arguments,
it becomes increasingly clear that there is a deep incoherence in our ordinary
way of looking at things. Our ordinary, intuitive belief that we exist as unitary
substances is not rationally credible.

One argument in support of the doctrine of no self goes as follows. All
composite things exhibit vagueness. Vagueness is a mark of conceptual construction. Therefore, all composite things are conceptually constructed.[13]

The first premise is surely true if it is being applied to the medium-sized
objects of our everyday life. Plants and animals, artifacts and natural objects, all
have vague spatial boundaries; once we look at them on the atomic level, they
are clouds of tiny particles, which constantly exchange matter with the environment in such a way that there is often no fact of the matter about whether a particular particle is part of them or not. Moreover, they begin, and often end, in
vague, gradual ways. The fact that the existence of a human being is vague is a
major source of controversies about abortion and assisted suicide. There is no
defensible way to resist the claim that our existence, and the existence of almost
all the things we normally believe in and talk about, is ineliminably vague. But
why should we believe that this vagueness entails that these things, and we
ourselves, are conceptually constructed? Why can't we just learn to live with
vagueness, while retaining a realist attitude toward composite things?

The trouble is that vagueness is not easy to live with: it keeps throwing tem-
per tantrums and breaking the dishes. Almost by definition, vagueness creates

the Sorites Paradox, a problem Western philosophers have been worrying about since classical antiquity. For example, suppose we assume that the distinctively human life doesn't start at conception. We may think that a single cell, like the fertilized egg, could not possibly have the level of complexity to be a human being. Even a sixteen-celled blastocyst does not seem like the kind of thing that could be a human being; biologically, it seems to be more on the level of pond scum. Suppose, then, we accept that the blastocyst is not a human being. Do we think that a thing that is not a human being could, by growing just one more cell, become a human being? Surely not; the addition of a single cell could not make such a huge and important difference. But then, if we added two cells, one after another, neither of them could make the crucial difference, since each of them is one; and the same goes for three cells. It follows that you and I are not human beings, since each of us grew from a blastocyst by a process of gradual addition of new cells. The things people believe about their own existence are not consistent.

Recently, vagueness has been causing more refined and even more difficult kinds of trouble. Parfit has shown that the vagueness inherent in people's conceptions of personal identity leads to the conclusion that, in some imaginable cases, there will be no fact of the matter about whether a particular person has or has not survived.[14] Consider the powerful example known as the Combined Spectrum. Suppose doctors suddenly replaced 1 percent of your body mass with new matter, in such a way as to make you look just slightly more like Marilyn Monroe, and simultaneously replaced 1 percent of your memories, beliefs, and desires with others that were like those of Marilyn Monroe. Surely you would survive. Suppose the doctors shot you, buried your body, and then made an exact replica of Marilyn Monroe. Surely you would be dead. In between these two cases are a continuous range of examples in which x percent of your body mass and mental states are suddenly replaced, making you more like Marilyn Monroe. If 52 percent were replaced, would you survive? How about 48 percent? Could a tiny difference, say 1 percent or 0.1 percent, possibly make the difference between whether you survive or not? People's ordinary way of thinking about their own existence does not allow for cases in which there is no fact of the matter about whether one has survived a certain procedure. The Combined Spectrum shows that this ordinary way of thinking is wrong.

Moreover, the vagueness of the boundaries of ordinary objects leads to a particularly puzzling metaphysical problem that Peter Unger calls "the Problem of the Many"[15] and that is also known as the Paradox of 1,001 Cats.[16] For any particular medium-sized composite thing, we can construct an astronomically large number of slightly different ways to draw its boundaries. It turns out to be difficult to resist the conclusion that each of these sets of boundaries defines a different object, and therefore that if you think you have one cat in your house, you really have 1,001—or perhaps even $2^{1,001}$.

Meanwhile, there's Gareth Evans's argument against vague objects to consider. Suppose it is indeterminate whether A = B. But it is determinate that A = A. So then A has a property, that of being determinately identical to A, that B lacks. So it is determinate that A ≠ B, contrary to the hypothesis.

In my view, there has been no satisfactory realist solution to the problems associated with vagueness—though there is certainly no shortage of attempts.[17] In the absence of such a solution, Buddhists can use vagueness as a powerful weapon against any kind of common-sense realist position. Some philosophers would refuse to accept Parfit's arguments for his reductionist view of people, on the grounds that all composite objects seem to exhibit vagueness. Unlike less ambitious reductionists, Buddhists would conclude that all composite objects are conceptually constructed. They do not exist in the world as it is in itself, independently of how we perceive it; but they do exist in the context of our everyday dealings with the world as we construct it, and can therefore be said to exist conventionally.

Even if some progress could be made on vagueness, there is another class of problems that result directly from issues about composition, time, and change. Thus we have the Ship of Theseus, and similar problems in which what seem to us to be sufficient conditions for the continued identity of a thing produce two equally good candidates to be identical with a single object in the past.[18] Parfit has shown us that humans are not exempt from such problems: if you identify with your body, you must face My Division;[19] whereas if you think you are your mind, you need to deal with the disturbing Branch-Line case.[20] In each of these cases, once we make heroic assumptions about future technology, we can show that a single human can divide into two, each with a good claim to be identical with the original.

And we shouldn't forget an ancient, simple, but still puzzling Buddhist argument. Suppose we believe that a whole and its parts are both really existent entities. Is the whole identical with its parts, or distinct from them? If we said that the whole was a distinct entity, we would be unable to describe what it was like, independently of its parts; we certainly wouldn't be able to see the isolated whole or interact with it causally, since it inherits all causal powers from its parts. But how can we say that the whole is identical with its parts, given that the whole and its parts have incompatible properties? For example, it is one, and they are many.

All of the arguments I have just canvassed could be resisted by someone who believes that she is her soul, an immaterial, spiritual substance, distinct from body and mental states, the owner of body and mental states, the agent of actions and the experiencer of happiness and suffering. But, of course, we have no evidence whatever that such an entity exists. Moreover, such an entity, in order to be the agent of actions, would have to be able to cause its body to move—which would require it constantly to violate the laws of physics, bringing about a vast number of tiny miracles. And if people think with their souls, it will be very difficult to explain a wide variety of evidence that people actually think with their brains. In particular, if the soul is what thinks, why do physical causes such as drugs, alcohol, Alzheimer's disease, and brain injuries have such a profound effect on people's thoughts and emotions? We can't say that these physical causes simply interfere with the soul's ability to control the body, since they also affect how things seem to people, and in ways inconsistent with the hypothesis that they merely interfere with the connecting links between a thinking thing and the rest of the body.

Taken together, these arguments, and others like them, seem to me to make up a powerful case against the supposition that there are really, ultimately existing selves in the world, whose existence is independent of the constructive activity of consciousness. Some readers may be less impressed, and may prefer to hold on to common sense in the hope that the problems and paradoxes may one day be resolved. This chapter is not the place for me to engage with the possible responses that might be offered to each of the arguments I have mentioned. My only intention is to show that the Buddhist doctrine of no self, however implausible it may initially seem, is not only a credible philosophical view, but can actually be supported by a wide variety of considerations. The ultimate nonexistence of people, sentient beings, and selves is a philosophical position that deserves to be taken seriously.

Damien Keown has written: "The discipline of ethics requires only that one individual can be distinguished from another: to pursue the issue of the ultimate ontological constitution of individual natures in this context is to confuse ethics with metaphysics, and does not make for a fruitful line of enquiry."[21] It is clear from chapter 8 of the Introduction that Śāntideva would disagree with this assessment. The doctrine of no self is at the heart of Mahāyāna ethics; it has far-reaching and dramatic normative implications. In particular, it implies that it does not matter who experiences benefits and burdens, since there are not ultimately any experiencers. This implication, in turn, leads to the claim that we can ignore the distributive effects of our actions and simply maximize the good. We can, in particular, morally endorse actions that produce a small total harm to one group of people and a larger total benefit to another group, balancing the burdens and benefits and choosing the actions that produce the greatest total of benefits minus burdens.

I showed in the previous chapter that Asaṅga does not offer any explicit or well-developed discussion of whether, and in what cases, the interests of different sentient beings may be balanced against, or sacrificed for, the welfare of others. In the writings of Śāntideva, we can find a number of passages that address issues related to balancing. Discussing whether and when to sacrifice one's body for others, Śāntideva writes:

> 5.86. The body serves the True Dharma. One should not harm it for some inferior reason. For it is the only way that one can quickly fulfil the hopes of living beings.
> 5.87. Therefore one should not relinquish one's life for someone whose disposition to compassion is not as pure. But for someone whose disposition is comparable, one should relinquish it. That way, there is no overall loss.[22]

This is an example of balancing between self and other, not between two others. Since I have shown that Mahāyāna texts sometimes treat the difference between the agent and others as morally relevant, this passage does not conclusively show that Śāntideva would countenance harming some innocent persons to benefit a larger number of others. But it seems that he is committed to allowing such an action by his strategy for justifying his ethical views. Śāntideva explicitly says that in the case of my own suffering I am rationally required to accept a lesser amount in order to prevent a greater.[23] Once we bring to bear on ethics the teaching that there are no metaphysically important differences between different sentient beings, it cannot ultimately matter whether harms are compensated by benefits to the same beings or to others; nor can it ultimately matter who it is that carries out a harmful action. This strategy inevitably leads to an ethical view that allows balancing.

It is not fully clear whether Śāntideva himself has thought through all the implications of this point. There are several passages scattered through his writings that make important moves in this direction. In the *Compendium*, Śāntideva quotes this fascinating scriptural passage:

> Moreover, he does not place his own burden on one who is unfit from fear of the loss of the interests of all beings. But where he sees no loss in the interests of all beings, what difference is there whether that which is good for the world be done by himself or another?[24]

This passage relates to beneficial, not harmful, actions. But it is hard to see how the same reasoning would not apply to actions whose immediate effect is to cause harm. And the principle that it does not ultimately matter who performs any action, beneficial or harmful, is a powerful form of agent-neutrality, capable of generating many of the most problematic cases that have been raised as objections against utilitarianism. For example, an agent following this principle would have to kill one innocent person if that was the only way to prevent another agent from killing twenty innocent people.[25]

In fact, Śāntideva seems to adopt a more wholeheartedly, or at least more explicitly, consequentialist ethical position than Asaṅga does. Such a position would clearly be entailed by a literal reading of *Introduction* 5.84: "Even what is proscribed is permitted for a compassionate person who sees it will be of benefit." We should be careful to note that Mahāyāna ethicists, including Śāntideva, do not extend the permission to break moral rules to just anyone. In this passage, Śāntideva requires that the person carrying out the proscribed action must be "compassionate"; moreover, she must actually see—not just theorize—that the action will be beneficial. Ordinary people, who neither understand the way things really are nor have the proper kind of motivation, are seen in this system in much the way everyone regards children and insane persons: they must strictly follow rules of conduct that have been designed for their benefit. Those with greater compassion and insight, though, may ignore these rules when doing so would be of benefit.

A universal permission to disregard moral rules when doing so would be beneficial, such as we seem to find in *Introduction* 5.84, directly implies act-consequentialism. In any given case, any rule we try to apply will either endorse the action that produces the best consequences—in which case following the rule coincides with act-consequentialism—or will endorse some other action, in which case the verse allows us to break the rule and do what act-consequentialism tells us to do. Thus, Śāntideva's view must coincide with act-consequentialism, at least as it applies to those who are truly compassionate. I will explore further what Buddhist ethics has to say about the moral status of very advanced practitioners, and the way ethical principles apply differently to people at different levels of spiritual development, in chapters 6, 7, and 11.

The flexibility that is endorsed at the level of theory in *Introduction* 5.84 is reflected in the discussion of at least two sets of practical ethical issues in the *Compendium.* First, Śāntideva has a broader conception than Asaṅga expresses of the circumstances under which a bodhisattva can make use of the property of others. He writes:

> If recognizing it for another's property, he consumes it for his
> own sake, he is guilty of the sin of theft. At the full penalty, in the
> Prātimokṣa he is liable to expulsion. But if he thinks that the body is

the servant of all creatures, and it is protected by using that which belongs to all creatures, there is no fault. For a servant always busy about his master's business does not always own that which he is busy with. . . . And when a servant is wholly devoted to his master's interest, and he is distressed with disease or the like, there is no fault if he eat even without asking his master's leave.[26]

This ingenious argument seems to be offered by Śāntideva as a way of showing that if a bodhisattva is genuinely motivated by compassion, he or she may ignore property rights, the topic of the Second Precept of Buddhism, whenever they interfere with working for the benefit of all beings. Śāntideva is also prepared to allow the Third Precept, which forbids sexual misconduct, to be overridden by the more fundamental significance of the welfare of all beings:

Also in the world, when a mother and father see their son being impaled on a stake, attachment to enjoyment is not observed in them, due to the power of innate compassion; at such a time, there would be no secret sexual misconduct with [any girl], married or unmarried, whether protected by her family, the Teachings, or the flag. [But] where there is benefit to beings [in such conduct,] and no harm to beings, having ascertained the consequences, there is no problem.[27]

The idea of this passage seems to be the following. A father whose son is being gruesomely executed would be so shocked and dismayed by the situation that he would not even think about engaging in sex, either legitimately with his wife or illegitimately with any other woman. Since bodhisattvas regard all beings as their own family members, their awareness of the terrifying sufferings of cyclic existence should drive all thought of attachment to lustful pleasures from their minds. But under exceptional circumstances, when for some reason engaging in socially forbidden sex would have good consequences and would not lead to any harm, compassion itself requires them to ignore the Third Precept.[28] Asaṅga might agree; he is simply not fully explicit on the range of cases in which a bodhisattva can break this precept, giving us only a single example in which such a violation would be permissible.[29]

This evidence is certainly suggestive, but it may not be enough to allow us to say unequivocally that Śāntideva is an act-consequentialist. If we interpret him in this way, we will have to account for passages such as 3.14: "Let there never be harm to anyone on account of me."[30] An act-consequentialist may sometimes have to inflict harms on some in order to prevent greater harms to others. Perhaps Śāntideva is expressing a wish or hope that he never be placed in such a situation. Alternatively, he is aspiring to attain a degree of moral skill so great that he can find actions that benefit all those involved in any situation, without having to harm anyone.

It appears we have some reason to regard Śāntideva as holding a somewhat different ethical position from Asaṅga, and one that is substantially closer to modern act-consequentialism. What theory of well-being does he hold? The verses I have quoted clearly tell us that the system of Śāntideva is no closer to situation ethics than is that of Asaṅga. Śāntideva's wish in chapter 3 of the *Introduction* to "avert the pain of hunger and thirst with showers of food and drink" is obviously an expression of compassionate love. But if that love is itself the only good, it would be fair to ask what the point of this generosity is. After all, according to situation ethics, being free from the pain of hunger and thirst is not genuinely a good. Why should one provide people with food and drink if doing so will not benefit them in any way? One might argue that food and drink would keep people alive so that they can develop love, but that doesn't seem to be what Śāntideva has in mind. He is trying to make beings happy. Thus, in the praise of the Awakening Mind that closes chapter 3, he writes:

32. For the caravan of humanity traveling the road of existence, hungry for the enjoyment of happiness, this is a feast of happiness offered as refreshment to all beings who approach.
33. Today I summon the world to Buddhahood and to worldly happiness meanwhile. In the presence of all the Saviours, may gods, titans, and all rejoice.[31]

Since it is generally recognized that it is difficult to regard happiness as an instrumental good, we should interpret Śāntideva as holding that it is an intrinsic good. Meanwhile, the verses from chapter 8 that appeal to the absence of any self also tell us that Śāntideva is explicitly interested in alleviating the suffering of all beings. This conclusion is clearly stated in the quotation from the *Compendium* I considered at the beginning of this chapter. There seems little room for doubt that Śāntideva, like other Mahāyāna Buddhists, regards happiness as good in itself, and suffering as bad.

Yet we might wonder whether these claims about his theory of well-being can be squared with what he says about Nirvana. It is a fascinating and disturbing feature of the bodhisattva ideal, as expressed by Śāntideva, that the goal of a bodhisattva is to bring about the end of the world. In a famous passage, which I quoted in chapter 1, Śāntideva expresses this aspiration:

10.55. "As long as space abides, and as long as the world abides, / So long shall I abide, destroying the sufferings of the world."[32]

The word for "world" in the Sanskrit is *jagat*, which refers to all sentient beings—literally, all moving things. In this passage, then, Śāntideva vows to remain in existence until space, and all sentient beings, cease to exist. He vows to lead all beings out of the trap of cyclic existence, and thereby eliminate cyclic existence itself. Now, one might wonder whether Śāntideva expects ever to succeed at this; perhaps his task will last forever. But at 3.21 he writes: "So may I be sustenance of many kinds for the realm of beings dwelling throughout space, until all have attained release."[33] It certainly sounds as if Śāntideva expects all beings to be freed eventually; and when that happens, the universe itself will be, as it were, no longer required. Through their actions, Śāntideva writes, beings themselves create the guardians of hell and the horrifying tortures there;[34] it seems to follow that if they ceased to perform such actions, hell, along with the other realms of the universe we know, would simply fade away. Once the last karmic hindrances had been eliminated, a world full of bodhisattvas would pass into Nirvana, beyond the reach of concepts of being.[35]

This kind of aspiration, though strange and somehow frightening, is not completely unintelligible in a Western context—it seems to have affinities to negative utilitarianism: the view that the sole moral priority is the eradication of suffering, which has negative value, and that nothing, either happiness or anything else, has any positive value. Negative utilitarianism shares with Buddhism a strong focus on alleviating the suffering of beings, so that Keown considers, though he ultimately rejects, an interpretation of Buddhist ethics in its terms. Negative utilitarianism can have a certain appeal; it sometimes does seem as if helping others to overcome their suffering is much more morally urgent than promoting their happiness. Nevertheless, many have regarded it as completely unworkable, above all because of a single objection. If a negative utilitarian had access to an enormously destructive weapon, a null-bomb capable of permanently annihilating all sentient life in the universe, she would jump at the chance to use it. Even if the death of all sentient beings would be very painful, still, it would be immediately followed by a state with zero suffering, the best state the universe could possibly be in. Since few people would be prepared to endorse the use of a null-bomb, negative utilitarianism has had few defenders.

It appears, though, that Śāntideva might agree with a negative utilitarian on goals, even if he would disagree about means. For Śāntideva, the null-bomb would not work, because the karma created by using it would immediately bring about an existence of suffering for the user, and because the unexhausted karma of the slain beings would, sooner or later, create another physical universe in which they could experience the results of that karma. But the goal of bringing an end to the universe seems to be shared between the two perspectives.

Does this key similarity show that bodhisattva ethics should be understood as a version of negative utilitarianism, and not, as I have claimed, a version of consequentialism with a complex objective list theory of the good? Probably not, or at least, not necessarily. The feature of negative utilitarianism that leads to the null-bomb is that according to negative utilitarianism, the universe is, on the whole, bad. Of course, for negative utilitarianism, everything is either bad or morally neutral, since it recognizes no goods. But even a theory that regards some things as good could still judge the universe to be bad, if the evils it contains outweigh the goods.

Even a cursory reading of Śāntideva's text makes it clear that he regards the universe, at least as it exists now, as bad. True, it contains the bliss of the heavenly worlds, but only a small number of beings at a time actually get to enjoy this bliss. Even the heavens contain very subtle forms of suffering; moreover, the gods who live in them must eventually die, and they suffer greatly when this happens. The vast majority of beings, meanwhile, exist in various realms dominated by suffering, some of which Śāntideva describes in absolutely horrifying terms. The tremendous risk of committing some wrong action that will plunge one into hell makes life as a human a tremendously dangerous affair. In the famous simile, seeking sensual pleasures in a universe of this kind is like licking honey off a razor blade. We should not be surprised, then, that even a consequentialist whose theory includes some goods would, if faced with such a monstrous universe, try to bring it to a halt.

The fact that Śāntideva wants to stop the world, then, is not evidence that his view should be interpreted as a kind of negative utilitarianism. But it is evidence that his view is some sort of consequentialism. Most Western virtue ethicists do not advocate bringing about the end of the world, and there is no obvious feature of their views that would lead them to advocate this, even if they accepted Buddhist descriptive premises. Śāntideva's view may seem quite alien and unappealing to modern American readers. But whether one finds it acceptable or not, it is a further piece of evidence for the consequentialist interpretation of Mahāyāna Buddhist ethics.

Given that Śāntideva is a consequentialist, is he a classical utilitarian, or does he hold the same theory of well-being I have attributed to Asaṅga and to the Theravāda tradition? It cannot be denied that Śāntideva frequently sounds like a classical utilitarian, as in the passage quoted at the beginning of this chapter. On the other hand, he does frequently emphasize the importance of virtue, often in extravagant terms: "If a virtue appears anywhere which is even an atom of those who are a unique mass of the very essence of virtue, then even the three worlds are not adequate for the purpose of worshipping

it" (6.117).[36] Yet there are indications in various places in Śāntideva that he sees
the promotion of virtue and the eradication of the afflictions as means to attain happiness without suffering. He explicitly says at 5.77: "Surely everything
is undertaken for the sake of satisfaction."[37] Repeatedly in the *Introduction* he
describes the suffering caused by the afflictions and the happiness produced
by the virtues.[38] Against this evidence, we may set the theoretical arguments I
canvassed in chapter 4, which presumably have as much force with respect to
Śāntideva's system as Asaṅga's.

Would it make sense, instead, to understand Śāntideva as accepting the
view, a view I rejected as an interpretation of Theravāda ethics, that Nirvana
is the good?[39] To evaluate this claim, we should keep in mind that Śāntideva's
views about the afterlife destiny of Buddhas are quite different from those
found in the Theravāda tradition. For Śāntideva, as for all other thinkers in the
mature Mahāyāna tradition, the life in which someone attains Buddhahood is
not that person's last life. From then on until the end of cyclic existence, this
individual will continue to manifest in various realms with the intention of
helping all other beings make spiritual progress. And we can describe Buddhas
as being both in cyclic existence and in Nirvana at the same time. Moreover, the
path that leads up to the attainment of Buddhahood and the state that results
from that attainment are filled with pleasure and happiness:

> 7.28. The body experiences pleasure as a result of acts of merit. The
>   mind is pleased through learning. When he remains in cyclic
>   existence for the benefit of others what can weary the
>   Compassionate One?
> 7.30. Proceeding in this way from happiness to happiness, what thinking
>   person would despair, after mounting the carriage, the Awakening
>   Mind, which carries away all weariness and effort?[40]

Here, the question we want to ask is this: is it the happiness resulting from
Buddhahood that is valuable, or is it Nirvana itself that has supreme intrinsic
value? Fortunately, Śāntideva gives us a fairly explicit answer to this question:
"Those who become oceans of sympathetic joy when living beings are released,
surely it is they who achieve fulfillment. What would be the point in a liberation
without sweetness?" (8.108).[41] It should be quite clear that it would be a mistake to say that for Śāntideva, Nirvana is the good. We may defensibly interpret
Śāntideva as either a classical utilitarian or a character consequentialist. But
in light of the evidence I have presented, that he is a consequentialist of some
kind seems difficult to deny.

Tibetan Path Literature

Some of the most important texts in the Tibetan Buddhist tradition are those
that describe the stages a spiritual practitioner must undergo on the way to
enlightenment. In the Geluk (dGe lugs) sect, the most revered such work is the
Great Treatise on the Stages of the Path to Enlightenment (Lam rim chen mo) of
Tsong kha pa. The Kagyu (bKa' rgyud) tradition relies for its presentation of the
path on the *Jewel Ornament of Liberation*, by sGam po pa; and in the Nyingma
(rNying ma) sect, the *Words of my Perfect Teacher*[42] (*Kun bzang bla ma'i zhal
lung*) plays a somewhat similar role. These texts consist largely of detailed explanations of how to practice the path, along with eloquent presentations of the
necessity and benefits of doing so. They therefore contain much information
about the ethical views endorsed by the different forms of the Tibetan tradition.
In what follows, I will briefly note a few passages from these texts that are particularly illuminating with respect to the issues I have been considering.

Since all sects of Tibetan Buddhism are forms of the Vajrayāna, and do
engage in Tantric practices, one might think that the texts I consider here
might more appropriately be considered in my discussion of Tantric ethics in
chapter 6. But the *Great Treatise* of Tsong kha pa, for example, is considered
by the Tibetans to be a text belonging to the Sūtra Vehicle or the Perfection
Vehicle—that is, the non-Tantric form of the Mahāyāna. *Words of My Perfect
Teacher*, on the other hand, does describe certain Tantric practices. But there is
a considerable amount of material in this text that in no way depends on distinctively Tantric doctrines. I shall therefore examine both of these texts in the
context of non-Tantric Mahāyāna.

The *Great Treatise on the Stages of the Path to Enlightenment*, in particular,
contains some interesting evidence in favor of the conception of well-being
that I attribute to the Mahāyāna. Tsong kha pa offers a summary presentation
of the kinds of gifts a generous bodhisattva should give. This discussion seems
to appeal to a conception of well-being—in this case, of what it is to benefit
someone—that has the structure I have identified as underlying character consequentialism. Tsong kha pa writes:

> In brief, bodhisattvas should give to others those things which
> immediately produce in the recipients pleasurable feelings that are
> free from the causes for a miserable rebirth and which ultimately will
> benefit them, either eliminating their sin or setting them in virtue.
> Even if these things do not immediately bring happiness, they should
> give them if they are beneficial in the end.[43]

This passage accords positive value to providing worldly "pleasurable feelings." But another, and perhaps more important aspect of benefiting other beings, in this passage, is helping them develop virtue and avoid vice.[44]

Another passage in the same work offers perhaps the best evidence I have yet been able to find in favor of the theory of well-being I wish to attribute to Mahāyāna Buddhists. Tsong kha pa writes:

> Besides this desire to attain buddhahood that comes from cultivating
> faith in a buddha's good qualities, there is no other way to stop the
> sense of contentment that thinks your peace alone is sufficient to
> fulfill your own aims. Indeed, you do need to overcome the sense of
> contentment that peace alone is enough to accomplish your own wel-
> fare because (1) Hinayana practitioners, who are merely liberated from
> cyclic existence, have only a partial elimination of faults and a partial
> knowledge, and thus lack the perfect fulfillment of their own aims.[45]

The attainment of Nirvana liberates one from the round of birth and death, eliminates all suffering, and at least for some Buddhists, involves the greatest possible degree of happiness. Yet in this fascinating passage, Tsong kha pa de- nies that individual Nirvana is the highest degree of welfare. Until a practitioner has attained the omniscience and other virtues of a Buddha, she has not reached the greatest possible degree of well-being. Here we have something close to an explicit assertion that knowledge and other good qualities are components of welfare. If we consider this passage together with the extensive evidence that the Mahāyāna regards happiness and the elimination of suffering as goods, we get the theory of well-being that combines happiness and virtue. If we then take into consideration the arguments presented earlier that indicate that the struc- ture of Mahāyāna ethics is consequentialist, we have arrived at the interpreta- tion I wish to defend. It may be that here, as arguably elsewhere, Tsong kha pa has uncovered ideas that are implicit in the thinking of Indian Mahayanists but that they only imperfectly grasped and did not make fully explicit.

Words of My Perfect Teacher, meanwhile, contains some evidence relevant to the question of whether we can appropriately attribute eudaimonism to the Mahāyāna Buddhist tradition. Recall that the issue here is the exact relation be- tween the altruistic actions a bodhisattva must perform and the welfare of that in- dividual bodhisattva. Since those who follow the bodhisattva path are said thereby to attain higher and higher degrees of definite goodness, along with high status, it is quite difficult to find passages that clarify the role of these benefits to the bodhisattva in justifying the practice of the path. Here, Patrul Rinpoche says:

> All the practices that Bodhisattvas undertake to accumulate merit and
> wisdom, or to dissolve obscurations, have but one goal: the welfare

of all living creatures throughout space. Any wish to attain perfect Buddhahood just for your own sake, let alone practice aimed at accomplishing the goals of this life, has nothing whatever to do with the Great Vehicle.[46]

This statement seems fairly clear, but it might still be possible to claim—on my view a bit perversely—that though it is psychologically necessary to focus on the welfare of all beings in order to attain perfect virtue, the foundational justification for the bodhisattva's actions is still her own virtue.

Valuable evidence against the eudaimonist interpretation is provided by Patrul Rinpoche's discussion of the three degrees of courage that a bodhisattva might possess. He distinguishes between those bodhisattvas who wish to attain Buddhahood first and then help others to attain it, those who wish to reach Buddhahood simultaneously with all other beings, and finally those who want to help all others realize Buddhahood and only afterward attaining it for themselves. Patrul Rinpoche claims that the last form of aspiration is the most courageous.[47] If we assume that Patrul Rinpoche, like Tsong kha pa, regards Buddhahood as the ultimate in welfare, then we may conclude that on his view, the most praiseworthy type of bodhisattva is one who postpones his own welfare for the longest. This claim seems very difficult to square with a eudaimonist interpretation.

One might, perhaps, argue that courage is a virtue, and that it is a benefit to a bodhisattva to develop the highest degree of courage. But Patrul Rinpoche seems to think that the aspiration to attain Buddhahood before leading others to it can be successfully fulfilled; and Buddhahood includes the highest possible degree of all virtues, as well as the greatest degree of bliss. On my view, there's no natural way to see the third form of aspiration as conducing to the greater virtue of the bodhisattva; its focus is on promoting the virtue of others.

Any attempt to understand the Mahāyāna in a eudaimonist way will also need to explain the important Tibetan Buddhist meditative practice called *tong-len*, or "taking and sending."[48] In this practice, with each in-breath, the meditator visualizes inhaling a hot, heavy, dark substance. This symbolizes all the pain, suffering, fear, anger, anxiety, and other negative feelings and emotions in the world, which the meditator visualizes taking upon herself. With each out-breath, the meditator imagines exhaling a cool, white, airy substance, which represents all of the pleasure, happiness, calm, compassion, peace, and other positive feelings and emotions she possesses. She thereby develops a state of mind which is as if she was giving all of these away to benefit all beings.

This practice poses the same philosophical problems for a eudaimonist interpretation as the ritual of the dedication of merit, but in a clearer and more severe form. If the ultimate goal is the practitioner's own welfare, why breathe in the suffering, and even the vices, of others? Tonglen also directly opposes many of the habitual psychological responses that are most characteristic of the human mind: it counteracts our tendency to protect ourselves from pain and to accumulate as much pleasure as possible. The practice is thereby supposed to clear away obstacles to the attainment of the highest welfare, the state of a Buddha; not just for the practitioner, however, but for everyone. The focus on the individual that we find in eudaimonism might plausibly be classified as one of these very obstacles.

Evidently, this brief discussion has only scratched the surface of what we can learn about ethics from the Tibetan Buddhist literature about the path to enlightenment. But I hope that what little I have said is enough to suggest that these Tibetan authors were worthy successors to Śāntideva, whose *Introduction* had a pervasive influence on their texts. In the Tibetan path literature, we can find an ethical perspective that, like other forms of Buddhist ethics, identifies the source of ethical norms and the best motivation for practicing the path with the happiness and virtue not just of the practitioner herself but of all sentient beings.

6

Transcending Ethics

On Having No Self

There is something a bit incongruous about the very idea of
attributing ethical theories to Mahāyāna Buddhism. I have presented
various texts that take moral positions, often with great earnestness
and rhetorical power. Yet innumerable passages in Indian Mahāyāna
Sutras and Tantras, not to mention Zen texts from East Asia, tell us
that this moral seriousness is an intermediate stage, very important
for beginners, but something that we must eventually transcend.
The idea that spiritual practitioners will eventually, in some sense,
go beyond ethics can be a very puzzling and disturbing one. To
a substantial extent, it is motivated by the Mahāyāna teaching of
emptiness, which I will discuss in the second section of this chapter.
But there is a form of transcendence that already arises from the
doctrine of no-self and the ethical teachings that flow from it, and
that is independent of emptiness. To put the point in the language
of my introduction, both the second stage of compassion, which
takes ever-changing mental states as its object, and the third and
highest stage, which operates in a vast field of emptiness, require
the practitioner to abandon certain aspects of the way ordinary
people relate to ethical requirements. But since these are still forms
of compassion, they do not make the practitioner into an amoral,
selfish, totally unconstrained exploiter of others. Rather, they make
her into a far more flexible, creative, and effective source of benefit

to all beings. They place the practitioner above and beyond ethical rules, not below them.

I am claiming that to transcend ethics is to make a transition from a state in which we frequently reflect on, and carefully try to follow, moral rules, to one in which we do not consciously think about the rules at all but obey them in a considerably more adroit way. Such a transition is not as mysterious and unusual as it sounds. Francisco Varela has pointed out that the same kind of transition happens to practitioners of perfectly ordinary skills, such as the game of chess. Beginners at chess need to think frequently about the rules, reminding themselves, for example, of which moves are legal for a particular piece. But chess masters don't explicitly think about the rules. Due to their long training, they see patterns in the positions of pieces, and intuitively recognize dangers and opportunities. Of course, these masters are still perfectly capable of formulating the rules of chess. When they teach the game to beginners, or explain the rationale behind their moves to those who are not at their level of skill, they will explicitly allude to rules. But their expertise is such that their decision-making processes don't any longer involve explicit consideration of the rules of chess. Varela makes an analogy to ethics: he argues that spiritual masters are relevantly similar to chess masters, in that they act skillfully for the benefit of all beings, without ever explicitly thinking about ethical rules.

This ethical expertise that goes beyond conscious adherence to rules seems to be connected in deep ways with the fact that advanced bodhisattvas neither have a self nor think that they do. It is risky to speculate intellectually about features of the awakened state, since spiritual exemplars in the Buddhist tradition regularly tell us that ordinary people can't really understand it conceptually. My remarks about awakening and having no self should be read as tentative and provisional; I cannot say with confidence what the enlightened state is like. Nevertheless, some possible ways in which transcending ethics could be connected with realizing no self can begin to emerge if we read Buddhist texts in the context of some of the remarks about identity offered by Charles Taylor in his book *Sources of the Self*. For Taylor, all humans have a deep psychological need for a sense of identity, a sense that depends on what he calls an "orientation to the good."[1] Such an orientation is a set of views about what has ultimate significance, and about how my life relates to that significance. Once I have such an orientation, I can tell a story about my life that portrays it not as a series of random events but as a journey, a narrative, that relates in some intelligible way to the things that really matter. For Taylor, my orientation to the good is what defines my identity, and therefore, my self.

What would it be like to lack an orientation to the good? Taylor paints a grim picture of someone who, in his sense of the word, has no self:

> Such a person wouldn't know where he stood on issues of fundamental importance, would have no orientation in these issues whatever, wouldn't be able to answer for himself on them. If one wants to add to the portrait by saying that the person doesn't suffer this absence of frameworks as a lack, isn't, in other words, in a crisis at all, then one rather has a picture of frightening dissociation. In practice, we should see such a person as deeply disturbed. He has gone way beyond the fringes of what we think [of] as shallowness: people we judge as shallow do have a sense of what is incomparably important, only we think their commitments trivial, or merely conventional, or not deeply thought out or chosen. But a person without a framework altogether would be outside our space of interlocution; he wouldn't have a stand in the space where the rest of us are. We would see this as pathological.[2]

On my view, there are important insights in Taylor's view of the self. Yet from a Buddhist point of view, Taylor is suffering from a failure of imagination. He describes the longing for identity as a "craving,"[3] and recognizes that it can cause considerable suffering. But he does not deeply understand what it would be like to transcend it.

That we must not only realize the ultimate nonexistence of any substantial self but also overcome the whole phenomenon of having an identity is an important message of the Mahāyāna scriptures. For example, in the *Diamond Sūtra* (*Vajra-cchedikā-prajñā-pāramitā-sūtra*), the Venerable Subhūti, a disciple of the Buddha and non-Mahāyāna practitioner, explains the proper response to being praised by his teacher:

> World-honoured One, when the Buddha declares that I excel amongst holy men in the Yoga of perfect quiescence, in dwelling in seclusion, and in freedom from passions, I do not say within myself: I am a holy one of Perfective Enlightenment, free from passions. World-honoured One, if I said within myself: Such am I; you would not declare: Subhūti finds happiness abiding in peace, in seclusion in the midst of the forest. This is because Subhūti abides no where.[4]

The best way to avoid pride and self-conceit, it seems, is not to have any self-image at all. But this passage tells us little about how someone with no conception of himself would behave. For a vivid picture of such a person, perhaps the best source in the Indian Buddhist tradition is the *Holy Teaching of Vimalakīrti* (*Vimalakīrti-nirdeśa-sūtra*).

Ironically, Subhūti himself is the target of criticism in a passage in the third chapter of this widely influential Mahāyāna scripture. There, Subhūti recounts what happened when he approached the Mahāyāna layman Vimalakīrti for alms. After filling Subhūti's begging bowl with food, Vimalakīrti told him, in part:

> Take this food, reverend Subhūti, if, entertaining all false views, you find neither extremes nor middle; if, bound up in the eight adversities, you do not obtain favorable conditions; if, assimilating the passions, you do not attain purification; if the dispassion of all living beings is your dispassion, reverend; if those who make offerings to you are not thereby purified; if those who offer you food, reverend, still fall into the three bad migrations; if you associate with all Māras; if you entertain all passions; if the nature of passions is the nature of a reverend; if you have hostile feelings toward all living beings; if you despise all the Buddhas; if you criticize all the teachings of the Buddha; if you do not rely on the Saṅgha; and finally, if you never enter ultimate liberation.[5]

This onslaught of words reduces Subhūti to a confused and embarrassed silence. Vimalakīrti has challenged every aspect of his identity, every way in which he takes himself to be related to those elements of the Buddhist spiritual path that he regards as ultimately significant. And the fact that Subhūti is troubled by this challenge reveals his limitations as a spiritual practitioner; if he were as enlightened as Vimalakīrti, he would have no identity to challenge.

Vimalakīrti's lack of any fixed identity is reflected not only in his words but also in his actions:

> He engaged in all sorts of businesses, yet had no interest in profit or possessions. To train living beings, he would appear at crossroads and on street corners, and to protect them he participated in government. To turn people away from the Hinayāna and to engage them in the Mahāyāna, he appeared among listeners and teachers of the Dharma. To develop children, he visited all the schools. To demonstrate the evils of desire, he even entered the brothels. To establish drunkards in correct mindfulness, he entered all the cabarets.[6]

Thus Vimalakīrti is able to take on a wide variety of social roles, even those that involve violating conventional moral standards — but always out of compassion for all beings, and without attachment to any of the profits or sensual pleasures that might flow from those roles.

The advantages of Vimalakīrti's lack of identity, and the resulting flexibility in dealing with ethical questions, are well illustrated by the story of his

encounter with the bodhisattva Jagatiṃdhara. The narrative begins as a standard example of a very common motif in Indian religious texts that might be
called the Temptation of the Ascetic. In numerous Hindu sources, the gods,
feeling threatened by the accumulated power of a spiritual practitioner, send
voluptuous supernatural females to seduce him. If he succumbs to the temptation, he will lose his power. This kind of story is found, variously transformed,
in Buddhist contexts as well; perhaps the most prominent example is Māra's
attempt to use his three daughters to tempt the Buddha, shortly before the Buddha's enlightenment.

In the story in question, Māra appears, disguised as the god Indra, and
offers to give Jagatiṃdhara twelve thousand divine maidens as servants. The
bodhisattva resists this temptation, however: "O Kauśikā, do not offer me, who
am religious and a son of the Śākya, things which are not appropriate. It is not
proper for me to have these maidens."[7] Notice that Jagatiṃdhara phrases his
refusal in terms of his identity: the rules appropriate to his status as a monk
forbid him from accepting the gift.

Just at this point, Vimalakīrti arrives, and exposes Māra's disguise. Then
the story begins to deviate from the standard Indian model: "Then the Lic-
chavi Vimalakīrti said to Māra, 'Evil Māra, since these heavenly maidens are
not suitable for this religious devotee, a son of the Śākya, give them to me.'"[8]
Vimalakīrti proceeds to exhort the heavenly maidens to become bodhisattvas.
He converts them to Mahāyāna Buddhism, and instructs them about how to
find joy in spiritual practice and not in sensual pleasures. He then gives them
back to Māra, on Māra's request, but only after encouraging them to "inspire
innumerable gods and goddesses with the spirit of enlightenment."[9]

Vimalakīrti's surprising response to the situation clearly produces better
results, from the point of view of the text, than Jagatiṃdhara's more conventional reaction. Vimalakīrti is able to convert the goddesses because he does not
take anything seriously: not his own sexual desires, or his own moral status, or
the opinion of others, or the moral rules of Buddhism. Unlike Jagatiṃdhara,
who is imprisoned by a conception of his own status and the moral rules that
flow from it, Vimalakīrti is able to respond creatively and flexibly, treating every
situation as an opportunity to lead others toward enlightenment. Even while
bending all his efforts to liberate beings from cyclic existence, Vimalakīrti does
not take even this goal seriously: after all, from the point of view of ultimate
reality, there are no beings to liberate.[10] He has no views about the good and
no orientation toward the good: therefore, in Taylor's terms, he has no identity and no self. Yet he is not exactly a madman, though he is not a normal
human either. Vimalakīrti is a model of what contemporary Buddhists call
"crazy wisdom."

It would certainly be possible to interpret Vimalakīrti as rejecting, along with the various particular moral rules that he is explicitly described as disregarding, the general moral rule of consequentialism, to always perform the action that will produce the greatest benefit for sentient beings. This reading would lead us to describe the *Holy Teaching of Vimalakīrti* as presenting a form of ethical particularism. But this line of thought, it seems to me, will not be very compelling unless we confuse consequentialism as a decision procedure with consequentialism as a structure of evaluation. As I understand Vimalakīrti, he is not consciously weighing consequences or explicitly reflecting on how to bring about the greatest total sum of welfare; but he is not thinking about these things because he has so fully internalized concern for the welfare of others that he can accomplish these things without thinking about them. He simply acts intuitively and spontaneously in a way that expresses the emotions of loving-kindness, compassion, and equanimity. An observer could interpret, evaluate, and justify his actions in terms of a consequentialist ethical perspective, since the Sutra makes it clear that Vimalakīrti does, in fact, work to promote the welfare of all beings; Vimalakīrti, therefore, is appropriately described as a consequentialist agent, even if he never consciously applies a consequentialist decision procedure. And the stories about Vimalakīrti give us a vivid sense of what it might be like to act in the world without being attached to any personal relation to the good.

The demand to act without attachment to any relation to the good—the demand to have no self, in Taylor's sense—might be seen as an idiosyncratic, and not particularly plausible, feature of Buddhist ethics. But this view would be seriously mistaken. The idea that we should be prepared, under some possible combinations of circumstances, to abandon the self is not restricted to Buddhism; it flows from the very structure of consequentialism. One of the best ways to establish this claim begins with the example of George the chemist, discussed in chapter 2. Recall that in this case, a young scientist must either accept a job designing chemical and biological weapons, to which he is morally opposed, or see the job taken by someone far more brilliant and motivated than himself, an evil genius whose weapons will end the lives of many.

If George has any degree of nonconsequentialist moral integrity—if he believes in side constraints that forbid certain actions, independently of the consequences—then he must give up that kind of integrity, or else allow a catastrophe to happen. Moreover, suppose that George is a consequentialist, and that part of his conception of his own identity is as someone who, through his work, is benefiting other beings. Once he takes up the job in weapons research, it will be true that he is benefiting all beings, but only in a subtle and indirect way. He must constantly devote intellectual effort to figuring out how to harm other people. One might say that George must give up his own conception of himself as someone who is doing good for the world precisely in order to do good for the world. To benefit all beings, he must give up his self.

Let us go beyond the details of Williams's case and suppose further that George knows that, as he spends years working, day in, day out, at this repellent job, the moral sincerity that he had at the beginning will gradually be eroded. His deep belief in consequentialist ethics will be hollowed out, and in the end he will come to accept a version of egoism whose only vestige of morality is a weak, defeasible presumption against harming others. Yet all the damage that George will do through the selfish actions he foresees that he will eventually perform pales in comparison with the devastation that would be caused by the weapons the evil genius chemist would develop if given the chance. So George, a consequentialist, has powerful consequentialist reasons for undertaking a course of action that he knows will eventually cause him to cease to be a consequentialist.

It would be fair to protest that this case has a very un-Buddhist flavor. Indeed, if we assume that George is a bodhisattva, and we take on board Buddhist descriptive assumptions about karma, reincarnation, and enlightenment, the right course of action in Williams's case becomes much less clear. What I am presenting is an analogy. Just as, assuming no reincarnation, George is required by consequentialist morality to begin a process that will destroy his belief in consequentialism, in the same way, Buddhists take themselves to be required by concern for the welfare of all beings to begin and pursue a process of development—namely, the path to enlightenment—that will ultimately cause them to lose all attachment to particular moral rules, and to cease to make decisions by consciously consulting any particular moral theory, even consequentialism.

Thus I turn Williams's *modus tollens* into a *modus ponens*—or better, into the proof of a conditional. If consequentialism is true, then, in order to act correctly in certain unusual cases, we must give up all attachment, even attachment to a sense of ourselves as acting morally. To bring about the greatest benefit to all beings, and thereby fulfill the substantive aims of consequentialism, we must be prepared, at least in special circumstances, to give up consequentialism itself. To many Western philosophers, even those who might be attracted to a consequentialist view of ethics, this is a serious and perhaps a decisive consideration against such a view. But for a Buddhist, this conclusion is acceptable, indeed welcome, and independently motivated. Thus, at least in this respect, the most philosophically defensible form of consequentialism would seem to be a Buddhist one.

This conception of how ethics can be transcended has numerous implications for the interpretation and defense of the Buddhist tradition. In particular, thinking of ethical transcendence in the way I have suggested may make it possible for us to understand Tantric ethics. Of course, not all scholars would be prepared to agree that there is any such thing as Tantric ethics.[11] Given the freewheeling spirit and the sometimes shocking excesses of Tantric texts, it makes sense to doubt whether the normative perspective of the Vajrayāna (that is, of Tantric Buddhism), insofar as there is one, can be seen as continuous in any way with the much more strait-laced, rule-based frameworks of Theravāda and non-Tantric Mahāyāna ethics. One advantage of the interpretive framework I have proposed, in which Buddhist ethical views are regarded as forms of consequentialism, is that it can represent all of these views as expressions of the same underlying ethical idea: that of the welfare of all sentient beings as the basis on which ethical views are built. Advanced Tantric practitioners — insofar as we can accept their own rhetorical presentation of their motives — can helpfully be regarded as behaving like act-consequentialists, but without actually believing any ethical theory, not even an act-consequentialist one.

It's not hard to understand why some writers would interpret followers of Tantra as amoralists. Ronald Davidson writes that in their texts, "they used erotic descriptions that framed in explicit language a series of rituals extolling everything from group sex to ritual homicide to cannibalism."[12] With great gusto, the iconic Tantric practitioners known as *siddhas* seem to take pleasure in trampling all rules, principles, and restrictions that might bind their freedom. Yet *siddhas* nevertheless try to justify their outrageous behavior as a form of skillful means that effectively promotes the welfare of others.[13] Keith Dowman makes this point quite clearly: "From the Buddha's point of view there is less virtue in the moralist's inflexible social and moral prescriptions than in the *siddha's* "sinful" attempts to induce awareness, with all the social and moral benefits that accrue, wherein enlightenment is the ultimate goal."[14] The altruistic motivation of Tantric practices, even the most shocking ones, is a consistent feature of Vajrayāna rhetoric; as Matthew Kapstein writes, "developed tantric Buddhism would always maintain its twin ends to be the attainment of benefit to others through proficiency in mundane rites and the attainment of one's own realization through insight born of yogic practice."[15] And, of course, since these Tantric practitioners are also Mahayanists, the attainment of enlightenment by the individual will then be of great benefit to others, as the realized practitioner continues to manifest illusory bodies throughout cyclic existence to lead others to their own awakening.

The most striking examples I have found of the relevant features of Tantric ethics come from a Tibetan Nyingma text called the *Copper Temple Life Story* (*rnam thar zangs gling ma*), a biography of the Tantric master Padmasambhava, who is said to have played a central role in the conversion of Tibet to Buddhism. This text was allegedly "discovered" (but actually composed) in the twelfth century; it was supposedly found in the Copper Temple in the monastery of bSam yas, having been written in the ninth century by Ye shes mtsho rgyal, one of Padmasambhava's consorts.[16] As a historical document, the value of the *Copper Temple Life Story* is essentially nil; we have no particular reason to believe that any of the events it recounts actually occurred as described. Nevertheless, it can give us quite a good indication of the forms of behavior that twelfth-century Tibetan Nyingmas considered acceptable in an enlightened spiritual teacher.

The picture of the master Padmasambhava that emerges from this text is of a man who is highly altruistic in his ends, but astonishingly ruthless in his means. In his youth, Padmasambhava is living as a prince in a palace; the king and ministers do not wish to allow him to leave and become a religious wanderer. Therefore, he kills the son of the most influential minister and is banished as a punishment, allowing him to seek ordination as a monk.[17] In order to survive a famine, Padmasambhava, while living in a charnel ground, eats human flesh and wears clothes made of flayed human skin.[18] He seduces the daughter of Arshadhara, the king of Sahor, and runs off with her without her father's consent, making her his partner in Tantric sexual rituals.[19] He kills four recalcitrant non-Buddhist teachers with a shower of meteors.[20] These actions, however shocking they may be, pale in comparison with the story of King Shakraraja. Since some might find it hard to believe that a passage of this kind could occur in any text purporting to be Buddhist, I will quote the story in full:

> During this time, in the district of Uddiyana known as Gaushö,
> there was an evil king named Shakraraja. He was forcing the people
> under his domain onto an errant path from which later they would
> go to the lower realms. The prince [Padmasambhava] considered that
> there was no other way to convert them than through subjugating
> and wrathful activity. He tied up the hair on his head with a snake,
> donned a human skin as his shirt, and made a tiger skin his skirt.
> Holding in his hands five iron arrows and a bow, he went to that
> country of evil deeds. The prince killed all the males he came across,
> ate their flesh, drank their blood, and united with all the females. He
> brought everyone under his power and performed the tanagana ritual
> of union and liberation. Therefore he was named Rakshasa Demon.[21]

On the basis of this passage alone, we may legitimately conclude that, at least according to the Nyingma sect, there are no limits to the destructive actions that are permitted to an enlightened Tantric master.[22]

Yet the text is at pains to emphasize that Padmasambhava is not really a demon, though ignorant people might mistake him for one. All of his most horrifying actions are justified by some greater good that he thereby achieves. Arriving in Tibet, he announces: "Embodying the aims of those who have great faith, I accomplish their welfare for both present and future lives."[23] Judged by Buddhist standards, the eventual results achieved are quite impressive, as we see from this stanza, attributed to the teacher Padmasambhava himself:

> I, Padmakara, came to benefit Tibet.
> By miraculous displays, I have tamed the vicious spirits
> And established many destined people on the path of ripening and
> liberation.
> The profound terma teachings shall fill Tibet and Kham
> with siddhas.[24]

Not only does Padmasambhava claim that his own actions benefit many people; he also exhorts others to do the same. When offering advice to the men of Tibet about how they should behave after his departure, he instructs them as follows: "Without losing your individual needs, Guard the general welfare of others with your lives."[25]

The events in the Copper Temple Life Story are obviously mostly fictitious, but for the sake of argument, let's assume they are known facts. If we are act-consequentialist, and we regard the spread of Buddhism and the achievement of the spiritual goals of Buddhism as goods, we must see Padmasambhava as having acted in a morally praiseworthy way, despite the reckless, chaotic, and merciless character of so many of his actions. If we do not see Padmasambhava as an act-consequentialist, we have little other choice but to regard him as completely immoral, or perhaps amoral; and such an interpretation would require us to ignore how careful the text is to point out that his actions produced more good in the end than harm.

How does the Tantric tradition describe the mental attitude of *siddhas* as they carry out their beneficial and highly unconventional activities? Keith Dowman offers a sympathetic summary:

> the siddha's behavior is characterized as unlimited and spontaneous,
> selfless and compassionate. After the initiate's experiential realiza-
> tion of pure awareness and emptiness in a mystical experience of
> union has determined constant, involuntary emanation of compas-
> sionate action, there are no restraints whatsoever upon the scope of
> the siddha's activity. With the experientially based conviction that the
> relative world is all vanity, and that any mundane ambition is a futile

waste of the opportunity afforded by this precious human body to attain spiritual liberation, together with a realization of the unity of self and others and the resultant benign empathy, the siddha cannot but act for the benefit of himself and others simultaneously. Thus insofar as the Bodhisattva Vow permeates his being, the siddha is driven to action uninhibited by any social or moral norm.[26]

I would argue that it is here, for the first time in the Buddhist tradition, that we encounter texts that have a clear, worked-out understanding of the implications of act-consequentialism. Note the role that Śāntideva's strategy plays in this passage: the absence of any individual self is once again being brought to bear on ethics. But here, the implications of the strategy are being allowed their fullest development. The constraint against harming and the strong emphasis on rules that we find in Asaṅga's form of Mahāyāna ethics have been swept aside, and all norms are to be broken if doing so promotes the welfare of beings. For example, if Padmasambhava, or any one of the *siddhas* to whom Dowman alludes, were reborn as George the chemist, it seems that he would not hesitate to participate in making chemical weapons — unless, as is likely, he could find some more creative response to that situation.

The passage just quoted also makes some very interesting remarks about the psychology of *siddhas*. According to Dowman, the *siddhas'* behavior is "involuntary"; it represents what they are "driven" to do and "cannot but" do. Though these terms are suggestive, it is not wholly clear what they mean. Ignoring the dangers involved in trying to describe the enlightened mind, I will now attempt to give a philosophically illuminating account of how *siddhas* relate to what we would call their actions.

I will begin with a saying of Nāgārjuna, from the *Fundamental Verses on the Middle Way*:

> The root of cyclic existence is conditioning.
> Thus, ignorant people form conditioning.
> The ignorant person, therefore, is an agent;
> The wise person is not, because he sees reality.[27]

Obviously, Nāgārjuna is not advocating a life of vegetating on the couch in front of the television: to him, that would be another form of action, and a rather destructive one. Like other Buddhist philosophers, Nāgārjuna thinks of enlightened beings, such as Buddhas and Saints, as behaving in such a way as to have an impact in the world. But they do so without acting, because the mental processes that lead to their behavior are utterly unlike the deliberation carried out by ordinary people. The enlightened don't have conditioning

(Skt. *saṃskāra*)—the habits and emotions that shape the decisions of ordinary people; moreover, they lack the delusive belief in a self. Their bodies move in such a way as to benefit all beings, and they are aware of what happens, but they never act, because they don't deliberate, and they don't identify with any decision procedures or long-term projects. To them, there does not even seem to be a self that makes choices; they just respond spontaneously to situations, out of pure, great compassion.[28]

What do I mean by saying that enlightened beings don't deliberate? I am not claiming that their bodies move in a totally random or unintelligible way. From the outside, we can make sense of them as acting for the benefit of all beings. However, on the account I am advancing, enlightened beings never go through the process that ordinary people call "deciding what to do." They can certainly spend time in theoretical inquiry into the facts of a situation, thereby ascertaining which movements of their bodies would produce the best consequences for sentient beings—though they wouldn't need to do so very often, as they would normally simply see, intuitively, what the best action is. But since the illusion of free will has disappeared for them, it no longer seems to them that they can do anything other than what would be best. Once they see what would have the best results, the corresponding movements just happen, without intervening states such as decisions and the formation of intentions. The cause of these movements is the unimpeded flow of natural great compassion. The abandonment of all selfish desires has removed all hindrances to the operation of this compassion, which now spontaneously produces bodily and vocal movements that cause the happiness and relieve the suffering of others.

According to Tantric Buddhists themselves, Vajrayāna practitioners do not always succeed in attaining this state of spontaneous great compassion; moreover, when the Tantric path is followed incorrectly, the consequences can be disastrous. The main reason why Tantric practice is dangerous is psychological. The use of sexual and violent imagery and ritual is intended to overcome all inhibitions, destroy all obstacles to complete spontaneity, and make room for perfect compassion. In the process, all forms of selfish desire are supposed to be purified and transformed into virtues, while their energy is tapped to power the entire process. His Holiness the Dalai Lama has explained the role of desire in the Tantric path as follows:

> According to the Mahāyāna sutras, if a certain situation suggests a positive outcome in terms of benefiting others the voluntary use of desire or attachment is allowable. However, in the tantras it is not merely that desire or attachment is permissible when beneficial, here one deliberately uses their energies as the path to purifying and consuming the dissonant states themselves.[29]

But this kind of practice can go terribly wrong. If the Tantric practitioner destroys all of his inhibitions but retains even one selfish desire, he will become a monster, ruled by an utterly unconstrained and destructive impulse. It is easy to understand why there are said to be special and particularly horrifying hells just for failed Tantrists.

If we adopt the act-consequentialist understanding of Tantric ethics I have proposed, we can offer another, complementary reason why the Tantric path is said to be dangerous. Act-consequentialism is itself dangerous. Since it removes all moral rules that might interfere with bringing about the welfare of all beings, it can require those agents who practice it to perform actions that directly cause serious harm or death to sentient beings, so as to prevent even greater harms, or to bring about very important goods. If the agent develops attachment to these ruthless actions, she could easily turn into a monster. And if the agent's information is inaccurate, she runs the risk of causing terrible damage without actually benefiting anyone. But a skillful act-consequentialist with correct information can prevent great disasters, and achieve great goods, in cases where other kinds of agents would be too scrupulous to act. Doing so requires overcoming our moral squeamishness, our attachment to our own integrity—indeed, all the inhibitions in human nature—precisely what the Vajrayāna path is designed to eliminate.

This brief discussion of Tantric ethics has shown, I hope, that we may be able to gain insight into the moral significance of the Tantra by bringing to bear our understanding of the form of moral transcendence associated with the second type of compassion, which takes momentary mental states as its object and results in universalist consequentialism. But this account cannot be the whole story, because a central part of the Tantric path is the realization of the emptiness of all things. Thus, the moral transcendence of Tantra must also involve the third type of compassion. Though my wisdom is hardly adequate to the task, I shall now attempt to offer what clarification I can of what it might be like to unite compassion with the realization of emptiness. Before I can do that, I must remove a very natural fear: that far from enhancing one's compassion and ethical discipline, emptiness might destroy it altogether.

Emptiness

I have argued in this and previous chapters that Mahāyāna ethics embodies an inspiring and philosophically powerful set of ethical ideas that bear a close resemblance to certain versions of Western consequentialism. However, these ideas, or indeed any conception of ethics, may be in tension with another very central Mahāyāna teaching: the doctrine of emptiness. This doctrine is set out in the *Perfection of Wisdom Sūtras* and defended philosophically by the Middle Way School, which many scholars consider to be the most important and influential form of Mahāyāna philosophy. The possibility that emptiness might pose a threat to ethics is not a modern misinterpretation. Central figures in the Mahāyāna tradition have recognized that there is a problem here that needs to be addressed. For example, Nāgārjuna, the founder of the Middle Way School, after offering an explanation and defense of certain aspects of emptiness, warns his readers:

> This doctrine wrongly understood
> Causes the unwise to be ruined
> Because they sink into the uncleanliness
> Of nihilistic views.[30]

Nāgārjuna obviously does not endorse the thought that emptiness will destroy ethical concern, but he sees that "the unwise" who do not grasp its proper interpretation might be tempted to draw this conclusion.

It's not hard to find passages that might be stumbling blocks for "the unwise." Numerous Mahāyāna scriptures say that sentient beings do not exist and that there are no actions at all, much less right or wrong actions. Sometimes we get explicit statements that apply these teachings to Buddhist ethics. For example, in the *Definitive Vinaya*, a part of the *Great Heap of Jewels Sūtra*, the Buddha tells his audience:

> I often praise the observance of pure precepts,
> But no being ever breaks any precepts.
> Precept-breaking is empty by nature,
> And so is precept-keeping.[31]

If there is no such thing as keeping the precepts, one wonders, why should the Buddha praise this nonexistent activity? Yet the text does not wish us to draw this kind of conclusion. The same Sūtra contains the statement that if someone "says, 'What is the use of practice, since all dharmas are empty?,' he is also arrogant."[32] It is not clear, though, how the conclusion is to be avoided.

We would, for example, be unable to avoid concluding that morality is pointless if we interpreted emptiness as absolute nonexistence. According to the nihilist interpretation of emptiness, the ultimate truth is that nothing exists. If nothing exists, then actions have no consequences; in fact, there are no actions, and so clearly there can be no ethical norms. Eminent Western scholars have defended this interpretation,[33] and there are some textual passages that appear to support it. Yet in many places, Mādhyamikas such as Nāgārjuna and Candrakīrti are at pains to deny that this is their position. Today, most scholars of the Middle Way School reject the nihilist interpretation.

What we need, then, is an alternative interpretation of the doctrine of emptiness that can be consistent with the ethical claims that defenders of emptiness continue to want to make. This is not the place to discuss the subtleties of the wide variety of philosophical interpretations of emptiness that have been proposed by scholars in India, Tibet, and the West. But I will make a few remarks that should be sufficient to suggest a particular interpretation, or a range of interpretations, that seem to allow some room for ethics.

When things are empty, what are they empty of? The answer, which can be found in any number of Madhyamaka texts, is that they are empty of *svabhāva* — a Sanskrit term that has no single equivalent in English. Its etymology is similar to the Latin derivation of the word "essence," and in fact, *svabhāva* is often used to mean something much like the Western concept of essence. Thus, the doctrine of emptiness can be viewed as a form of antiessentialism. But the doctrine goes beyond the denial of essence. *Svabhāva* can also mean "intrinsic character." Thus, for things to be empty of *svabhāva* is, in part, for all their characteristics to be defined and constituted by their relations to other things, and not by what they are in themselves, independently of anything else.

Svabhāva can have another meaning, one too complex to be expressed in any simple English phrase. With respect to this third meaning, to have *svabhāva* is to be a posit of a prestige discourse, one that expresses the true nature of reality, one that carves nature at the joints. From the point of view of this meaning of the term, the things that have *svabhāva* are the things that exist ultimately. That is, they are in the world as it is in itself, independently of the constructive activity of the mind. To say that all things are empty is to say that nothing has this kind of objective, independent, ultimate existence. Instead, everything we believe in exists in a way that depends, in part, on conceptual construction. This is not a perspective on which ordinary things, such as chairs, trees, and people, are utterly nonexistent. Indeed, they do exist, but they exist conventionally, not ultimately. On the Madhyamaka view, conventional existence is a type of existence, and it is the only type of existence that anything could possibly have.

Though these views are, in a sense, quite radical, they should not be utterly unfamiliar to Western philosophers. They bear a striking similarity to the views held by contemporary American neopragmatists, such as Richard Rorty and, during some parts of his career, Hilary Putnam. These thinkers are skeptical of the concept of essence, affirm the relational nature of entities, and reject the concept of a special, prestige discourse that uniquely describes reality as it is in itself. So far, in asserting the emptiness of all things, we have not gone beyond the range of views current in Western analytic metaphysics.

There are, however, other features of the teaching of emptiness that, at least initially, appear much more strange. For example, the texts of the Middle

Way School frequently compare all entities to deceptive phenomena such as mirages.[34] These similes should not be interpreted nihilistically: a mirage is not something that absolutely does not exist. Rather, it is an entity that appears to be real in a way in which it is not; the manner in which it seems to exist is not the same as the manner in which it exists. In a similar way, according to the teachings of the Middle Way School, ordinary objects such as chairs and people are not utterly nonexistent, but neither are they real in the way we think they are. We take them to exist independently of human concepts; but they do not. In fact, they exist only relative to one or more conceptual schemes. Since we take them to be more real than they are, we are deceived; this deception is the cause of a subtle kind of attachment and suffering, and an obstacle on the path to Buddhahood.

Thus, the endless litany of negations we find in the *Perfection of Wisdom Sūtras* does not amount to nihilism. When a text such as the *Definitive Vinaya* says "No being ever breaks any precepts," it is speaking at the ultimate level. The scripture is telling us that incidents of precept-breaking, like chairs, rocks, elementary particles, people, and mental states, do not have the kind of objective, independent, ultimate existence that we instinctively take them to have. Instead, they have a conceptually constructed, perspective-dependent, conventional existence—just like everything else.

Some Mādhyamikas are also prepared to make another kind of claim not found in the writings of pragmatists. On their view, it is possible to hold your mind in such a way as not to have any concepts. Anyone who does this no longer perceives any things, since the things exist only in relation to particular conceptual schemes. Rather, someone who is aware in a nonconceptual way will be conscious without being aware of any objects of consciousness. This is not an awareness of an ultimately existing absolute; that is ruled out by the emptiness of emptiness. But having the experience of seeing nonconceptually can set us free of attachment to particular concepts, and make it possible flexibly to change conceptual schemes whenever this is appropriate.

What is the status of ethics on this view? If we adopt this interpretation of emptiness, we must say that ethical judgments do not have the kind of robust, full-blooded objectivity we might be tempted to assign to them. On the other hand, we can say that ethics is as objective as any conceptual scheme gets; indeed, it is as objective as physics. The idea will be that the conceptual scheme of ethics answers to certain purposes. If we want to achieve these purposes, we must think ethically; but the insights we derive from doing so can transcend the contexts in which they were originally introduced. Ethics demands a kind of impartiality and universality that can lead human societies in surprising directions.

What purposes does the conceptual scheme of ethics serve? One of the most important such purposes would seem to be that of offering justifications of one's actions to others. My discussion earlier of the views of Francisco Varela can shed light on this issue. For Varela, experts in any practice can often act without having to reflect explicitly on the rules they are following; but if someone else asks them to explain why they acted in a certain way, they can offer an explanation in words. Similarly, on the account I am discussing, enlightened beings act fully spontaneously, out of innate great compassion, without having to engage in practical reasoning. But if someone requests an explanation of why they behaved in a certain way, these beings would be able to adopt the conceptual scheme of Buddhist ethics in order to offer such an explanation. Other purposes of thinking ethically might include offering moral advice to, and criticizing the actions of, others who are not yet at the stage of being able to behave spontaneously and correctly in every situation. Those who have realized emptiness will still think ethically, if they need to accomplish these purposes. But they will not be attached to ethical thinking, since they see it as conventional, perspective-dependent, and in the final analysis, optional.

Mādhyamikas can use the conceptual framework of ethics, but there is room for disagreement about whether they can try to revise it. As I have argued, Buddhist thinkers such as Śāntideva make crucial use of the strategy of criticizing ordinary intuitions about morality on the basis of the doctrine of no self. This strategy is central to my account of Mahāyāna ethics, and it is therefore important for that account that the use of this strategy can be endorsed, in some sense and at some level of truth, by the Middle Way School. Yet some interpreters of Buddhism would argue that the version of Middle Way School philosophy advocated by Candrakīrti — regarded by the Tibetan tradition as the most profound version of that philosophy — is not consistent with this strategy. His *Introduction to the Middle Way School* (*Madhyamaka-avatāra*) contains passages that seem to suggest that it can never be acceptable for a philosophical theory to be allowed to override the collection of everyday common sense and practical experience that goes to make up conventional truth: "If everyday experience poses no threat to you, then you may persist in the denial of the evidence provided by such experience. Quarrel with the evidence of everyday experience, and afterward we will rely on the winner."[35]

Several philosophers of the Middle Way School in India identify conventional truth as that which "satisfies without analysis."[36] That is, so long as we do not attempt to reason about the manner in which things exist, we will be content to operate according to conventional truth. But once we examine this question, we will begin to discover that the existence of ordinary things cannot withstand critical examination. By doing so, we can transcend our attachment to the conceptual schemes that endorse their existence, and move toward the level of ultimate truth. But for Candrakīrti, the ultimate truth is not something that can be expressed in words or in concepts. If we can be aware of it at all, this can only be possible through a nonconceptual, unmediated awareness.

One problem with this philosophical approach is that it seems to leave no room for rational criticism of commonly held ethical beliefs. At the level of conventional truth, no philosophical theory can overthrow the common-sense beliefs of ordinary people. But no moral criticism can be brought at the level of ultimate truth, since at that level there are no concepts of happiness or suffering and no distinction between good and bad. Indeed, no human concepts operate there. So there is no point of view from which the common-sense moral perspective of ordinary people can be criticized.

Compelling as this line of reasoning might seem in elucidating the implications of Candrakīrti's philosophical commitments, it is not a line Candrakīrti himself could have taken. In his commentary on the *Four Hundred Stanzas* (*Catuḥśataka*) of Āryadeva, Candrakīrti offers numerous criticisms of normative views that are taken for granted by the society in which he lives. In a single chapter of this commentary, the fourth, Candrakīrti denies that kings have reason to be proud,[37] that criminals should be harshly punished,[38] and that it is honorable to sacrifice one's life in battle.[39] In each case, he rejects these beliefs on the basis of rational argument.

We therefore need to interpret Candrakīrti as holding that criticizing commonly held moral beliefs is not the same as rejecting conventional truth. We should not, on Candrakīrti's view, hold any philosophical theory that requires us to reject descriptive aspects of the experience of everyday life, such as the existence of external objects and of causal relations. These matters must be accepted conventionally, though they no longer exist once we take up the ultimate perspective. But it is perfectly consistent with Candrakīrti's philosophy that we should criticize normative beliefs; these are not endorsed by everyday experience in the same way, and they do not receive the same immunity to criticism at the conventional level.

Moreover, Candrakīrti distinguishes between conventional truth and conventional falsehood. If many people believe that the earth is flat, their beliefs do not make the earth actually become flat; that would be an implication of some versions of relativism, but it does not follow from Madhyamaka. If the kind of evidence and arguments that are relevant to ascertaining conventional truths can demonstrate that the earth is round, then it will be conventionally true that the earth is round, even if no one yet realizes this truth. Similarly, people's normative beliefs may be invalidated by reasoning that conforms to the standards of conventional truth. This reasoning might be used either to criticize these beliefs directly or to knock out the descriptive presuppositions on which they rest. These considerations show that, contrary to what we might initially think, a member of the Middle Way School can indeed analyze and reject the morality of common sense from the perspective of Buddhist philosophy.

Is it possible, though, for that analysis to involve Śāntideva's strategy? Powerful considerations suggest that the answer is no. If mental states were more real, if their existence were more fundamental, than that of the person, then it would make sense to infer from that claim that genuine moral significance must attach to mental states and not to persons. But if there is no asymmetry — if both mental states and persons are empty of any real, ultimate existence — then the strategy seems to be unusable.

We may be induced to look harder at the question once we notice that Śāntideva himself was a Mādhyamika. If his strategy is incompatible with the Madhyamaka view, then his position is inconsistent. Of course, this situation might actually be acceptable to Śāntideva, who would have seen it as permissible to use any form of words, accurate or not, that is likely to help people make spiritual progress and weaken their afflictions.

However, there may be a way to reaffirm Śāntideva's strategy even from within the Middle Way School. We could claim that the conception of a self can interfere with compassion by creating selfishness and partiality only if it is taken fully seriously, as ultimately established. Happiness and suffering, on the other hand, can motivate a compassionate response even if they are seen as merely conventional. After all, on the Madhyamaka view, conventional existence is a kind of existence. Pain that is not ultimately real still hurts; and those who see that pain as empty can still move to relieve it.

There is another issue about emptiness that needs to be considered, and that can be framed in terms of an objection to my interpretation of Buddhist ethics. All forms of consequentialism centrally involve the concept of intrinsic value, for it is intrinsic value, whatever they take it to be, that consequentialists try to maximize. And I have been trying to attribute a specific view about intrinsic value to Buddhist thinkers. But the distinction between intrinsic and instrumental value seems never to appear in Indian texts, at least explicitly. It is very far from clear how to say "intrinsically valuable" in Sanskrit.[40] The best we can do, perhaps, would be something like *svabhāvataḥ kuśalam* or perhaps *svataḥ kuśalam*. From these proposals, it might seem that the Mādhyamikas would be inclined to reject the whole concept of intrinsic value if it were presented to them.

The terms *kuśala* and *svabhāva* are prominently linked in verses 52–56 of Nāgārjuna's *Vigraha-vyāvartanī*.[41] Here Nāgārjuna attacks the view of an unnamed opponent who holds that some of the basic constituents of the universe, the *dharmas*, are skillful (*kuśala*) or unskillful (*akuśala*) in virtue of their essence (*svabhāva*). The opponent in these verses is almost certainly a non-Mahāyāna advocate of the Abhidharma. As usual, Nāgārjuna is terse and difficult, but his basic objection to this view is clear. According to Nāgārjuna, an essence is something permanent and unchanging. His Sarvāstivādin opponents were explicitly committed to this view, and he attempts to show that anyone who accepts essences is implicitly committed to it. However, according to Nāgārjuna, if these *dharmas* had such an essence, they, too, would be permanent and unchanging, contrary to the opponent's view.

It will not be necessary for us to evaluate the success of Nāgārjuna's arguments here; rather, I am concerned with what he is trying to establish. Is he trying to show that the concept of a skillful essence is not viable as an ultimate truth, but can still be maintained at the conventional level? Or does he hold that the notion of an essence must be discarded both ultimately and conventionally? Famously, the great Tibetan philosopher Tsong kha pa interprets the Indian philosophers belonging to what he calls the Middle Way Autonomous School (Tib. *dbu ma rang rgyud pa*), such as Bhāvaviveka, as holding the first position, and those belonging to what he calls the Middle Way Reductio School (Tib. *dbu ma 'thal 'gyur pa*), such as Candrakīrti, as holding the second. It is far from clear whether Tsong kha pa was correct in advancing this interpretive claim.[42] If we assume that he was correct, then the Reductio School might reject the concept of intrinsic value. But the Autonomous School, who regard ethics as in any case operating at the conventional level, might be happy to accept intrinsic value as an ethical concept, while not allowing it any ultimate validity.

Though this line of reasoning is tempting, I think it would be a mistake to adopt it. The sense of "intrinsically valuable" that is needed for consequentialism is quite different from the one that the Middle Way School criticized. Consequentialism needs to appeal to features of the world that have their value independently of what they can be used as a means to produce. What the Middle Way School would object to is the idea of features that are valuable independently of any conceptual scheme. It seems perfectly possible for a kind of value to be intrinsic in the first sense but not in the second.

An analogy might help to illustrate this point. Suppose that in a discussion of naval architecture, an engineer asserts the following: "Wooden ships can be difficult to sink, because the material they are made of is less dense than water, and the intrinsic buoyancy of wood keeps them afloat. But the sides of metal ships are denser than water; they have no intrinsic buoyancy. Metal ships are able to stay afloat only because of the air trapped inside them, which is much less dense than water and prevents the ship from sinking." Do these assertions conflict with emptiness? I answer that Mādhyamikas should not be afraid of the mere word "intrinsic." There is no reason for denying that the engineer's statement could be conventionally true. The buoyancy of wood can be intrinsic in one sense, since it does not depend on some other substance trapped in the wood, but not intrinsic in another sense, since buoyancy can be defined only in terms of a conceptual framework involving a large number of concepts all of which are understandable only in relation to each other, such as mass, volume, gravity, force, and so on. In the same way, the value of happiness can be intrinsic in the sense of not depending on the causal consequences of being happy, even if it is not intrinsic in the sense that it is established only in relation to the conceptual framework of ethics.

More research needs to be done into the question of whether the distinction between intrinsic and instrumental value can legitimately be used to understand Buddhist ethics. If not, then at least to that extent, the Mahāyāna Buddhist view was quite different from any modern consequentialist theory. Of course, that view would also be at the same remove from that of Aristotle, who accepts and frequently appeals to the intrinsic/instrumental distinction. But I think that when we distinguish between two relevant senses of "intrinsic" as I have done here, it becomes clear that there is no particular reason for Mādhyamikas to object to the distinction. And the possibility of confusion between the two senses might go a long way toward explaining why the Western distinction is not explicitly found in Buddhist sources. The crucial point is that emptiness poses no threat to our ability to distinguish between instrumental and intrinsic goods, a distinction we must make to do consequentialist ethics.

Suppose, then, that I have succeeded in showing that there is no conflict between emptiness, properly understood, and Buddhist ethics. Nevertheless, I have not begun to explain how the realization of emptiness can actually make us morally better, as Mahāyāna Buddhists claim it can. An important part of the explanation of the relation between emptiness and moral perfection could run as follows. By showing us that the conceptual structures we use to navigate ordinary life are merely conventionally, and not ultimately, valid, the realization of emptiness makes us much less attached to those structures. It can thereby make us much more creative, by allowing us to, in Robert Nozick's words, "break frame." Nozick writes:

> Breaking out of an established framework of thinking or perceiving occurs in creating a theory or artistic object, yet it is not restricted to these; it is important to be able to "break frame" in our everyday lives also. Sometimes the breaking of frame will be a direct action, violating a previous framework of expectations that defined which actions

were admissible or were allowed to occur, but which excluded the
most functional actions or even effective ones.[43]

This, of course, is just what Vimalakīrti does when he asks Māra for the divine
maidens. Instead of following the well-known script of the Temptation of the
Ascetic story, Vimalakīrti moves in a new and unexpected direction, thereby
creating a better outcome.

Meanwhile, by showing us that ethically relevant properties, like everything else, do not ultimately exist, a realization of emptiness can dispel the
excessively grim and serious attitude that can result from reflecting on the vast
amount of suffering in the world. As Winston Churchill said, "A fanatic is one
who can't change his mind and won't change the subject." Moral fanaticism
can be as unappealing as any other form, and is not a useful tool for achieving
the welfare of all beings. Moreover, it is exhausting. To struggle against the vast
mass of the world's suffering without realizing emptiness will lead to the form
of burnout known as compassion fatigue. But, as the *Vimalakīrti Sūtra* tells us,
the great compassion that results from seeing emptiness does not exhaust the
practitioner, precisely because it doesn't take itself as seriously. For that reason,
those who possess great compassion can accomplish varied and limitless bodhisattva deeds for the benefit of all sentient beings.

To perfect ethics, we must transcend the explicit use of ethical rules and
ethical theory. This realization is already built into the structure of consequentialism, whose determined pursuit of the good subverts itself in a bewildering
variety of ways. Western consequentialists and their opponents have typically
regarded this self-subversion as a source of important reasons to reject consequentialism. But from a Buddhist point of view, the requirement of transcendence isn't a bug, it's a feature. Buddhists can and do embrace the idea that we
must overcome our attachment to ethical rules and theories if we are to become
the best that we can be. To do this in the right way, we must realize, first, the absence of any self, and then, the emptiness of all things. Having fully integrated
insight into reality with liberative technique, those who realize these truths can
lead all beings toward the good.

7

Buddhist Ethics and the Demands of Consequentialism

Utilitarianism was once dominant in the ethical thought of the English-speaking world, but this theory, along with its consequentialist relatives, has now declined in popularity due to a number of serious objections. One of the most important of these objections is that consequentialist theories are excessively demanding, that they ask more sacrifices from us than it is reasonable to expect us to give. The source of consequentialism's very severe demands lies in a deep feature of moral thought: the idea of equal concern for all sentient beings.[1] As consequentialism interprets this idea, it implies that we must assign no greater weight to a benefit to ourselves or our loved ones than to an equal benefit to a stranger living far away. As Peter Singer has argued,[2] this feature of consequentialism seems to lead irresistibly to the conclusion that most of us spend far too little of our time and money assisting others who are in desperate need. It might even imply that we are morally required to give away so many of our resources to benefit famine victims in other parts of the world as to be reduced to a condition almost as destitute as the famine victims themselves.

Like Western consequentialists, Buddhists have had to struggle with the problems created by an ethical theory that demands more effort and sacrifice than most people are willing to give. Recall the discussion of the *Mahāsattva Jātaka* in chapter 3. Those who wish to attain moral perfection, it seems, must be prepared to sacrifice their bodies and lives for the benefit of others.

Let us examine how consequentialist thinkers in the Western tradition have tried to deal with the difficulties of this position, and produce a realistic response to the extreme, and to common sense excessive, demands that their moral theory seems to make. Two approaches are often used to blunt the force of these demands. First, if one applies a consequentialist criterion directly to acts of praise and blame, it will clearly follow that not all those who do the wrong thing should be blamed for it. It might be counterproductive in the extreme to blame and criticize people who show a significant and unusual degree of generosity and self-sacrifice for not manifesting the even greater degree of these qualities that would be necessary to maximize overall welfare. The best consequences might be obtained by praising those who do better than average, and only blaming people who fall well below the usual standard. Thus, though consequentialists hold that almost all people fall short of their moral obligations, it is no part of consequentialists' view that almost everyone should feel guilty about this.

The second solution Western thinkers frequently propose to the problem of the extreme demands of consequentialism involves noting that people who act out of their own particular goals and desires, or who act to benefit people who are near and dear to themselves, can often do more good than if they tried to act out of universal benevolence. It is well known that consequentialists do not always advocate taking conformity to moral duty as one's motive for acting. The greater spontaneity and wholeheartedness of benefiting those we love, along with the superior knowledge we have of the needs of those close to us, can lead consequentialists to endorse acting out of more particular motives such as familial affection. Indeed, as has often been pointed out, if we contrast a society in which people refrain from violating common-sense morality and are kind to those close to them with a society in which everyone tries to be a selfless do-gooder, the first society may well realize the good far better than the second. It can make sense, therefore, for consequentialists to recommend a way of life that involves close personal attachments as opposed to a life of incessant activism on behalf of everyone.

But is this contrast the correct one to draw? Utilitarian writers such as Scarre consistently write as if the only choice was between a society in which everyone tries to become a moral saint and a society in which no one at all makes this attempt.[3] Consider an intermediate case: a society in which there are a large number of ordinary people who follow the common-sense rules of morality and have close personal attachments, along with a small number of extraordinary individuals who devote themselves full-time to the welfare of all. Perhaps this society would do better than either of the two models in the more usual comparison. The happiness that comes from loving families and loyal friendships would still exist in abundance in this sort of society. Meanwhile, there would be a few people who would be working selflessly, and full-time, to resolve problems and make the society a better place. It may well be that most people are not capable of such devotion to all beings. But surely some people are, and it would probably be better if they were to actualize this potential. If able to choose this kind of society, it seems that a consequentialist would do so.

Of course, introducing this element into the comparison appears to suggest that even sophisticated consequentialism may still be extremely demanding. For if you realize that you are capable of being one of the elite of extremely altruistic people, and that there seems to be a shortage of such people in your society, it appears that you should try to become one. So for those who have reason to suppose that they are able to be paragons of altruism, sophisticated consequentialism may be as demanding as the plain variety.

In fact, the demanding nature of consequentialism is not the only feature of the view that seems to push it in the direction of advocating the creation of a moral elite. If ordinary people are told that the only moral imperative is to bring about the best consequences, they might start to produce specious and self-serving pseudoconsequentialist justifications for doing whatever it is in their perceived interest to do at the time. Many ethicists have reasoned that the best consequences will result if the only people who are taught to apply the consequentialist test are those who are capable of applying it in a rational and impartial way.[4] Thus, a consequentialist theory should be, in Derek Parfit's phrase, "partly self-effacing and partly esoteric."[5] For a small elite, consequentialism will be esoteric: they are allowed to believe it, but should keep its tenets secret from the masses. Most people are in a stranger position, though: for them, consequentialism is self-effacing. If they should come to believe consequentialism, it would tell them to stop believing it. Instead, consequentialism would require them to try to cause themselves to believe some other theory, perhaps some version of common-sense morality.

For several reasons, consequentialism seems to endorse an arrangement in which a moral elite are the only people in society who know the truth about ethics. Yet many writers have found this idea deeply unappealing, and it's not difficult to see why. The members of the elite have to engage in deception, since they conceal their true moral beliefs from the unsuspecting multitude. In order to get the multitude to go along with the reforms whose ultimate justification is consequentialist, they will quite likely have to use some kind of coercion. This leads to the image of the consequentialist elite as an isolated class of colonial rulers tyrannizing over an ignorant native population. This image of "government house utilitarianism" is only reinforced by the fact that certain prominent nineteenth-century defenders of utilitarianism, such as

John Stuart Mill and his father, James Mill, were actually employed as colonial administrators by the British East India Company.[6]

Philosophers in the tradition of analytic ethics have thus tried to find ways to mitigate the problems associated with the demanding nature of consequentialism. By making consequentialism self-effacing, it is possible to make it livable for most people, while also avoiding the problems arising from biased or ignorant attempts to apply the consequentialist test directly. But this solution requires a degree of coercion and deception that is unacceptable to many ethicists. Moreover, some might find the very notion of a self-effacing theory problematic; there is need for careful exploration of whether any self-effacing theory can be acceptable. Western consequentialists have thus not fully succeeded in replying to the problem of consequentialism's demands. Is it possible to do better?

Suppose we had a version of rule-utilitarianism with two sets of rules. There would only be one overarching rule that would apply to everyone: "Choose either the rules on list A or the rules on list B, and then always follow whichever set of rules you have chosen." The choice between one or the other set of rules might be left completely free, or it might be constrained in some way by the number of other people who have already chosen one option or the other. This might seem like a strange way to set up a moral theory, and so far as I know, no recent Western thinker has proposed it. But, I claim, it is an appropriate model for Theravāda Buddhist ethics, and for Asaṅga's version of Mahāyāna Buddhist ethics; moreover, this model can give us insight into how these perspectives deal with the demands of morality.

The two sets of rules, of course, are the Five Precepts that apply to the laity and the Prātimokṣa code that governs the lives of the monks and nuns. In an ideal society, there is a division of labor between those who follow these two sets of rules, a division of labor described by Buddhists as follows. The laity work, produce resources, form close relationships, and raise families. They are deeply involved in the particular attachments that characterize most healthy human lives. They strive to follow the Five Precepts, which forbid killing, stealing, sexual misconduct, lying, and excessive use of intoxicants. They cultivate a limited but significant form of generosity that is compatible with family life, and in doing so, they provide the material resources that enable the monks and nuns to survive.

The monks and nuns, meanwhile, devote themselves to spiritual practice and to the welfare of all sentient beings. By renouncing all individual property, they separate themselves from greed for material possessions. By renouncing marriage and taking vows of celibacy, they remove the possibility of romantic attachments to particular people, thereby leaving emotional space for the great compassion (*mahākaruṇā*) that embraces all of life. By renouncing worldly concerns, they are able to devote their energies to seeking those spiritual attainments that are the basis of blissful happiness for themselves, and that enable them to teach others the way to happiness. Meanwhile, monastic institutions play a more mundane role in succoring the desperately poor, providing a haven for children whose parents cannot support them, and protecting the interests of nonhuman animals. If the infrastructure of society is not sufficiently developed to deliver medical care and education, the monks may step in as doctors and educators.[7] In these ways, they promote the happiness of the most vulnerable members of society, and even of the animals that live nearby.

If it turns out that a society with both of these groups will attain the highest level of welfare, then rule-utilitarians would have reason not to seek for a simple rule that gives everyone exactly the same guidelines, and instead to adopt an overarching rule with a disjunctive form. All citizens of the society, whether lay or monastic, can follow the overarching rule by following the particular set of rules they have chosen to adopt. This system can make room for everyone, whether they are capable of the highest form of life or not.[8]

In the Mahāyāna versions of this view, it will turn out that once practitioners are sufficiently advanced in their spiritual development, they will be authorized to break the rules in certain extreme circumstances, when doing so will be of benefit to sentient beings. In the Theravāda, truly advanced practitioners never knowingly break the rules. But they may reach a point at which they no longer need to consciously follow them, since they have developed such a high degree of virtue that their actions spontaneously accord with what the rules prescribe. So although there will be only two sets of rules in the system, there will be different attitudes to and ways of following the rules, depending on the level of spiritual development of the practitioners in question.

This approach to the problem of consequentialism's extreme demands can work, of course, only for those Buddhists whose form of ethics is rule-utilitarian. How could Buddhist act-utilitarians, such as Śāntideva, deal with the problem? Here it is relevant to notice that Buddhist societies tend to develop an ideology of the "transfer of merit," in which the karmic benefits from the practice of the monks are shared with the laity. If we ignore the topic of reincarnation and look at the situation from a moral point of view, there is nothing magical about this teaching. The monastic institutions could not possibly continue to exist without the support of the lay community. If it is indeed true that these institutions bring great benefits to society, the credit for bringing about these benefits must be shared with the laypeople who provided the support and resources that made them possible.[9]

Lay Buddhists usually do not make a very impressive effort to become as morally good as they could possibly be. But they have no defensible reason to feel guilty, if they provide indispensable support to those who are making that effort. And in return, they will receive guidance, advice, and fellowship from the monks and nuns who depend on them. Meanwhile, according to the Mahāyāna tradition, rare exemplars of lay practice, such as P'ang and Vimalakīrti, somehow find time in the midst of worldly distractions to develop their compassion and wisdom to dazzling levels of accomplishment.

Buddhist act-consequentialists could adopt another feature of sophisticated Western consequentialism: the concept of a consequentialist elite. For Buddhists, consequentialism can be partly self-effacing without being coercive or deceptive. They can conceive of the members of the consequentialist elite in a different way: rather than being a secret cabal of governors tyrannizing over the rest of the population, the elite members could be monastic religious professionals.

From the perspective of Mahāyāna Buddhist act-consequentialists, the direct application of the consequentialist criterion is primarily a matter for monks, nuns, and a small minority of spiritually advanced laypeople. The mass of the laity, who are powerfully motivated by particular worldly attachments, would have a strong tendency to misinterpret the consequentialist principle to allow actions shaped by those attachments. Lacking in insight, they might not properly understand the needs and interests of others. Lacking in compassion, loving-kindness, and sympathetic joy, they might not be sufficiently motivated to give those needs and interests their proper weight. Lacking in equanimity, they would tend to count the welfare of their close relatives and friends far more heavily than that of strangers or foreigners. For all these reasons, most of the laity should not be expected to do a good job of deciding which of many available actions would have the best consequences. Buddhist texts make it clear that their best course is to rely on simple moral rules that are easy to understand and apply, rules summarized in numerical lists such as the Five Precepts and the Ten Good Paths of Action.[10] These rules express the accumulated ethical knowledge of many generations. They often resemble the analogous rules offered by other religious and secular traditions. Such straightforward guidance is much more helpful to those of limited moral and spiritual attainments than the highly abstract and easily misapplied consequentialist principle could ever be.

But although this division of society does imply an elite that accepts different moral views from everyone else, it requires no deception to maintain itself. The laity can be explicitly told that monks and nuns have a more nuanced and accurate understanding of the Buddha's doctrines than they do. The Buddhist tradition has maintained from the beginning that the truths realized by the enlightened are "profound, hard to see and hard to understand . . . subtle, to be experienced by the wise."[11] Laypeople who wish to gain a deeper understanding of their tradition need not be denied the opportunity to do so; the monks must only make sure, as numerous Buddhist texts urge, that the teachings are given in the proper order. Buddhists should learn the consequentialist basis of their ethical rules of thumb only once they are ready to reflect in a mature way about how this basis should be put into practice.

Nor does the Buddhist version of self-effacing consequentialism involve the element of coercion that is perhaps the least attractive feature of what has been called government house utilitarianism. It is precisely because Buddhism is a religion that it has developed such effective forms of persuasion, both rational and nonrational, to induce people to follow the moral guidance of its authoritative texts. When laypeople encounter moral dilemmas that cannot be resolved on the basis of the simplistic rules they have learned, they can do what followers of many religious traditions have always done: voluntarily consult clergy members for moral guidance. If this moral guidance is provided on the basis of an underlying consequentialist ethical theory, then consequentialism will be able to shape and to reform the moral practices of society without having to arrange for its dictates to be imposed by force.[12]

I expect that these suggestions will strike many readers as distinctly premodern in flavor. But on reflection, it may be difficult to pinpoint what is objectionable about them. After all, the majority of American citizens are surely unable to cite any of Kant's formulations of the categorical imperative. But the failure of American education to inculcate Kantian ethical theory surely does not make our social system illegitimate, even from the point of view of Kantians. Our schools do teach students a number of values that are reflected in Kantian ethics, such as the importance of rights, the equality of citizens, respect for the law, and so on. The fact that they do not provide a deep theoretical justification for these values does not generate a serious objection to our education system; not everyone needs to know what the deep theoretical justification is.

The democratic project of a state that is justified to its citizens by reasons should not be taken to presuppose the existence of high school classes in ethical theory. I do not see why a Buddhist system of education that offers simple moral guidance to beginning students, withholding the underlying ethical justification, should be any more objectionable than teaching false theories such as Newtonian mechanics to those without the mathematics to understand modern physics. And since the Buddhist society I have proposed does not require coercion to keep the laity in line, it should be fully compatible with democratic governance, especially if the scope of government power is limited and the range of free personal choice is wide.

I have offered a highly idealized description of the relations between the monks and the laity, which I do not claim is an accurate description of the historical reality of any actual Buddhist country. Of course the monasteries have always contained spiritually unimpressive, corrupt, and power-hungry individuals. Perhaps every human institution fails to achieve its own ideals. I do want to suggest, however, that describing this ideal allows us to see that it is conceivable for there to be a society of sincere consequentialists who are also human beings, and yet who give the demands of their moral theory all the respect due to them.

Indeed, there may be systematic reasons why the proposed division of labor, if implemented in practice, would generally tend to fall short of the ideal. Members of a self-proclaimed moral elite may, just in virtue of that proclamation, develop a kind of pride that would by itself undermine any real moral superiority. And insofar as membership in this elite is a privileged position, elite members may become an inappropriately conservative force, struggling even against needed social changes that appear to threaten their status. I do not wish to deny that these are real problems for the Buddhist vision of society. But they are both shared with government house utilitarianism, which has been thought to result from the self-effacing character of consequentialism. Buddhist ethics may not be able to solve all, or even most, of the problems facing consequentialism. But it seems to me that the idea of a society with a consequentialist moral elite will face fewer objections, and be at least less unappealing, in its Buddhist version.

A very important aspect of the issue that still needs discussion is the question of the appropriate attitude toward those texts that express the total, self-sacrificing love of the bodhisattva ideal through stories about the gift of the body, in which the bodhisattva sacrifices his own flesh and blood, his limbs, or even his life to benefit others. Though a number of Buddhist texts extol the gift of the body, many others recognize that this ideal is not realistic as a model for the actions of the overwhelming majority of humans.[13] The attitude of commentators to the stories of the bodhisattva's gift of his body can be summed up in the television slogan "Don't try this at home." According to these commentators, it would be a foolish and excessive action to give away one's body or body parts before having cultivated the immensely advanced state of mind that makes such gifts a free and spontaneous action of generosity. Thus, Buddhist ethicists seem to be in a position similar to that of most Western consequentialists: wanting to shower praise on spectacular acts of self-sacrifice for the benefit of others, without actually expecting most people to perform such acts.

Indeed, from Śāntideva's point of view, trying to engage in extreme acts of generosity before one is ready is positively destructive to the bodhisattva path. He writes:

> What is the joyous perseverance on account of which you become dispirited? It is when one who has little strength undertakes activity that is weighty or that extends over a long period of time; or when those lacking fully mature belief undertake difficult tasks like, for example, giving away their own flesh and so forth. Though these beginning bodhisattvas have given away their own body to all beings, still they turn away from untimely uses of it. Otherwise they would despair about these beings who ask for flesh, and thereby squander huge masses of good results due to wasting the seed of their spirit of enlightenment. Therefore, the *Questions of Sky Treasure Sutra* says: "Untimely wishes are demonic activity."[14]

Notice that Śāntideva, as I have already often mentioned, mirrors sophisticated Western consequentialists in appealing to indirect effects of actions. From Śāntideva's point of view, it seems, it would be inappropriate for us to try to act like moral saints right now. Instead, what morality demands of us is that we should strive to change our psychology so as to become more like moral saints.

How should we begin to carry out this transformation? Śāntideva gives us a clear answer to this question: Start with vegetables. He writes, in the *Introduction to the Bodhisattva's Way of Life*:

> 7.23. All doctors use painful treatments to restore health. It follows that to put an end to many sufferings, a slight one must be endured.
>
> 7.24. Though such treatment is appropriate, it is not what the best doctor prescribed: he cures by sweet conduct those with the greatest illness.
>
> 7.25. The Guide enjoins giving only vegetables and the like at first. Later, by degrees, one acts in such a way that one is even able to give up one's own flesh!
>
> 7.26. When the understanding arises that one's own flesh is no more than a vegetable, what difficulty is there in giving away one's flesh and bones?[15]

Thus, at no stage does the path of the bodhisattva place demands on us that we are unable to bear. At first, we give away things we are able to give away. We give away our own flesh only when it becomes easy to do so. If we have not yet completed this change, we have no reason to blame ourselves or feel guilty, so long as we are on the path.

I have argued that different forms of Buddhist ethics have a variety of strategies for negotiating the tension between the demands of consequentialism and the realities of ordinary people's lives. These strategies offer us ways to hold up moral sainthood as an ideal and maintain consequentialist understandings of ethics without lapsing into paralyzing guilt or a sense of personal worthlessness. But is moral sainthood an appealing, or even a defensible, model of the best human life? To most people, a person who has found inner peace, who has renounced selfish desires, and who is motivated by great love for everyone would be a profoundly appealing figure. This fact is a small part of the reason for the continuing popularity of the great world religions. But not everyone agrees that this kind of life is genuinely valuable. Many analytic philosophers are now persuaded that this is not a worthwhile goal to pursue, under the influence of certain arguments offered by Susan Wolf.[16]

Wolf not only rejects the ideal I have been describing, which she calls the Loving Saint. Her argument also operates at another, and even higher, theoretical level. Wolf actually denies that anyone ought to be, or has most reason to be, as morally good as possible: "moral perfection, in the sense of moral saintliness, does not constitute a model of personal well-being toward which it would be particularly rational or good or desirable for a human being to strive."[17] This will feel like a paradoxical claim to anyone who is attracted to the idea of the sovereignty of morality: the idea that moral reasons can override, or trump, other kinds of considerations. If morality has this kind of overriding force, Wolf's unflattering portrayal of moral sainthood must leave something out. Buddhists, it turns out, can uphold the sovereignty of morality; the Buddhist tradition contains numerous descriptions of what it would be like to be a moral saint that are far more appealing than Wolf's. These descriptions may also increase the plausibility of the view that the characteristic Buddhist virtues really are intrinsic goods.

Philosophically, the most powerful consideration Wolf advances against the ideal of moral sainthood is the claim that there are other, nonmoral excellences of character that have their own kind of value, a value that is lost or demeaned if these excellences are abandoned for moral reasons, or even if they are pursued for moral reasons. But much of the emotional force of Wolf's case seems to me to arise instead from the ways she suggests that it would be unpleasant to spend time with a moral saint, that such a person would be a "nauseating companion."[18] Not only do moral saints make other people uncomfortable about pursuing their own private goals; as Wolf portrays them, they also have no sense of humor at all: "A moral saint will have to be very, very nice. It is important that he not be offensive. The worry is that, as a result, he will have to be dull-witted or humorless or bland."[19] And this lack of humor actually makes such a saint less appealing as a moral exemplar: "one prefers the mischievousness and the sense of irony in Chesterton's Father Brown to the innocence and undiscriminating love of St. Francis."[20]

Wolf's account of moral sainthood can be seen as a manifestation of an Anglo-American tradition that appears in the repudiation of the "monkish virtues" by such Enlightenment figures as David Hume and Adam Smith, and that ultimately springs from the Protestant Reformation.[21] As she describes moral saints, modern Americans would indeed not see them as appealing objects of emulation. But there are other, and far more compelling, ways of imagining what sainthood would be like.

Consider a story about Patrul Rinpoche, the author of the *Words of my Perfect Teacher*, as told by Pema Chodron:

> A hermit well known for his austerity had been practicing in a cave
> for twenty years. An unconventional teacher named Patrul Rinpoche
> showed up at the cave, and the hermit humbly and sweetly welcomed
> him in. Patrul Rinpoche said, "Tell me, what have you been doing in
> here?" "I've been practicing the perfection of patience," the hermit
> answered. Putting his face very close to the hermit's face, Patrul
> Rinpoche said, "But a pair of old scoundrels like us, we don't care
> anything about patience really. We only do this to get everyone's
> admiration, right? We just do this to get people to think we are big
> shots, don't we?" And the hermit started getting irritated. But Patrul
> Rinpoche wouldn't stop. He just kept laughing and patting him on
> the back and saying, "Yeah, we sure know how to dupe people, don't
> we? We really know. I'll bet they bring you a lot of gifts, don't they?"
> At this point the hermit stood up and screamed, "Why did you come
> here? Why are you tormenting me? Go away and leave me in peace!"
> And then the Rinpoche said, "So now, where is your perfection of
> patience?"[22]

The protagonist of this story is not the watery, inoffensive figure of Wolf's caricature. Yet the Tibetan tradition holds Patrul Rinpoche up as one of the highest expressions of the human spirit—and as a great benefactor of humankind. No social worker or Oxfam employee, if constrained by the limitations of an ordinary human mind, could accomplish any appreciable fraction of the benefit Patrul Rinpoche is regarded as having conferred on the generations of Buddhists who have studied his teaching. And the Rinpoche's offensiveness is not an accident. A crucial goal of a Buddhist teacher's activity is to show us, vividly and repeatedly, those flaws of character and limitations of understanding that we would prefer to conceal even from ourselves. Seeing these defects in ourselves can be very unpleasant, but it is a central part of the process of spiritual growth. Buddhist teachers can be sweet and gentle, at the right time; they can also be harsh and critical, at the right time.

It would be easy to reply that the use of humor by Buddhist masters simply suggests that they are not moral saints. It might appear that they disregard the feelings of their students to make themselves appear witty and sophisticated. But the Tibetan tradition, like the Zen tradition, understands this use of humor as neither detrimental to nor independent of the project of mind training. The fundamental tendencies in the personality of most humans that are opposed to morality, such as greed, hatred, and pride, are for Buddhists dependent on basic misunderstandings of our relation to the universe. They can be undermined far more powerfully by laughter than by hours of earnest moral exhortation. By showing their students — and through them, future generations — how to laugh at their own delusions, the great figures of Tibetan Tantra and East Asian Zen made them far less likely to be violent, selfish, or conceited. And as I pointed out in the case of Vimalakīrti in chapter 6, a crucial aspect of enlightenment is the ability not to take oneself too seriously. Someone trying to help others develop this mental state might find humor to be the most natural vehicle for many teachings. The kind of laughter produced by an ordinary clown or comedian would not necessarily have the same beneficial effect, of course; only when the mischievous sense of humor found so plentifully in traditions such as Zen is combined with profound intuitive wisdom can it change minds and lives. And, for the Buddhist tradition, anyone who wants to be a friend to all sentient beings should first set out to acquire just this wisdom.

Nor does the bodhisattva path require giving up one's sense of beauty. Many Buddhist teachers have excelled in fields such as poetry, visual art, and Chinese calligraphy. Through these arts, they have been able to manifest a combination of skill and spontaneity that mirrors, and thus guides us toward, enlightenment itself. But in the lives of masters themselves, the appreciation of artistic beauty is regarded by the tradition as being of small importance compared to a constant awareness of the beauty of ordinary, everyday things. The ability of masters to find great beauty in the ordinary is a central component of the supreme happiness Buddhists attribute to them. As Śāntideva writes, "Today I summon the world to Buddhahood and to worldly happiness meanwhile."[23] I would argue that it is precisely because enlightenment represents such an unexcelled degree of well-being that the Buddhist tradition gives such great importance to activities that make it possible for students to attain it.

Wolf's way of imagining what moral saints would be like does indeed seem to justify the thought that one would not want one's children to join their ranks. But I see no compelling reason not to want one's children to emulate Patrul Rinpoche. The value of a Buddhist master's life may depend in part on highly controversial Buddhist descriptive premises. But if, for the sake of argument, we grant those premises, it seems difficult to avoid the conclusion that the life of a Buddhist saint is the best kind of life to lead. And even if we jettison the more problematic descriptive claims, such as reincarnation, the idea of a life full of humor, the appreciation of beauty, happiness, and service to others must surely be appealing, even if pursuing it requires giving up such goods as family and wealth. Meanwhile, laypeople can keep the latter goods and escape blame. Theravādins can think of laypeople as pursuing one of the two sets of rules that, when each of them is pursued by some members of society, will produce the best consequences. Mahāyānists can point out that laypeople should receive their share of the moral credit for making the lives of spiritual masters materially possible. Thus, Buddhism can offer a conception of moral sainthood that we have every reason to pursue—while making it possible to be excused from guilt and blame if we find ourselves unable or unwilling to pursue it.

Most Western ethicists seem entirely unaware of the important contributions Buddhist literature has to offer them. The project of forming an ethical theory and an ethical sensibility based on the welfare of all beings is far older in Asia than in the West, and it has a rich and vast literature there. In particular, if Western consequentialists were better poets, surely they would sound like Śāntideva. If a consequentialist genuinely wants to arouse the altruistic motivation necessary for heroic acts of benevolence, she could hardly do better than to echo the words of the *Introduction*:

> 3.17. I am the protector of the unprotected and the caravan-leader for travelers. I have become the boat, the causeway, and the bridge for those who long to reach the further shore.
> 3.18. May I be a light for those in need of light. May I be a bed for those in need of rest. May I be a servant for those in need of service, for all embodied beings.
> 3.20. Just as earth and the other elements are profitable in many ways to the immeasurable beings dwelling throughout space,
> 3.21. So may I be sustenance of many kinds for the realm of beings throughout space, until all have attained release.[24]

Any people who actually aspire to become moral saints can find inspiration in these evocative words. More important, perhaps, Buddhists claim that their techniques of meditation have the power to effect, over a long period of time, profound changes in the motivational structure of their practitioners, so that a few of them will actually attain the saintly altruism that consequentialism seems to demand.

Not all people will attain this level of moral development. Not all will even try to do so. But in addressing the nonsaintly majority, Buddhism has strategies for mitigating the extreme demands it shares with consequentialism. By defending this claim, I hope to suggest that Buddhist ethics is much more interesting than many contemporary ethicists have supposed. It can supply possible solutions to important and difficult philosophical problems, even those that have led some writers to reject consequentialism entirely. Analytic ethicists concerned with these problems might learn more by reading Buddhist texts than most of them would expect.

8

Buddhism on Moral Responsibility

Buddhists have always been interested in freedom, but only recently have they begun to think about free will.[1] Concepts closely related to freedom—spontaneity, independence, self-mastery—have been central to Buddhism since its beginnings. Serious Buddhist reflection on the problem of free will and determinism, however, is a product of dialogue between Asian and Western cultures. Unfortunately, this dialogue has barely begun, and very little is known about what a Buddhist position on free will might be like. Thus, Galen Strawson has argued that at least "certain schools of Buddhists" are committed to the nonexistence of free will and the incoherence of moral responsibility.[2] Mark Siderits, meanwhile, claims that at least "early Buddhists" are, or should be, defenders of a particular kind of compatibilism.[3] And Paul Griffiths asserts that Buddhism involves a version of libertarianism.[4] We can hardly expect to compare two traditions when one of them is as badly understood, from a philosophical point of view, as Buddhism still is.

Although Buddhist scriptures and philosophical texts never explicitly confront the issue of free will, at least in the form in which we know it, there are passages in various of these texts that deal with related issues. These passages, taken from a number of texts that differ greatly in other ways, can be used to construct a Buddhist position about the problem of free will. This view about free will stems from deep features of Buddhist thought that are largely held in common by different articulations of the tradition. Therefore, most or all philosophers in the highly diverse Buddhist tradition would probably have been prepared to agree with it. This position is importantly different from what most Western thinkers say, but it doesn't represent an entirely new answer to the problem. Rather, Buddhist writers describe a way to live with the practical consequences of the absence of free will. As Strawson repeatedly points out, Western thinkers who have denied the reality of free will have continued to apply notions of moral responsibility in their own lives. Their practice is thus inescapably inconsistent with their theory. By drawing on Buddhist ideas, however, it is possible to develop a view on which perfect people do not ascribe moral responsibility.

To see why it makes sense to explore a view of this kind, consider the dilemmas faced by Peter van Inwagen, one of the most prominent writers on free will. Van Inwagen is an incompatibilist: he thinks that, if everything that happens is entirely determined by the past and the laws of nature—that is, if determinism is true—then there is no free will.[5] And, really, if everything you do is determined by antecedent conditions, namely the laws of nature and various events that happened before you were even born, and if you have no control over these antecedent conditions, how can you claim to be the ultimate source of your own actions and decisions? Of course, there are various philosophers, called compatibilists, who say that free will is compatible with determinism. They say, roughly, that you are free if you do what you want to do and you aren't being coerced or compelled. Now, certainly, not being coerced or compelled is a kind of freedom, and a very desirable one; but many people think that when they want free will, they want something *else*, a kind of ultimate responsibility for what they do, and even who they are. And you can't have that kind of ultimate responsibility if everything you do is determined by things over which you have no control. This kind of argument is the basis of hard determinism, the view that because determinism is true, free will does not exist.

Although van Inwagen believes in free will, he agrees with hard determinists that if determinism is true, free will is impossible; free will is only able to exist, on his view, because the world is not deterministic. But van Inwagen admits that even if determinism is false and there is a certain amount of complete randomness or chance in the world, the existence of free will is still a complete mystery. After all, if what you do is caused by some random quantum-mechanical event in your brain, how can *you* be responsible for it? Some philosophers, called libertarians, argue that free will exists, and that indeterminism in the world is crucial to its existence. Most libertarians, however, defend this claim by assuming the existence of a very special entity, a self or soul, that has the power of agent causation, which enables it to cause actions independently of the ordinary natural order and independently of the flow of event causation.

This kind of self or soul doesn't fit well into a scientific worldview, and even if it does exist, no one has any idea how it manages to affect the body, how it goes about coming to one decision rather than another, or how its behavior could be distinguished from simple randomness. To explain free will in terms of a soul is to wallow in mystery.

Apparently, then, if determinism is true, free will is impossible; but, if determinism is false, free will is incomprehensible. Van Inwagen recognizes this situation, but argues that there is no choice but to believe in free will.[6] If free will does not exist, then the practice of holding people morally responsible for their actions is unjustified. But this practice is deeply embedded in everyday life. Could anyone really give it up? Certainly, the Western philosophers who have denied the existence of free will have not given it up, and have not really even tried. Van Inwagen mentions a hard determinist philosopher of his acquaintance who, when his books were stolen, complained "That was a *shoddy* thing to do." But if this philosopher thinks that moral responsibility doesn't exist, why is he getting angry at the thief, who wasn't really responsible for the theft? This example illustrates the close connection between the concept of moral responsibility and certain of our attitudes, such as anger and resentment.

P. F. Strawson forcibly defended the idea that we have no choice but to accept free will, because of the connection between free will and some of our emotions or attitudes.[7] Strawson argues for a version of compatibilism, on the ground that the truth of the general metaphysical thesis of determinism cannot, and should not, affect our commitment to what he calls the "participant reactive attitudes." These attitudes include resentment, gratitude, anger, and certain other emotions, which Strawson regards as central to the interpersonal relationships on which our social life is based. Intuitively, it seems that one cannot feel resentment, for example, toward beings to whom one does not ascribe agency and moral responsibility. In fact, in particular cases where circumstances uncontroversially override people's agency, no one feels resentment for the actions of those whose will has been overridden.[8] If determinism is a threat to agency and moral responsibility, then it should call into question the appropriateness of these attitudes.

According to Strawson, determinism can pose no such threat, because abandoning these attitudes is not a real possibility. About the possibility that general acceptance of determinism might undermine the participant reactive attitudes, he says:

> I am strongly inclined to think that it is, for us as we are, practically
> inconceivable. The human commitment to participation in ordinary
> inter-personal relationships is, I think, too thoroughgoing and deeply

rooted for us to take seriously the thought that a general theoretical conviction might so change our world that, in it, there were no longer any such things as inter-personal relationships as we commonly understand them; and being involved in inter-personal relationships as we normally understand them precisely is being exposed to the range of reactive attitudes and feelings that is in question.[9]

This argument does not show that free will exists, or that determinism is compatible with moral responsibility. At most, what it shows is that there is no choice but to believe that humans are, somehow, free, since the contrary belief would be in such hopeless tension with the stance that people do, and must, take toward themselves and toward other people. Nevertheless, if Strawson is right, the position of any disbeliever in free will is a highly problematic one.

Anyone who doesn't believe in free will, it seems, faces an irresolvable conflict between theory and practice. Anyone who does believe in free will has to accept a complete mystery that no one can think of any way to justify, or even to understand. The Buddhist tradition offers a way out of this difficult predicament: a way to give up both the theory and the practice of moral responsibility, and thereby to escape the need to believe in the indefensible notion of free will.

This approach to the problem of free will depends on the Buddhist doctrine of no self. This doctrine is subtle and complex, and different Buddhist philosophers interpret it differently. In particular, the version of it defended by early Buddhists and explained in the Abhidharma[10] is somewhat different from the even more subtle and more general doctrine of emptiness, which was taught by Madhyamaka philosophers such as Nāgārjuna and which I discussed in chapter 6. Even the early Buddhist doctrine of no self has profound implications for the topic of free will, however. The *Treasury of Metaphysics,* a work from the fifth century CE in the tradition of the Vaibhāṣika Abhidharma, quotes a Buddhist scripture that explains this doctrine:

> There is no sentient being here, nor is there a self, but simple entities, each with a cause. There are twelve categories of being, the spheres, and there are aggregates, and components; having thought about all these, one still doesn't perceive any person. Everything that belongs to you is empty. Perceive it as empty; perceive it as external. He who meditates on emptiness does not exist.[11]

According to early Buddhists, then, the world is not what you think it is. Ordinary people believe that the world is mostly made up of composite, macroscopic entities that persist through time and can undergo change, such as rocks, tables, cats, and people. But Buddhists hold that these entities do not ultimately exist. According to these Buddhists, the really existing entities are simple, momentary, localized things, interrelated by a web of causal connections. On this view, the world is made of tiny, momentary entities, examples of which would be colors, sounds, thoughts, and sensations. These entities can be classified in a number of ways: into aggregates, into spheres, into components, and so on. But nowhere in this universe of momentary things is there room for a soul, an enduring self, or a sentient being. In particular, you do not really exist, and neither does any other person.

One may wonder how any sane people, much less an entire religious tradition, could hold a view this strange. Isn't there very strong reason to reject, even to dismiss, a view with such counterintuitive consequences? In fact, doesn't anyone who defends such a view automatically run into contradictions just by referring to himself, his audience, other authors, various texts, and other nonexistent entities?

The Buddhist answer relies on a distinction between ultimate and conventional truth. On the most plausible interpretation of this distinction, ultimate truth is just truth. Statements that accurately describe the tiny, momentary entities that make up the world are ultimately true. Statements that talk about composite, macroscopic, enduring substances are not ultimately true. However, some of them have conventional truth, which is something like approximate truth and something like fictional truth. For practical purposes, saying something that is false, but conventionally true, can be more useful and effective than saying what is ultimately true, which might be too long, detailed, and incomprehensible to be useful. Therefore, even enlightened beings would sometimes make use of conventionally true expressions.

Philosophers associated with the Mahāyāna go even farther than this in their rejection of common sense. They argue that even the momentary elements of existence are themselves empty and without any essential nature. Exactly what this doctrine of emptiness comes to is difficult to understand; I have offered a sketch of an interpretation in chapter 6. As I will show later, though, Mādhyamika philosophers such as Śāntideva, when they discuss free will, rely on the early Buddhist doctrine of non-self. The additional claims contained in their more radical version don't seem to bear directly on free will. Leaving aside the disagreements about non-self between different Buddhist philosophers, the crucial point is what they agree on: that people, subjects, agents, are not really existing entities.

Suppose the Buddhists are right about the nonexistence of the self. What would follow about free will? Here's one simple answer: if you don't exist, then nothing is up to you. If there is no autonomous self, there is no autonomy. If there is no genuine boundary between self and other, there can be no genuine distinction between actions that flow from the self and motions imposed on the self from outside. Galen Strawson uses these sorts of considerations to defend the idea that according to Buddhists, the notion of free will is a myth arising from the deluded belief in a self. Unfortunately, Strawson does not attempt to provide any support from Buddhist texts for his hard determinist interpretation. Moreover, many people would resist the notion that Buddhists repudiate free will. Don't Buddhists believe we have some control over our own destiny? Isn't it necessary to make some kind of individual effort to purify people's minds and lives? Starting from this intuitive response, Paul Griffiths has argued that Buddhists hold a form of libertarianism. But his arguments do not hold up well under close scrutiny.

Griffiths explains the Buddhist view of free will as follows:

> Things like personal appearance, physical defects, mental capacity, place of birth, social class, moral character of one's parents—all these are determined by karmic effect. But within these parameters it is still possible to act well or badly, to make the best possible use of what has been determined for one or to make things still worse by bowing to one's limitations. So Buddhist karmic theory is certainly not a strict determinism.[12]

This claim puts Griffiths in a difficult position. If the parameters are all determined by karma, then people's actions must be caused by the parameters, by something else, or by nothing. If actions are caused by the parameters, then they are determined. If they are caused by nothing, they are utterly random, and therefore not free. If they are caused by something else, this something else must either be the self or something other than the self. If the something else is not the self, then either determinism or randomness will result. But the something else can't be the self, because according to Buddhists, there is no self. Therefore, Griffiths's interpretation is untenable.

Griffiths claims that Buddhists don't accept determinism, but his case for this claim is weak. He offers only one argument:

> It is going to be very difficult in any given instance to calculate the karmic effect of any particular action; no one—except of course a Buddha–is likely to have enough data at his disposal to make the necessary calculations. This should be further warning that Buddhist karmic theory is no open-and-shut determinism wherein it is possible to calculate with precision the karmic accounts, as it were, of any given individual.[13]

Now this argument seems to rest on an elementary confusion between predictability in principle and predictability in practice. Few determinists, if any, have held that it is usually possible for humans, equipped with the kind of knowledge humans usually have, to predict what complex systems will do. Even those determinists who have explained their view in terms of predictability have done so in terms of predictability in principle, by hypothetical beings whose cognitive and epistemic resources far exceeded those of ordinary humans.

Moreover, by making an exception for Buddhas, Griffiths seriously undermines his case. In the Mahāyāna Buddhist scriptures, Śākyamuni and other Buddhas constantly make predictions about the future status and accomplishments of various people around them. If Griffiths is right, that fact should give rise to a serious philosophical problem exactly analogous to the conflict between divine foreknowledge and human freedom in Christianity. The fact that Mahāyāna Buddhists never so much as mention this problem suggests that it doesn't arise for them, and therefore that they are determinists of some kind.

Of course, prophecies of enlightenment are not a common feature of the earliest Buddhist scriptures, transmitted by the Pāli Canon of the Theravāda sect. And although Abhidharma texts such as the *Treasury of Metaphysics* describe the Buddha as omniscient about the future, the nature of his knowledge in the Pāli Canon itself is less clear. Thus, for instance, in the *Tevijja-vacchagotta Sutta*, the Buddha gives an account of his own knowledge as consisting in, first, the ability to remember his past lives; second, the "divine eye" that allows him to see the death and rebirth of beings; and third, the direct realization that liberated him from all afflictions.[14] This account does not seem to ascribe to the Buddha any special knowledge about the future. Nathan Katz uses passages like this one to develop a rather restrictive account of the Buddha's omniscience that might not result in problems for libertarian free will.[15] But in the *Cūḷasakuludāyi Sutta*, the Buddha claims that he, or anyone else with the divine eye, can answer any question about the future.[16] Theravāda thinkers have tended to interpret the Buddha's omniscience as the ability to call to mind any fact he wishes about past, present, or future. Their denial that the Buddha has simultaneous occurrent knowledge of all facts seems irrelevant to our concerns here. It appears, then, that Buddhist thinkers, whether Mahāyāna or non-Mahāyāna, held a doctrine of the Buddha's omniscience that should have given them a reason to question libertarian free will.

Besides, we can be independently sure that Buddhists should not be interpreted as libertarians. As Siderits points out,[17] they clearly affirmed a version of determinism: that any psychological or physical event has a cause. In fact, they held that everything that has a beginning has a cause, and that at most a few special entities (such as space and Nirvana) have no beginning. Although it is controversial whether or not universal causality entails the other theses called "determinism," I know of no reason to believe that Buddhists would have tried to reject these other versions of determinism.

There are, moreover, many passages in Buddhist philosophical texts that explicitly reject the notion of agent causation that is so crucial to libertarianism. For example, Vasubandhu, the author of the *Treasury*, gives an account of action that, while scientifically obsolete, manifests an instantly recognizable commitment to the universality of event causation: "From memory arises intention; from intention, thought; from thought, exertion; from exertion, a current in the body; and from this current comes the action. What does the self do in this process?"[18] Meanwhile, the "timing objection" to agent causation, which is often attributed to C. D. Broad,[19] appears in several Buddhist texts. This objection, which involves claiming that a permanent self or soul would be unable to fix a specific time for an action to occur, is central to the Buddhist rejection of the soul[20] and of God.[21] It is clear, then, that Buddhists, while explicitly rejecting agent causation, accept both the universal causality and predictability-in-principle forms of determinism. Thus, if the Buddhist view can be classified at all in the Western taxonomy, it must be either a version of compatibilism or of hard determinism.[22]

According to Siderits, early Buddhists were committed, explicitly or implicitly, to the compatibilist option. He describes what he takes to be the Buddhist position using the distinction between conventional and ultimate truth. At the level of conventional truth, it is correct to say that persons exist and that they carry out actions. At the level of ultimate truth, it is correct to say that there are no persons, that the only entities that exist are momentary simples, and that everything that happens is a result of causes. Siderits argues that the hard determinist rejection of free will is a result of mixing these two levels. At the conventional level of truth, free will exists, since persons are not being broken down into their components, but are being considered from the point of view of common sense, as responsible agents. And at the ultimate level of truth, since there are no persons, there are no unfree persons. Siderits writes that "since psychological determinism is not true of persons, its truth poses no threat to the freedom of persons."[23] Psychological determinism, he holds, is true only at the ultimate level, not the conventional level. He also argues that the problem causality poses for free will arises only when one of the terms of the causal series is a person. "But the causal relations that psychological determinism asserts to obtain among certain physical and mental events do not have persons as relata. Hence it does not follow from the truth of psychological determinism that a person's actions are not freely performed."[24]

How does Siderits know that a compatibilist interpretation is appropriate? In setting out the details of his view, he admits to "striking out on my own, for on this issue the Buddhist texts are silent." But, he argues, "it is clear that the early Buddhists are committed to some form of compatibilism."[25] This is because, as Siderits points out, the Buddhists "claim, against the fatalists, that humans are free in that they are able to act on those choices reached through deliberation."[26] The fatalists in question are such thinkers as Makkhali Gosāla. According to the unfriendly account of this teacher's views that we find in the *Sāmaññaphala Sutta* of the Pāli Canon,[27] he held that the religious life is useless because human actions have no causal efficacy. Whatever one's actions are, the result is the same; whether one is wise or foolish, one remains in cyclic existence for the same amount of time. This fatalist view is often criticized in the *Majjhima Nikāya* section of the Pāli Canon, where it is expressed in the following terms:

> There is no cause or condition for the defilement of beings; beings are defiled without cause or condition. There is no cause or condition for the purification of beings; beings are purified without cause or condition. There is no power, no energy, no manly strength, no manly endurance. All beings, all living things, all creatures, all souls are without mastery, power, and energy; moulded by destiny, circumstance, and nature, they experience pleasure and pain in the six classes.[28]

Unfortunately for Siderits's argument, the fatalist view criticized in the Buddhist scriptures is nothing like modern hard determinism. The claim that defilement and purification occur without a cause conflicts directly with determinism, according to which every event has a cause. Hard determinists would also deny the view that human actions have no causal efficacy; they know that human actions have effects. Rather, they claim that since those actions also have causes, they are not genuinely free. A hard determinist who accepted ancient Indian factual premises might say something like "Good actions are highly effective at promoting one's future welfare, but only some are fortunate enough to be determined to perform them." Hard determinists also hold the view that Siderits thinks distinguishes Buddhism from fatalism: that humans can do what they choose to do. True, it is a central part of a compatibilist account of freedom that a free agent can do what she chooses to do. But hard determinists agree that people can do what they choose to do. Their claim is that since people's choices are determined, they are not free even when they do what they choose to do. The Buddhists' reasons for rejecting fatalism simply are not reasons for rejecting hard determinism. Thus, Siderits's argument for a compatibilist interpretation depends on failing to distinguish clearly between hard determinism and fatalism.

Once this argument has been rejected, and given the absence of any explicit consideration of the problem of free will in Buddhist texts, it is not easy to determine what views about free will, if any, should be attributed to Buddhist thinkers. The best way to proceed is to recall that if there is no free will, attributions of moral responsibility are unjustified. One way to discover the Buddhist view about free will, then, is to examine what Buddhists say about moral responsibility and the associated reactive attitudes.

What would be the consequence of rejecting the notion of moral responsibility? Such a rejection would not overthrow morality: actions can be good or bad even if no one is ultimately responsible for them. Of course, some might ask what the point would be of calling certain actions good and others bad once we have rejected moral responsibility. The answer would be that in doing so we ascribe to those actions a certain property that they objectively have. If we are viewing the question from a Madhyamaka perspective, this is not the most robust form of objectivity that philosophers have proposed: moral properties are only as objective as the properties physics talks about. But the claim that describing an action as good or bad is ascribing an objective property to it is required not just by my interpretation of Buddhist views on moral responsibility, but by my more general interpretation of Buddhist ethics as consequentialist. This is because consequentialism forces certain notions to come apart that we would intuitively expect to go together. Thus, for instance, from a consequentialist point of view, not all wrong actions are blameworthy, and not all right actions are praiseworthy. The blameworthy actions are not those that are wrong, but those that it would have good consequences to blame. Rejecting moral responsibility does not take anything away from the concept of a good action that has not already been removed from that concept by accepting consequentialism.

To the extent that our morality is consequentialist, denying moral responsibility will not undermine it. Instead, rejecting moral responsibility would have *affective* consequences: it would render certain emotions, such as anger and resentment, irrational and inappropriate. That's what gives philosophical interest to van Inwagen's story of the hard determinist philosopher who, "when certain of his books were stolen, said, 'That was a *shoddy* thing to do!'"[29]

Now, most people know that Buddhists don't approve of such emotions as anger and resentment. The Buddhist scriptures often state that anyone who is "given to anger and revenge" is far from liberation.[30] The ideal the Buddha held up to his students goes rather far in the opposite direction:

If anyone should give you a blow with his hand, with a clod, with a stick, or with a knife . . . you should train thus: "My mind will be

unaffected, and I shall utter no evil words; I shall abide compassionate for his welfare, with a mind of loving-kindness, without inner
hate." . . . Bhikkhus, even if bandits were to sever you savagely limb
by limb with a two-handled saw, he who gave rise to a mind of hate
towards them would not be carrying out my teaching.[31]

Several Buddhist texts describe meditative practices that are intended to help
students progress toward this almost superhuman degree of compassion and
forbearance. The content of these meditative exercises is very helpful for understanding Buddhist attitudes toward free will and moral responsibility.

Buddhaghosa, the fifth-century Theravāda Buddhist philosopher and author of the *Path of Purification*, has some advice for van Inwagen's friend:

If resentment arises in him when he applies his mind to a hostile
person because he remembers wrongs done to him by that person,
he should get rid of the resentment by entering repeatedly into
loving-kindness meditation . . . But if irritation still arises in him in
spite of his efforts, he should admonish himself thus: . . .

Since states last but a moment's time
Those aggregates, by which was done
The odious act, have ceased, so now
What is it you are angry with?[32]

In ultimate truth, the action of stealing the books was caused by a collection
of momentary mental and physical simples, all of which have since ceased to
exist. The term "aggregates" in the text should be understood as just referring
to these simple entities, not to a composite entity constructed out of them,
since Buddhaghosa does not believe in the real existence of composites. And
because the simple entities exhaust reality, there is no person to have committed the act; no person who can be held responsible; no person, in fact, who
could have free will.

This strategy for undercutting resentment depends on rejecting the ultimate reality of the persistence of persons through time. Another strategy, also
found in Buddhaghosa, depends instead on rejecting the unity of persons at a
time:

But if he is still not able to stop it in this way, he should try resolution
into elements. How? Now you who have gone forth into homeless-
ness, when you are angry with him, what is it you are angry with?

Is it head hairs you are angry with? or body hairs? or nails? . . . Or among the five aggregates or the twelve bases or the eighteen elements with respect to which this venerable one is called by such and such a name, which then, is it the materiality aggregate you are angry with? . . . For when he tries the resolution into elements, his anger finds no foothold, like a mustard seed on the point of an awl or a painting in the air.[33]

None of the parts of a person seems like an appropriate object of resentment. Only the whole person, or perhaps the self of a person, could be the kind of thing toward which resentment could appropriately be directed. (The only part of the body that might perhaps be an object of resentment is the brain—and then only if the brain is thought of as a self.) If, in ultimate truth, there are no people and there is no self, then since none of the parts of a person can be resented, there is nothing to resent.

Though these arguments may be compelling, at least to some, it would be easy to protest here that simply having these thoughts occur to one would not be sufficient to overcome the deeply ingrained human tendency to anger and resentment. It is crucial, however, that Buddhaghosa is not only presenting philosophical arguments but also describing a meditation practice. If, through mindfulness meditation, a person attains the ability to focus and reflect on her passing thoughts, and if, using that ability, she always responds to an angry or resentful thought by reflecting on the absence of any self, she might, over a long time, be able to weaken or even eliminate her angry impulses. Such is the hope of Buddhist thinkers and practitioners.

Thus, Buddhaghosa exemplifies a tradition of philosophical arguments being used as instructions for meditation. The same sort of dual-purpose text is found in a much later work, the *Introduction to the Bodhisattva's Way of Life* by the Madhyamaka philosopher Śāntideva. As the title suggests, Śāntideva is concerned to describe and advocate the life of boundless compassion and self-sacrificing altruism characteristic of a bodhisattva, an enlightened being who, instead of passing into Nirvana, remains in cyclic existence to work for the benefit of all beings. But Śāntideva also has the goal of telling readers how, over a long period of time, they, too, can become bodhisattvas and embody the highest ideal of Mahāyāna Buddhism.

The one emotion that is the most destructive to the bodhisattva's way of life is hatred. Therefore, in his chapter "The Perfection of Forbearance," Śāntideva offers his readers a series of arguments, again doubling as subjects for meditation, about the inappropriateness and rational indefensibility of anger and resentment. Although they differ significantly from those offered by

Buddhaghosa, they have a similar structure, and a similar basis: the negation of what is recognizably the notion of free will. Śāntideva writes:

> 6.22. I feel no anger towards bile and the like, even though they cause intense suffering. Why am I angry with sentient beings?
> They too have causes[34] for their anger.
> 6.25. Whatever transgressions and evil deeds of various kinds there are, all arise through the power of conditioning factors, while there is nothing that arises independently.
> 6.33. Therefore, even if one sees a friend or an enemy behaving badly, one can reflect that there are specific conditioning factors that determine this, and thereby remain happy.
> 6.39. If it is their very nature to cause others distress, my anger towards those fools is as inappropriate as it would be towards fire for its nature to burn.
> 6.41. If, disregarding the principal cause, such as a stick or other weapon, I become angry with the person who impels it, he too is impelled by hatred. It is better that I hate that hatred.[35]

Śāntideva makes exactly the same argument as Western hard determinists. Unlike them, however, he advises his readers to strive to eliminate anger and resentment from their psyche by repeated, even continual, reflection on the philosophical reasons for rejecting these emotions. Meanwhile, he compares the proper attitude toward other people with the one most people are inclined to take toward such nonsentient things as bile, fire, or sticks. Even if they cause harm, people do not become angry because no one ascribes agency to them. Anyone who ceased to ascribe true agency or self-determination to people would no longer get angry at them; and Śāntideva urges his readers to make this change in themselves.

How does Siderits's interpretation hold up in the face of these passages? The Buddhist tradition clearly seems to hold that at least some of the participant reactive attitudes are neither rational nor appropriate. In fact, it's clear from Śāntideva's tone that he would describe the moral emotion of resentment as a very grave danger: "When the mind is catching alight with the fire of hatred as a result of contact with something, it must be cast aside immediately for fear that one's body of merit might go up in flames. . . . On account of anger, I have been placed in hells thousands of times."[36] Getting rid of the resentment that arises from the illusion of free will, according to Śāntideva, is not just an intellectual requirement, but a pressing practical necessity.

On the other hand, there are certain passages in the *Introduction* in which Śāntideva seems to be evoking reactive attitudes. Though he never tries to inspire his readers with resentment toward any other person, in 6.41, quoted earlier, he does say "It is better that I hate that hatred." This passage does not necessarily mean that hating the hatred is entirely justified, but it does clearly state that this emotion would be preferable to hating the other person who inflicted the suffering. Moreover, at 6.42, he says, "Previously, I too caused just such pain to living beings. Therefore this is just what I deserve, I who have caused distress to other beings." And there are other passages in which Śāntideva is clearly trying to produce the emotion of remorse. In chapter 2, "Confession of Faults," he offers this meditation to his readers:

> 2.28. Throughout the beginningless cycle of existence, and again in
>   this very birth, the evil I, a brute, have done or caused,
> 2.29. Or anything that I, deluded, have rejoiced in to my own
>   detriment, I confess that transgression, tormented by remorse.[37]

Should we conclude from these passages that a compatibilist interpretation of Śāntideva is required?

Note first that it would be perfectly consistent for Śāntideva to hold that some reactive attitudes are useful on the spiritual path, while others are not. The useful emotions might include remorse, gratitude, and certain forms of aggression that are directed toward bad mental states.[38] At the early stages of one's spiritual journey, one should not try to eliminate these emotions, and in fact, it might be helpful to increase them. They operate in the practitioner's mindstream in a way that promotes progress toward enlightenment, so retaining them can be justified by the consequences of doing so. Meanwhile, other reactive attitudes, such as anger and resentment, are completely unhelpful and should be ruthlessly eliminated. And the useful emotions themselves must be held in check, so that healthy remorse, for example, does not develop into pathological guilt.

Since a position of this kind implies that it can make sense to have certain reactive attitudes, it has some compatibilist elements. But it involves proposing a drastic revision to the set of reactive attitudes that ordinary people have; so it does not imply that the range of emotions that ordinarily arises from ascriptions of moral responsibility is, as a whole, compatible with the truth about the causation of actions. It would make sense to describe a position that is so revisionist about everyday life as a form of hard determinism.

Moreover, a position that accepts the pragmatic utility of a subset of the reactive attitudes at an early stage of the path is quite consistent with the view that at the end of the path, all the reactive attitudes have been abandoned. According to traditional Buddhist beliefs, a Buddha can remember innumerable past lives; in many of these, especially those very far in the past, he can remember committing destructive and terrible actions. But it would be wholly inconsistent with the tradition's understanding of Buddhahood to say that this Buddha is "tormented by remorse" about these actions. Nor would a Buddha ever feel gratitude, or have any kind of aggressive emotional reaction to anyone's afflictions. From a Buddha's point of view, all the reactive attitudes are entirely irrational and unjustified.

How can I claim that reactive attitudes such as remorse and gratitude are always irrational and unjustified, and also claim that it is good for certain people to have them? I interpret the Buddhist view of emotions to be that emotions centrally involve descriptive and normative judgments about the world. Like Stoics, Buddhists hold what Martha Nussbaum calls a "cognitive" or "evaluative" view of emotions.[39] And like Stoics, Buddhists maintain that the judgments involved in a wide range of emotions, including almost all the emotions experienced by ordinary people, are comprehensively false. Anyone who is experiencing any of these emotions is, just in virtue of that fact, confused about the way things are. The reactive attitudes, in particular, presuppose a commitment, at some deep psychological level, to the illusion of free will. Of course, emotions also typically involve many other more particular false beliefs. Hatred, for example, may trick me into thinking that someone who has harmed me is a very bad person, a conclusion that may not be remotely warranted by my evidence. These considerations explain why Śāntideva describes hatred as a "deceiver."[40]

Enlightened beings are free from all deception, and therefore don't have most of the emotions with which we are familiar. The only emotions an enlightened being would ever feel are the Four Divine Abidings: loving-kindness, compassion, sympathetic joy, and equanimity. These are emotions that don't depend on mistaken conceptions of the world, such as the illusion of free will.[41]

An enlightened spiritual teacher might sometimes praise or criticize others, in order to cause them to feel emotions that would be helpful to them at their stage on the path. But she would never feel any resentment about their mistakes, or regard them as genuinely responsible for their successes; all praise and blame, for such a teacher, would be merely an expression of skillful means (upāya). Once the students are far enough along, the teacher will show them how to see the inappropriateness of all emotions that are in any way connected with praise and blame. I understand that these statements may seem strange, so I pose a question here: suppose you desperately need to learn a certain subject or skill, and you have to choose between two teachers. The first teacher praises his students whenever they do well and blames them whenever they do poorly. The second teacher is much more subtle and manipulative; she praises and blames the students in just that way that maximizes the rate at which they learn, even sometimes making false statements in the process. If the subject or skill is important, it could well make sense to study with the second teacher. And for Buddhists such as Śāntideva, nothing could be more important, either to you personally or to your ability to help others, than your progress toward enlightenment.

I maintain, therefore, that the *Path* and the *Introduction* contain passages we should read in a way inconsistent with Siderits's compatibilist interpretation. Siderits does cite one Buddhist text that seems to support his view: the *Questions of King Milinda (Milindapañha)*.[42] In this relatively early work, which I discussed in chapter 1, the Greek king Milinda questions a Buddhist monk, Nāgasena, about various problems in Buddhist thought. One of these is how it can be possible, given that personal identity is an illusion, for a person to suffer adverse consequences from his actions in a previous life. Nāgasena replies with a series of similes, intended to illustrate the idea that responsibility can, as it were, flow down the stream of causality. Here is one such example:

> It is, O Great King, like the case of someone who lit a lamp and took it with him to the terrace roof of his home to have his dinner there. And suppose that as the lamp burned it ignited the thatch on the roof of his house, and the fire spread to the rest of the house and from the house it spread to the rest of the village. Then the villagers would seize him and take him before the king, and they would then say, "Your majesty, this man here set fire to our village." [Imagine that the first man] said, "Your majesty, I did not set fire to the village. The flame on the lamp under whose light I had my dinner is one thing, the fire that burnt the village is another thing. I am not guilty of any offense."[43]

Asked how he would decide this case, Milinda says he would rule for the villagers; Nāgasena then claims that, in the same way, karma from past lives applies to one's present life. Siderits's interpretation of the Buddhist attitude toward responsibility is based on passages such as this one. Nevertheless, I believe it is possible to interpret the *Questions of King Milinda* consistently with the hard determinist views of Buddhaghosa and Śāntideva. (This had better be possible, since both Buddhaghosa and Śāntideva face the same problem about reincarnation as the author of the *Questions*.) The key to this passage is that it deals, like the rest of the relevant passages in the text, not directly with moral responsibility, but with *legal* responsibility. Nāgasena can be read as saying something like "Just as the king's law will punish someone for an event that is linked to him through an appropriate causal series, so will the Law of Karma."[44]

This interpretation is significantly strengthened by the observation that Indian Buddhists had the same kind of attitude toward many of their doctrines as modern philosophers do to the laws of nature discovered by science. The Law of Dependent Arising (*pratītyasamutpāda*) is an example. Many scholars would hold that the Law of Karma is in the same category;[45] it is, after all, considered a form of causality. Thus, the Law of Karma is not analogous to a normative law set down by the king but to a reliable description of what the king will do if you transgress. Now, what if the Law of Karma fails to track a robust notion of moral responsibility, because no such notion exists? Well, tough. No one created the Law of Karma, so no one is to blame if it doesn't assign destinies according to desert; there can be no analogue here of the problem of evil faced by theists. For Buddhists, the Law of Karma is just a description of how the universe works, and insofar as people are concerned about their future lives, recognizing its operation will motivate them to do the right thing.[46]

There is another important reason, a moral reason, why Buddhists should not regard karma as tracking a robust sense of desert along the lines advocated by Kantian philosophers. Those who regard desert as having intrinsic significance as a moral concept typically think that if we know that someone's suffering is deserved, we should take a different attitude toward it than we do to undeserved suffering. According to a moderate version of this view, suffering that is deserved is less bad than it would otherwise be, and we have less reason to relieve it. Some philosophers have maintained the stronger thesis that deserved suffering is actually good: it is better if the wicked suffer than if they are happy. Consequentialists, of course, would disagree; they might use the word "desert" to refer to a kind of appropriateness of criticism, punishment, and so on that is wholly based on the consequences of these reactions, but they wouldn't think that the suffering inflicted by the criticism or punishment was good in itself—merely that it was a necessary evil, justified by its good consequences.

If we conjoin a strong, Kantian-style view of desert to the claim that we deserve the effects of karma, that claim will turn out to undermine our compassion. Different Buddhists have different attitudes to the question of whether all of the suffering we see, or just a major part of it, is caused by karma.[47] But on either view, we have far less reason than we thought to relieve the suffering of others, since much or all of the suffering that we would intuitively think was undeserved is actually deserved. Versions of this attitude, which I would regard as based on a misinterpretation of karma, have had very unfortunate consequences in some historical periods. Thus, in certain parts of Buddhist Asia, disabled people have been treated badly, even ostracized, because their relatives and others have interpreted their disabilities as deserved on the basis of their wrongdoing in previous lives. Compassion is at the center of Buddhist ethics, especially in the Mahāyāna, and I would argue that no doctrine that is so opposed to compassion should be regarded as part of Buddhism—especially when we have a superior account available that doesn't have these consequences.

It seems, then, that the Buddhist texts cited above support Strawson's hard determinist interpretation much more than they do Siderits's compatibilist one. In particular, Buddhists seem to have a response to the objection that if free will does not exist, it will be necessary to abandon the practice of ascribing moral responsibility: namely, that abandoning this practice will actually help people to achieve the compassion, generosity, and forbearance needed to make themselves, and others, happy. Though Buddhists would acknowledge that the task of abandoning anger and resentment is difficult, they think it can be achieved through meditation on recognizably philosophical objections to the appropriateness of these emotions.

This view of free will receives support from a variety of different Buddhist texts, and therefore has some claim to represent the tradition generally. It is quite different from the attitude most Western philosophers have taken toward the problem. However, it does resemble the view recently developed by Derk Pereboom in his *Living without Free Will*. Pereboom, though not a determinist, rejects free will. He argues that neither determinism nor quantum randomness leaves space for free will, and that there is no evidence of the existence of agent causation. He calls his view hard incompatibilism, not hard determinism, but the difference is not very important from the point of view of questions about emotions and moral responsibility. Pereboom thinks it may not be possible entirely to overcome feelings of resentment and anger, but to the extent that it is possible, he regards the decay of these feelings as on balance a good thing. He argues that in contemplating the fact that a wrongdoer's actions were wholly determined by events and circumstances not under his control,

> indignation gradually gives way to a kind of moral sadness—a
> sadness not only about his past but also for his character and his
> horrible actions. This kind of moral sadness is a type of attitude that
> would not be undermined by a belief in determinism. Furthermore, I
> suspect that it can play much of the role that resentment and indig-
> nation more typically have in human relationships.[48]

Pereboom further asserts that a reduction in anger and resentment might lead to better interpersonal relationships and to a more just and compassionate social policy. The reform of our moral emotions that Pereboom advocates is somewhat less ambitious than the transformation of the psyche at which Buddhists aim, but it seems to go some distance in the same direction.

Finally, how would a defender of this kind of psychological transformation reply to P. F. Strawson's claim that given the way of life that people in fact lead, they are psychologically incapable of rejecting the participant reactive attitudes? Pereboom claims, with some plausibility, that many of the attitudes Strawson discusses could survive the acceptance of hard determinism, and that those that would not survive, mainly anger and resentment, are not as central to interpersonal relationships as Strawson thinks. But even if Strawson were right about the cost to be paid for rejecting free will, Buddhists would still be willing to pay it. Many modern analytic philosophers seem to think that philosophy must accept society's way of life as it is, and restrict itself to clarifying the conceptual presuppositions of that way of life. But in Buddhism, rational thought can be part of a process that leads people to turn against the way of life they know, and to seek spiritual values instead of worldly ones. For Theravāda Buddhists, those who wish to bring their minds into accord with reality, and thereby attain true inner peace, will normally have to become monks or nuns, thereby severing their ties to the interpersonal relationships of worldly life. But for Mahāyāna Buddhists, it is possible to live as a layperson, in the midst of the demands and distractions of work and family life, while attaining the perfect wisdom that destroys hatred and leads to perfect compassion. From a Buddhist perspective, ordinary interpersonal relationships, though they may have some value, are pervaded with greed, anger, and delusion. To live the best kind of life, a Buddhist must transform the functions of his mind, as well as his relationships to others and to the world. The confidence Buddhists have in the power of their meditative practices leads them to be very optimistic about the practical possibility of such a transformation, despite the obvious difficulty of the task.

Some Western philosophers have regarded philosophical critiques of free will as a danger to religion and morality. But according to Buddhists, these critiques can be incorporated into a meditative methodology that can lead toward compassion and inner peace. Discovering the beliefs and values of Buddhist philosophers may not by itself resolve the problem of free will; but it can suggest options that might otherwise not be discovered, or might otherwise seem much less plausible. This process illuminates how comparative philosophy can lead not only to intercultural understanding but to philosophical understanding as well.

9

Punishment

Nāgārjuna on Punishment

Few scholars of Buddhist ethics have devoted much attention to
questions about the criminal law and the punishments it metes
out. Yet several Indian Buddhist texts contain very interesting
remarks about punishment; of these, the most detailed and revealing
treatment is found in an important Mahāyāna work, Nāgārjuna's
Precious Garland (*Ratnāvalī; Rin po che'i phreng ba*), lost in Sanskrit
and preserved only in Tibetan. This text is a letter of advice to a king.
Along with discussions ranging from the disadvantages of hunting
to the most subtle principles of Buddhist metaphysics, Nāgārjuna
gives the king advice about how to conduct social policy, and in
particular how to treat criminals. These remarks are very interesting
for the light they shed on general issues in Buddhist ethics. They
provide additional evidence for two interpretive theses that we should
believe anyway, on independent grounds: that Indian Buddhists are
consequentialists, and that they are hard determinists.

Moreover, Nāgārjuna's views about punishment have practical
relevance to issues of punishment in modern society. A critic who was
following the principles of Nāgārjuna would certainly render a harsh
verdict on the American penal system. From a Buddhist perspective,
our criminal justice system often punishes the wrong people, to the
wrong extent, and for the wrong reasons. Buddhists should regard
American criminal law as having been substantially shaped by hatred

and ignorance. A legal system that was instead shaped by compassion and insight would still punish, but it would do so very differently from the society we presently live in.

Western philosophers who have reflected on the practice of punishment have been primarily interested in two questions, which can be seen as related or treated independently: the questions of the justification of punishment and of the right to punish. Punishment often involves inflicting great suffering on the guilty. What reasons can be given for such a harmful practice? Even if we can show that some people ought to be punished, not everyone is equally entitled to punish them. Who can legitimately carry out punishment, and what gives them the right to do so?

Buddhist writers do not directly address the question of the right to punish. This is an understandable omission, since the concept of rights is not a feature of their moral discourse. They do advance a political theory that is relevant to this issue. According to Buddhist sources that go back to the Pāli Canon, the original source of royal power is the consent of the governed. The first king, known as Mahāsammata ("great appointee"), was chosen by the people to protect the fields. The kings ruling today, though they were not literally chosen by their people, should still be morally regarded as the people's employees, and the taxes they receive as their wages.[1] There has been some debate about whether it would be inappropriately anachronistic to identify this view as a social contract theory,[2] but any differences between the Buddhist view and Western social contract theory are unlikely to affect the question of the right to punish. Beyond offering the foregoing account of political legitimacy, Buddhists have nothing more to offer that relates to this question. I propose to focus, therefore, on the issue of the justification of punishment, since a number of passages can be found that relate directly or indirectly to this issue.

Philosophers of law have long recognized several main ways punishment can be justified. The simplest is incapacitation: the criminal who is being punished may thereby be prevented from committing further crimes. People who are in prison are generally unable to commit crimes against the general population, though they may, of course, harm each other in various ways. The death penalty is an even more effective method of incapacitation. Perhaps the most important justification for many punishments is deterrence. People who have been punished may refrain from offending in future out of fear of further punishment. And those who have never committed crimes may avoid doing so as a result of reflection on the consequences inflicted on others. Punishment may also be justified by the optimistic consideration of rehabilitation. Perhaps penal institutions can be set up so as to reform the character of inmates, so that the vicious traits that led them to commit crimes are replaced with more socially beneficial ones.

All three of these attempted justifications appeal to beneficial consequences that result from the practice of punishment. Therefore, to regard some or all of these three as together providing sufficient justification for the practice of punishment is to take a consequentialist attitude toward that practice.

All three of the consequentialist reasons for punishment are inherently forward-looking: they appeal to the good consequences that punishment will have in the future, and don't seem to make essential reference to what has happened in the past. Many ethicists and political philosophers have therefore regarded them as missing an element that is essential to the justification of punishment: that in order for punishment to be appropriate, the offender must somehow merit or deserve punishment by his own past actions. The view that some such backward-looking considerations are required to justify punishment is called retributivism.

Retributivism is not a single view but a complex family of views about punishment. For example, some retributivists would claim that the good consequences of punishment can go some of the way, but not all of the way, in justifying the practice, whereas others insist that only backward-looking considerations can legitimately justify punishment.[3] The latter retributivists might argue that to punish a person in order to deter others from committing crimes is to use that person as a means to promote social order and harmony, and that using persons as means is inconsistent with a proper respect for human dignity.[4]

Many ordinary Americans who hold attitudes related to retributivism seem to be motivated, at least in part, by anger toward criminals. They seem to hold not only that criminals deserve to suffer but also that it is better if this suffering is inflicted by an appropriate agent, and that it is fitting for such an agent to be motivated, in part, by righteous indignation toward the criminal.[5] Most philosophers, including those who endorse versions of retributivism, would wish to distance themselves from this kind of claim. However, a few retributivists have accepted it, such as the Victorian legal theorist James Fitzjames Stephen, who writes about criminal acts that

> it is not, however, difficult to show that these acts have in fact been
> forbidden and subjected to punishment not only because they are
> dangerous to society, and so ought to be prevented, but also for the
> sake of gratifying the feeling of hatred—call it revenge, resentment,
> or what you will—which the contemplation of such conduct excites
> in healthily constituted minds.[6]

Stephen is a fairly obscure figure, best known for his criticisms of John Stuart Mill. A more central figure in the Western tradition who also clearly held this view was the economist and moral philosopher Adam Smith. I do not expect ever to read a clearer or more eloquent expression of the position in question than the one Smith offers in his *Theory of Moral Sentiments*:

> Our sense of the horror and dreadful atrocity of such conduct, the delight which we take in hearing that it was properly punished, the indignation which we feel when it escapes this due retaliation, our whole sense and feeling, in short, of its ill desert, of the propriety and fitness of inflicting evil upon the person who is guilty of it, and of making him grieve in his turn, arises from the sympathetic indignation which naturally builds up in the breast of the spectator, whenever he thoroughly brings home to himself the case of the sufferer.[7]

Adam Smith, then, connected desert of punishment closely to the anger and righteous indignation that the crime arouses in an impartial spectator. But this position is not an obligatory view for a retributivist. Other retributivists could reject this view about the moral emotions, but nevertheless hold that criminals deserve to be punished, and that their desert creates reasons to punish them that are independent of the consequences of doing so. These philosophers might say, for example, that by breaking the rules that govern social cooperation, criminals have taken unfair advantage of their fellow citizens, creating a moral imbalance that needs to be righted by punishment.

Utilitarian legal reformers have always opposed the various forms of retributivism. Sidgwick wrote that he had "an instinctive and strong moral aversion to it."[8] It's not difficult to see why. Consequentialism is in tension with the idea that it could make sense to inflict suffering just because of things that have happened in the past; for a consequentialist, reasons that could justify the infliction of suffering have to invoke future benefits to be gained or harms to be avoided. Sidgwick also pointed out that "if we scrutinize closely the common moral notion of Retributive Justice, it appears, strictly taken, to imply the metaphysical doctrine of Free Will."[9] In particular, the view about free will that seems to be most consistent with the retributivist account of punishment is the Kantian version of libertarianism, or one of its relatives. Since, by definition, they reject libertarianism, hard determinists would have reason to oppose a retributive conception of punishment. They could, however, use the other three types of reasons—deterrence, incapacitation, and rehabilitation—to provide justifications for penal institutions.

These connections between moral philosophy and the justification of punishment make it possible to use Buddhist writers' remarks about punishment as evidence relevant to the interpretation of their ethical commitments. By themselves, the comments of Nāgārjuna and others about punishment would not be sufficient to establish any particular account of Buddhist views about ethical theory or the freedom of the will. But if, as I have argued in previous chapters, we have independent evidence that supports a view of Buddhist thinkers as consequentialists and as hard determinists, examining Buddhist views on punishment can reinforce that case.

Hard determinism is not itself a Buddhist concept, and it has no Sanskrit equivalent. Yet, as I discussed in chapter 8, Buddhists do accept claims that we can identify as the universal causality and predictability-in-principle forms of determinism. They explicitly repudiate the concept of agent causation that plays a central role in libertarian views on free will. Buddhists are specifically hard determinists, not compatibilists, because they claim that anger and resentment are never justified, and that these negative emotions can be undermined by reflection on the impersonal causal processes that underlie the production of other people's harmful actions.

The English word consequentialism has no Sanskrit equivalent either. But, as I have argued in previous chapters, the various forms of Buddhist ethics found in South Asian and Tibetan texts can nevertheless appropriately be interpreted as different varieties of consequentialism. Most fundamentally, the reason is that these ethical systems all take the welfare of all sentient beings as the ultimate source of ethical norms. But I have also tried to offer various forms of supporting evidence to buttress this set of interpretations.

If I am right in these interpretive theses, then Buddhists should reject the retributive justification of punishment. And this is indeed the attitude we find in Indian Buddhist texts such as the *Precious Garland*. In particular, Nāgārjuna offers the following advice:

> 331. O king, through compassion you should
> Always generate just an attitude of altruism
> Even for all those embodied beings
> Who have committed awful ill deeds . . .

Nāgārjuna recognizes the necessity for punishment; he advises the king to "eliminate robbers and thieves / in your own and others' countries."[10] But he clearly regards punishment as a necessary evil, to be moderated if possible. The claim that the king should generate altruism toward the criminal presumably entails that the interests of the criminal must be taken into account in setting his punishment—a claim with which utilitarians would, of course, agree. The idea that one's motive for punishing a criminal is compassion, whether to the criminal himself or to other members of society, is also entirely consistent with the utilitarian view, but in tension with the more extreme versions of retributivism. Nāgārjuna also writes:

> 336. Just as deficient children are punished
> Out of a wish to make them competent,
> So punishment should be carried out with compassion,
> Not through hatred nor desire for wealth.[11]

Some retributivists would object to this analogy. Children who have broken their parents' rules, they would argue, are not capable of fully comprehending the moral implications of their actions; nor have they developed the degree of free will that normal adults possess. Thus they are not capable of deserving suffering in the same way adult criminals do. Hence, the reasoning that justifies punishing delinquent children must be quite different from that which justifies punishing adult criminals.

We have antecedent reasons to believe that Buddhists would be unsympathetic to retributivism, at least in those versions that endorse the idea of righteous indignation. The claim that anger can sometimes be warranted is alien to Buddhist thought, and is repudiated by both Mahāyāna and Theravāda thinkers.[12] As Bhikkhu Ñānamoli, for example, has taught, "there is no righteous anger in the Buddha's teaching."[13] And we read in the *Sumangala Jātaka*:

> King I am, my people's lord;
> Anger shall not check my bent:
> When to vice I take the sword,
> Pity prompts the punishment.[14]

The *Precious Garland* shares this rejection of anger, especially when it is prompted by wrongs done to oneself. Nāgārjuna's advice is as follows: "considering the harm others do to you / as created by your former deeds, do not anger."[15] This suggestion to dispel anger by examining the causes of wrong actions should certainly remind us of Western hard determinism—though with the difference that karma is seen as central to those causes. As I showed in chapter 8, even closer parallels can be found in other Buddhist texts.

The retributivist view, which I claim the Buddhist tradition is committed to rejecting, has important practical consequences when it comes to the treatment of prisoners. If criminals deserve to suffer, and punishing them is justified by responding to this feature of desert, then their punishment should take place under harsh conditions, so as to ensure that the required suffering in fact occurs. On the other hand, consequentialist justifications of punishment imply that prisoners should not be treated any more harshly than is required to achieve deterrence and incapacitation. If prison is more pleasant than life on the outside, then no one will be deterred by the threat of prison. And security measures in the prison are necessary to prevent escape and thereby make sure that prisoners don't harm the general population while they are serving their sentences. But to make prisons worse than these goals require them to be is to inflict needless suffering with no moral justification.

It's not hard to discover which side of this dispute would be supported by Buddhist thinkers. Nāgārjuna writes:

> 335. As long as prisoners are not freed,
> They should be made comfortable
> With barbers, baths, food, drink,
> Medicine, and clothing.[16]

This does not seem like a very ambitious set of suggestions to us, but in the materially far poorer society of ancient India, these recommendations probably went well beyond what would actually have been provided in most prisons. In any case, Nāgārjuna clearly thinks that compassion requires the king to make the prisoners comfortable, and not to torment them unnecessarily.

He also advocates clemency whenever possible:

> 333. Free the weaker prisoners
> After a day or five days.
> Do not think the others
> Are not to be freed under any conditions.

Thus, shorter sentences are to be preferred to longer ones. It is important to note that Nāgārjuna lists physical weakness as a relevant factor in deciding whom to release early. In his society, where most violence was carried out with such weapons as bows and swords, physical strength was a good proxy for danger to society. All retributivists, though, would object to the idea that the degree of punishment should be based on how dangerous the criminal is to society, rather than the severity of the crime or the degree of culpability of the criminal.

The compassionate concern that leads to these recommendations, moreover, extends even to those guilty of the worst crimes:

> 332. Especially generate compassion
> For those murderers, whose sins are horrible;
> Those of fallen nature are receptacles
> Of compassion from those whose nature is magnanimous.

This verse makes a strong claim, but one that is entirely consistent with both Asian and Western understandings of compassion. Elizabeth Anderson, for example, has remarked that "compassion seeks to relieve suffering wherever it exists, without passing moral judgment on those who suffer. International humanitarian organizations such as the Red Cross offer aid to all the victims of war, including even the aggressors."[17]

Though the king should feel compassion for all prisoners, Nāgārjuna recognizes that not all of them can realistically be expected to reform. His recommendation for dealing with incorrigible prisoners is this:

> 337. Once you have analyzed and thoroughly recognized
> The angry murderers,
> Have them banished
> Without killing or tormenting them.

Thus Nāgārjuna is an opponent of capital punishment. Banishing these prisoners would seem to show a lack of compassion for the inhabitants of neighboring countries; but permanent banishment might at least have the virtue, in a society with primitive means of transportation and communication and strong ties to local communities, of being a fairly effective deterrent.

Notice that Nāgārjuna advises the king to think carefully about the prisoners and try to understand them. Buddhist texts often advise trying to see situations from various points of view, including the points of view of others who may be causing trouble for you.[18] Doing so, Buddhists would claim, can reduce your anger, and thereby undermine the strongly punitive attitudes that arise from that anger.

This picture has recently received some support from empirical research. Psychologists Arthur G. Miller, Anne K. Gordon, and Amy M. Buddie asked experimental subjects to read accounts of crimes and then write explanations of the causes of the criminals' actions. The subjects were also asked to offer judgments about the criminals, expressed in a numerical scale. Some were asked to do so before, and others after, writing the explanations. The results were as follows:

> Participants who generated explanations before indicating their rating-scale judgments took a relatively more exonerating stance toward the perpetrator. They displayed more empathy, attributed more influence to the perpetrator's socioeconomic status, and rated the perpetrator as a better person than did participants who made these ratings immediately after reading the scenarios. They also recommended less punishment and saw the perpetrator as being less of a threat to society.[19]

The same authors cite other recent experiments that suggest that when subjects are caused to be angry by such means as being asked to imitate angry facial expressions, and are then exposed to scenarios that resulted in harm to someone, they are more likely to blame the negative outcomes on agents in the scenarios and to adopt punitive attitudes toward those agents.[20] Psychological evidence, it seems, is beginning to appear that supports the Buddhist tradition's views that to understand is to forgive, and that the desire to inflict harsh punishment often flows from a form of anger that cannot withstand rational scrutiny.

In American politics, religious voices are often heard on both sides of debates about capital punishment and prison reform. It is clear, and should not be surprising, that the Buddhist tradition weighs strongly on the side of clemency and moderation in punishment. Some students of Buddhism might be surprised, though, that Nāgārjuna tells the king to use punishment at all, under any circumstances. A very strict, absolute interpretation of the concept of nonviolence, after all, would not allow the punishment of criminals. Indeed, some South Asian Buddhist texts adopt this kind of extreme attitude. The different views about punishment and nonviolence expressed in Theravāda Buddhist texts have been ably discussed by Steven Collins.[21] He cites, for example, the story of Siri Sangha Bodhi, a Sri Lankan king who completely ceased to implement punishments,

> secretly releasing prisoners after giving them money, and having
> corpses burnt publicly in their place. His treasurer Gothābhaya, how-
> ever, assembles the released criminals into an army and threatens
> Siri Sangha Bodhi, who not only renounces the crown in his favor to
> avoid war, but also, when later Gothābhaya puts a price on his head,
> decapitates himself in front of the poor man so that he can take his
> head and obtain the reward. . . . The text has him do this specifically
> "for the sake of attaining Omniscience (i.e. Buddhahood)."[22]

Siri Sangha Bodhi is held up as a kind of ideal of nonviolence and detachment from worldly concerns. Yet from this story, it is clear that the South Asian sources recognize the potentially disastrous consequences to society of abandoning the practice of punishment. The people of Sri Lanka are left to be ruled by an unscrupulous tyrant, backed by an army of criminals. In general, if the state fails to punish, crime will increase to the point at which social order completely breaks down. There are Buddhist texts that make this very point; for example, we read in the *Sutra of Golden Light* that

> when a king overlooks an evil deed in his region and does not inflict
> appropriate punishment on the evil person, in the neglect of evil
> deeds lawlessness grows greatly, wicked acts and quarrels arise in

great number in the realm . . . whoever has accumulated wealth, by
various evil acts they deprive one another of them.[23]

This text clearly recognizes the need for deterrence and the disastrous consequences of its absence. Long before this kind of chaos reaches its maximum,
the government that refuses to function as a government will be replaced by
another that will.

The behavior of Siri Sangha Bodhi makes sense only in a vaster, cosmic
context, in which the training in renunciation he undergoes will make possible
the immense benefits he can bring to sentient beings as a Buddha. Perhaps
these consequences, viewed in a broader perspective, can outweigh the catastrophic social effects of unqualified nonviolence. But a writer inspired by the
Mahāyāna would be likely to object that if Siri Sangha Bodhi, as a bodhisattva,
really feels compassion for the people in his kingdom, this compassion should
lead him to choose a path that will promote their welfare, not their misery.
From this point of view, unqualified nonviolence represents one extreme on
a spectrum at the other end of which lie the vengeful excesses of the harsher
versions of retributivism. Nāgārjuna, here as elsewhere, steers a middle path
between these extremes.

A Buddhist defender of unqualified nonviolence might try to avoid reading the text this way. Perhaps Nāgārjuna's advocacy of the moderate and compassionate application of punishment is no more than an exercise of skillful
means, an upāya. Perhaps the Precious Garland is a text of provisional meaning (neyārtha), presenting a limited and unsophisticated interpretation of the
Dharma for the benefit of a spiritually undeveloped layperson. This is a standard interpretive strategy used by Buddhists to avoid accepting the literal sense
of texts that seem in tension with other sources in the tradition.

But there is a major bar to relegating the Precious Garland to this lower status. The work contains an extensive explanation of the doctrine of emptiness.
Nāgārjuna and other members of the Middle Way School make it clear that one
should not explain emptiness to those who are spiritually unprepared to hear it.
The king to whom the Precious Garland is addressed must therefore be a fairly
advanced spiritual practitioner. It is unlikely that he is getting anything less
than the best possible explanation Nāgārjuna can give about how a king should
behave. This explanation may, of course, differ quite substantially from a presentation of how a monk should behave.[24] Nevertheless, the Precious Garland
constitutes significant evidence that entirely unqualified assertions of nonviolence do not express the consensus of the South Asian Buddhist tradition.[25]

We can still ask, from a more theoretical standpoint, how any view that was
legitimately Buddhist could ever endorse the kinds of violence that are needed

to establish and maintain the practice of punishment, given the prohibition against violence embodied in the First Precept. But the answer is not far to seek, if we refer back to Asaṅga's explanation of when precept-breaking can be justified. In chapter 4, I showed that for Asaṅga, the precepts can be broken whenever doing so benefits everyone, including the person who might at first seem to be the victim of the precept-breaking. But from a Buddhist point of view, specific deterrence and incapacitation are a benefit to the criminal. If we forcibly stop someone from performing karmically destructive acts, we protect that person from having to suffer the consequences of those acts in future lives. Rehabilitation, if we can achieve it, is an even greater benefit to the criminal, since it removes him from a state of vice to one of greater virtue, therefore (according to the theory of well-being I have attributed to the Buddhist tradition) making him considerably better off. On Asaṅga's view, it seems, we may permissibly use violence against someone in order to benefit him in these ways.

This view of punishment is interestingly similar to that presented by Plato in the *Gorgias*.[26] On both views, punishment benefits the criminal, no matter how much he may seem to be harmed by it. It is not difficult to understand why this similarity exists, if, as I have argued in earlier chapters, Plato and the Buddhist tradition agree that virtue is intrinsically good and is a crucial component of human well-being. It may also be relevant that both Plato and the Buddhists maintain that there will be future lives in which our fate will be determined by the moral quality of our actions in this one.

This account of punishment finds a striking instance in the conduct that later Indian Buddhist traditions attribute to the Buddha himself. I refer to the story of Hariti, dramatically depicted (along with numerous other Buddhist narratives) in the rock-cut temples of Ellora and Ajaṇṭā in Maharashtra, India. Hariti, a demonic female being with hundreds of offspring, amused herself by carrying off and killing human children. The Buddha, seeking to correct this behavior, kidnapped one of Hariti's children. The demoness, filled with rage, found the Buddha and attempted to slay him, but was unable to overcome his supernatural powers. The Buddha then pointed out to her that her feelings of rage and distress were just like those experienced by the human mothers whose children she had killed. Filled with remorse, Hariti accepted the Buddha's request to cease her wicked deeds and become, instead, a divine protector of children.

From the point of view of the history of religion, this story reflects the process by which an Indian folk deity associated with infant mortality was incorporated into the Buddhist canon. If we look at the story from the point of view of ethical theory, though, it looks quite similar to more standard (and nonmagical) cases of punishment. Using coercive force, the Buddha shows a wrongdoer why her actions are morally reprehensible, and induces her to change her ways and reform. In carrying out punishments out of a motivation to benefit both the criminal and other sentient beings, Buddhists who accept the traditions in question can regard themselves as emulating the best of all possible models.

Asaṅga's view not only makes possible the justification of punishment but also quite elegantly handles a standard objection to consequentialist views of punishment: that they might justify punishing the innocent. Those who are innocent are in no need of reform; therefore, punishing them cannot benefit them, and would only harm them for the benefit of others. Indeed, being punished for crimes they didn't commit might well cause them to become bitter, resentful, contemptuous of authority, and in general, less virtuous. In Asaṅga's version of rule-consequentialism, this kind of balancing is generally not allowed. So we can rule out the possibility of punishing the innocent without having to accept that the guilty deserve punishment. It appears that Asaṅga's complex rule-consequentialism may be better suited to provide a coherent justification of punishment than either direct or indirect Western forms of consequentialism.

The early Buddhist tradition and Śāntideva's system do not share this advantage. On the Theravāda view, which implies that morally ideal people do not ever break the precepts, the violence inherent in punishment will always represent a questionable compromise with how one really ought to live. This fact may explain the currency of the story of Siri Sangha Bodhi in that tradition. Śāntideva's form of act-consequentialism shares with its Western relatives the problem that in special cases, it might require punishing innocent people. Śāntideva would probably need to fall back on the fact that such cases would be very rare. As just noted, rehabilitation would be highly unlikely ever to justify the punishment of the innocent. Moreover, the innocent do not need to be incapacitated. And if the fact that punishment was inflicted on the innocent ever becomes generally known, then deterrence will be severely undermined. Deterrence cannot work if people believe they are in danger of punishment whether or not they break the law. Any widespread social practice will eventually become generally known. So Śāntideva would have to endorse punishing innocent people only in extremely rare cases in which doing so was necessary to prevent some terrible catastrophe. Though some might still consider this a grave objection, others might find it an acceptable consequence of Śāntideva's views.

Practical Implications

The evidence I have discussed is highly relevant to interpreting general Buddhist views about how we should relate to each other. But its relevance transcends this historical context. The moral standpoint of the *Precious Garland* straight-forwardly generates specific criticisms of the American penal system.

These criticisms are based on distinctively Buddhist normative and descriptive premises; some will have little or no force for non-Buddhists. Thus, in countries where Buddhists are in a minority, it will be useless to advance these criticisms as a contribution to public debate about the legal system. Even where Buddhists are in a majority, respect for their fellow citizens who hold different beliefs may oblige them to advance, within the public sphere, only arguments that can be defended entirely on secular grounds. Therefore, the criticisms I shall present should be viewed within the context of the Buddhist comprehensive doctrine, in Rawls's sense.[27]

One obvious point is that a follower of Nāgārjuna would wish to encourage the United States to join most other industrialized nations in abolishing the death penalty. The argument just given that Asaṅga's system can justify punishment clearly does not extend to capital punishment. It does not seem likely that we could reform a criminal by executing him. Moreover, since life imprisonment in solitary confinement is available as a highly effective form of incapacitation, if a prisoner is in police custody, we cannot justify killing her by appealing to the necessity of preventing her from incurring more bad karma by committing more crimes. Public support for the death penalty in the United States seems to be based mainly on the retributivist attitudes that Buddhist thinkers reject.[28]

Those Buddhists who, unlike Asaṅga, are act-consequentialists, need to take into account recent empirical work suggesting that the death penalty may, in fact, be a more effective deterrent than any alternative punishment.[29] For a Buddhist act-consequentialist, saving the lives of many potential victims through deterrence would be a valuable enough goal to justify harming the criminal. In reply, Buddhists might wish to endorse the argument of Catholic death penalty abolitionists who point to the value of creating a "culture of life" in which the government encourages respect for life by refraining from killing whenever possible. Buddhists would also attach great importance to the possibility that a prisoner who is incarcerated for life instead of being executed may have the opportunity to repent of his crimes. Paradoxically, for someone who accepts the traditional Buddhist worldview, saving a murderer's life may even be more important than saving the lives of his victims through deterrence. His possible victims, if they are killed, may have a reasonable chance of being reborn as humans; whereas the murderer, if he does not repent, is almost certain to spend an extremely long (though finite) time in a terrible, hellish realm of suffering. A punishment that gives him any realistic chance of avoiding this destiny through repentance is thus morally very important.

The relevance of Nāgārjuna's views to modern society goes well beyond the death penalty. A Buddhist thinker reflecting on the U.S. criminal justice system would probably be alarmed at the fact that in 2002, U.S. state and federal prisons held 54,400 inmates aged fifty-five or older.[30] The vast majority of crimes are committed by young men. Most of these inmates probably do not represent a serious danger to society, no matter how terrible their earlier offenses. Nāgārjuna's injunction to "free the weaker prisoners" would surely apply to the majority of these elderly inmates.

They could, perhaps, be released by acts of executive clemency. The exercise of such clemency would be politically difficult in the current climate of opinion; Buddhists engaged in social activism might take on the task of altering that climate. But a better solution would surely be to change the harsh laws that are responsible for the current situation. When Nāgārjuna says "Do not think the others / Are never to be freed," we may deduce that he would oppose the imposition of the sentence of life imprisonment without the possibility of parole. There may be some criminals, sociopathic mass murderers for example, who are so dangerous to society that they should in fact be kept in prison for life. Parole boards can make such decisions in particular cases. But a penal system inspired by the values of the *Precious Garland* would not foreclose the possibility of rehabilitation by deciding in advance that a prisoner could never be released.

These considerations would imply that the "three strikes" laws in many states, which provide that those who commit three felonies are put in prison for life without parole, are ethically unacceptable. California's law is especially bad, since it allows the third "strike" to be a nonviolent crime. Most people, on reflection, do not regard it as appropriate that a person could be imprisoned for life after being convicted three times for forging checks, for instance. Yet in practice, "three strikes" laws are very popular. A plausible explanation is that those who support these laws have little concern for the welfare of criminals, and are primarily motivated by hatred and fear toward them. These problems are exacerbated, of course, by racial patterns of criminal activity and incarceration that tap into long-standing problems in U.S. society.

It is instructive to reflect on why Buddhists should advocate harsher penalties for violent offenses than for nonviolent ones. One obvious reason is that violent offenses normally cause more harm, and from the point of view of the potential victims it is therefore more important to deter or incapacitate those likely to commit them. But Buddhists have a reason to claim that in general, a violent crime should be punished more than a non-violent one, even when they cause equal harm. Recall that, for Buddhists, deterrence is also a benefit to the potential criminal: if he is stopped from committing crimes, he will not suffer the karmic consequences of doing so. Now Buddhists believe that actions taken out of hatred are much more karmically damaging than those taken out of greed. Since violent crimes are more likely to be performed out of hatred, they should be more severely punished.

I have shown that Nāgārjuna seems to advocate a substantial amount of discretion on the part of the king, acting here as judge, to allow the king to show mercy to some criminals. It would be appropriate to infer, I think, that Buddhists should oppose harsh mandatory minimum sentences, which are deliberately designed to prevent compassionate judges from exercising clemency. Some defenders of mandatory minimum sentences have argued that they are necessary to produce consistency in sentencing. Although this reasoning may have force as a legal argument, it would not be as powerful if offered in the context of Buddhist ethics. Buddhist texts do not seem to assign fairness any intrinsic weight in moral judgments. A situation in which some of those who have committed the same crime are punished enough and others too much would be better, from a Buddhist point of view, than a situation in which all were punished equally excessively.

Those who have a retributive conception of punishment may well believe that all those who commit a certain crime should receive a certain minimum punishment, since they have deserved that punishment through their wrong actions. But those who wish to justify punishment through rehabilitation, deterrence, and incapacitation will say instead that circumstances alter cases, and that these goals do not require all criminals to be punished equally harshly. However, these consequentialist aims do rule out a totally unpredictable system in which there is no regularity at all in the application of punishment. If prisoners see that there is no rhyme or reason to the length of sentences that are assigned, they may come to believe that punishment is merely the unjustified infliction of suffering on them by those who have the power to do so.[31] This belief would prevent the punishment from having any rehabilitative effect. Moreover, if the degree of punishment for a crime is very unpredictable, people may be less deterred, thinking that even if caught, they could be punished only lightly. These considerations show that some degree of consistency is necessary, but they do not seem to me to require the high degree of rigidity embodied by legal mandatory minimum sentences.

For Buddhists, being a judge is a morally perilous position. Those who pass sentences out of hatred toward those they punish will receive bad karma from doing so. Judges themselves need some legal space to show mercy and compassion if they are to preserve their own psychological and moral well-being. And Buddhists and Western utilitarians would argue that to punish criminals more harshly than necessary is simply to bring about needless suffering.

In addition to reinforcing public support for mandatory minimum sentences, the retributivist beliefs of many Americans seem also to have undermined confidence in the value of prison education programs. Retributivists may well hold that there is no urgent need to provide educational opportunities for prisoners; indeed, they may not deserve to receive such opportunities, especially if they are valuable and not available to all nonimprisoned persons. The prevalence of such sentiments has meant that these programs, where they exist, are often severely underfunded. On a Buddhist conception of the function of punishment, on the other hand, programs such as GED courses and prison libraries are a highly desirable use of resources. For one thing, empirical evidence shows that prison education programs reduce recidivism, thereby contributing very materially to the central goal of reducing crime.[32] Moreover, these programs are the best hope society has for achieving the elusive goal of rehabilitation. The present system not only fails abjectly to rehabilitate prisoners but, sadly, seems in many cases to make prisoners worse. The inevitable consequences of long-term association with hardened criminals, the general climate of fear and violence in prisons, and the lack of a realistic hope for a better life after getting out of prison all contribute to making rehabilitation unlikely. Even if extensive educational opportunities are provided to prisoners, only a minority will probably take full advantage of them; the grim reality seems to be that without a profound transformation nobody really knows how to bring about, our prisons will remain more likely to make prisoners worse people than to make them better ones. But insofar as prison education programs can partially counteract this general trend, Buddhists should support them and do what they can to contribute to them.

This dreadful situation in U.S. prisons provides a powerful argument against using prisons as instruments of drug policy. A case can be made on Buddhist grounds that currently illegal drugs, especially marijuana and certain hallucinogens, should not be illegal at all. But if possession of these drugs is to be punished, treatment would seem to be a much more appropriate form of sentence than prison, given that perfectly ordinary young people who experiment with drugs, once sentenced to prison, may be turned into hardened, lifelong criminals. The sale of drugs is motivated by greed, not by hatred; thus the reasoning canvassed above suggests that from a Buddhist point of view, the current, often extremely harsh punishments for selling drugs should be reduced, and that the sale of drugs should, at the very least, be punished less harshly than violent crimes.

I have explained several consequences that follow from the application of Buddhist values and beliefs, as found especially in the *Precious Garland*, to the contemporary American criminal justice system. Those who do not share these values and beliefs may have little reason to endorse the details of their consequences. But Buddhists' rejection of retributivism, the core of their position in this area, can be justified independently of their less plausible traditional beliefs. Retributivism is not viable without a robust notion of free will, and such a conception of free will is extremely difficult to defend. Some might argue that without the concepts of desert and moral responsibility, the practice of punishment would disintegrate, leading to catastrophe and social chaos. Those Buddhist texts that appear to completely reject punishment can only reinforce this impression. But insofar as some Buddhists, such as Nāgārjuna, have been able to develop a coherent view of the role of punishment in society that does away with concepts of free will, desert, and retribution, they may help us to see the practical relevance of a compassionate worldview that can be defended with powerful theoretical arguments.

10

Objections and Replies

Interpretive Objections

In this chapter I consider several different objections that can be raised against the points I have been making. First, I consider some interpretive objections, whose purpose is to cast doubt on the possibility of interpreting the Buddhist tradition in terms of consequentialism. Next, I address a substantive objection that has been raised against classical utilitarianism. By showing that the Buddhist ethical view, as I interpret it, is immune to this objection, I hope to show that this view is in some respects preferable to at least some Western versions of consequentialism. Finally, I discuss substantive objections that can be raised specifically against character consequentialism. In trying to answer these objections, we may be able to clarify the nature of that theory and assess its plausibility.

In chapter 7 of *The Nature of Buddhist Ethics*, Damien Keown offers a series of objections against the interpretive claim that Buddhist ethics is best understood as consequentialism. Most of these objections have little force. If we adopt a sufficiently general and sympathetic understanding of consequentialism, we see that a consequentialist who accepted the appropriate factual premises could agree with Buddhists in each case in which Keown sees a disagreement. There is no conflict between the evidence Keown brings forward and the texts I have presented in support of a consequentialist interpretation.

In replying to Keown's objections, I will need to make use of a distinction between two kinds of act-consequentialism: objective and subjective. Objective act-consequentialists say that the right thing for an agent to do in any situation is whatever action will, in fact, have the best consequences in that situation. But many writers believe that this version of the theory is less plausible than the alternative: subjective act-consequentialism, according to which the right thing to do in any situation is whatever action the agent expects to have the best consequences, given the agent's beliefs. The subjective version of act-consequentialism is stronger because the objective version seems to imply that morality sometimes tells people to act on information they don't have.

This distinction among utilitarian theories enables us to dispose of Keown's "formal considerations" against a utilitarian account of Buddhist ethics. Keown points out that according to Buddhists, "wrong (akusala) acts cannot turn out 'in the event' to have been right by virtue of their proximate or remote effects; nor can right (kusala) acts turn out to have been wrong in view of their consequences."[1] Although objective utilitarians think that acts that appeared to be right could later turn out to have been wrong, since they happened to have bad consequences, subjective utilitarians, like Buddhists, would hold that if you do what you expect to have the best consequences on the whole, your action is morally right, no matter what its actual consequences are.

Keown's other "formal consideration" is based on an elementary misunderstanding. According to Keown, "Buddhism does not define the right independently of the good"[2]—but neither does utilitarianism, which defines right actions as those that are expected to maximize the good. Indeed, this way of defining the right in terms of the good is distinctive to consequentialism.

Keown later says that a utilitarian who accepted Buddhist factual premises about the blissfulness of a heavenly existence would judge that "this is the highest good achievable through ethics and acts which produce it are by definition right."[3] But Keown presents an example from the Pāli Canon in which the Buddha discusses the non-Buddhist story, going back to the Rg Veda, of the gods, who gained heavenly bliss by defeating the asuras. Since the Buddha disapproved of the violence the gods used in this struggle, he offered a negative assessment of their actions. Therefore, Keown concludes, "pleasant and unpleasant consequences do not lie at the root of Buddhist moral evaluation."[4]

This example is very weak. A Buddhist might certainly say that though the gods temporarily gained heaven, their violence against the asuras would lead them to a large number of lives in hell after they died in heaven, and the sufferings of hell would more than outweigh their impermanent heavenly happiness. Moreover, Keown is focusing only on the consequences experienced by the gods, and forgetting about the suffering inflicted on the asuras, both during and after the battle. A universalist consequentialist would take this suffering into account in evaluating the gods' actions.

Keown worries about how a consequentialist could explain the actions of enlightened beings. He asks:

> Once the *Arhat* has transcended karma, what is there now to deter-
> mine his moral conduct? If moral acts no longer have consequences
> for him, then consequences cannot be the criterion of rightness. So
> why should he continue to follow rules which are fashioned on the
> basis of a utility in which he no longer has any interest?[5]

Directed at a universalist consequentialist interpretation, this objection is surprisingly flatfooted. The actions of a Saint no longer have any consequences for
him, since he is wholly happy and peaceful no matter what happens to him. But
surely they continue to have consequences for others. Since the Saint is perfectly compassionate due to his repeated practice of the Four Divine Abidings
(loving-kindness, compassion, sympathetic joy and equanimity), he will pay
attention to those consequences. In fact, not having any desires of his own, he
will devote all his efforts during the remainder of his final existence to teaching
the Dharma and promoting the good of other beings. Surely the canonical descriptions of the behavior of Saints are just what a universalist consequentialist
would expect.

Keown's attempts in *The Nature of Buddhist Ethics* to discredit a consequentialist interpretation of Buddhist thought are, then, quite unsuccessful. Some
rest on a failure to recognize the distinction between subjective and objective
utilitarianism. Others seem to require not noticing the universalist nature of
the consequentialist theories that might plausibly be used to interpret Buddhism. In a more recent article, "Karma, Character, and Consequentialism,"[6]
Keown offers further arguments against the consequentialist interpretation,
some of them directed at a view not completely dissimilar to the one I am advocating. Though he repeats some of the same misunderstandings found in his
book, there are additional points that need to be considered.

The theory Keown is concerned to attack is an application of ideas from
P. J. Ivanhoe's article "Character Consequentialism"[7] to Buddhist ethics. The
theory Ivanhoe puts forward in this article is rather complex and, as I explained
in chapter 3, involves repudiating certain features of consequentialism that I
believe Buddhism would want to retain. But at its core, the theory of character
consequentialism involves taking virtues to be intrinsically valuable—that is,
adding them to the objective list of intrinsic goods—and then maximizing the
good thus defined. Keown thinks that this view is either ill-defined or reduces
to virtue ethics. He complains that

this amounts to the suggestion that a means (in this case virtue) is inherently valuable because it is the only way to secure the utility sought. But for consequentialism no *means* can have inherent value. A wrench may be the only tool which will get the job done, but it is still only a tool. For consequentialism, *nothing* has inherent value other than the utility produced.[8]

Ivanhoe may have been incautious in expressing his view here, and Keown is right that even an indispensable means has only instrumental value, for a consequentialist. But the main idea of character consequentialism is that the "utility" we are to use for evaluating consequences itself includes a consideration of how much virtue there is in the world. Thus, for a consequentialist who includes virtues on her objective list of goods, these virtues are not mere means, but ends in themselves. Yet we can still attach quite a bit of content to the claim that this theorist is a consequentialist, and not a virtue ethicist, because her theory might come out consequentialist on the various tests I discussed in chapter 2.

In his criticism, Keown focuses on egoistic, rather than universalistic, forms of character consequentialism. He does this even though he admits that an egoistic interpretation "is a gross distortion of Buddhism, which constantly emphasizes compassion and concern for *others*." His reason for focusing on this "distortion" is that "it has been entertained seriously by several authorities as representing the Buddhist position."[9] Though any egoist interpretation of Buddhism clearly misses the mark quite badly, Keown fails to realize, as I have repeatedly pointed out above, that the Buddhist emphasis on universal compassion is in fact one of the strongest reasons for understanding Buddhist ethics as consequentialist.

Many of Keown's criticisms of consequentialist interpretations of Buddhism are, as I have shown, strikingly inept. But he has one objection that, it seems to me, has real force, at least if developed in the right way. Keown claims that in Buddhism the rightness or wrongness of an action depends on the intention of the action, rather than the actual consequences. Thus, for instance, Channa, who donated the food to the Buddha that gave him dysentery and thereby caused his death, was acting rightly, according to the Buddhist scriptures, because he did not know that the food was contaminated. According to Keown, utilitarians care only about the actual consequences of actions, and not about their motives.[10] Thus, Buddhist ethics cannot be utilitarian.

Keown is correct, but only about objective utilitarianism. Thus, an objective utilitarian would condemn Channa for an action that resulted in the Buddha's death. But a subjective utilitarian could praise Channa for acting rightly, since he thought his action would have the good consequences of sustaining the Buddha's life and making merit for himself. Keown's point, as stated, shows only that Buddhists would reject the objective version of utilitarianism; they might still have accepted the more plausible subjective version.

However, the role of intention in Buddhist ethics goes well beyond cases similar to Channa's, and it may well appear that this role is not one that intention could play in any genuinely consequentialist theory. So, for example, the *Chapter on Ethics* of Asaṅga repeatedly discusses how the different motives that one might have for performing an action can affect the moral status of that action. According to Asaṅga, performing a given action out of malice can count as a "defiled fault," whereas performing that same action out of laziness would be an "undefiled fault."[11] In a consequentialist theory, on the other hand, the moral weight of an action can depend only on that action's consequences—whether actual or expected—and not on the motivation for performing the action. How, then, can I claim that Asaṅga is any kind of consequentialist?

We can begin to answer this objection by noting that consequentialist evaluation of an *agent* can be different from consequentialist evaluation of an *action*.[12] Performing an action out of malice can reveal serious flaws in a person's character; perhaps it is to these flaws that Asaṅga is alluding with the term "fault" (*āpatti*). On the other hand, doing the action out of laziness may still manifest an undesirable character trait, but it is not a trait that is likely to cause nearly as much damage. There is nothing to prevent consequentialists from noticing or discussing these points.

Given the particular theory of well-being I have attributed to Buddhists, when they discuss the motives behind actions, they may be as interested in what acting out of a particular motive *does to* your psyche as in what it *reveals about* your psyche. Buddhists would agree with Aristotle that, over time, habitual actions can shape your character, for good or bad.[13] Since, as I have claimed, Buddhists consider character traits to be intrinsically morally important, they will regard effects on character as among the more important consequences of many of our actions. Insofar as similar actions performed out of different motives have different effects on character, they have different consequences.

And let's not forget, in this connection, about the Law of Karma. The Buddha famously identified karma with intention. If motives and intentions control what kind of karma we receive from an action, and karma is a powerful source of future happiness and suffering, then obviously Buddhists should be concerned about it. But the role of karma in moral evaluation does not make Buddhist ethics nonconsequentialist; rather, on my interpretation, karmic consequences are among those that need to be considered in evaluating an action.

These considerations can be used to answer another possible objection to my interpretation of Buddhist ethics. Writers on ethics often note that consequentialist theories seem to make no distinction between doing harm and allowing harm to happen. They seem, for instance, to regard letting someone die as being just as serious as killing him. However, it is evident that Buddhist ethics makes a distinction between killing and letting die. How, then, can Buddhists be consequentialists?

My reply is that the typical motivations of a doer are different from those of an allower, so that when people cause harm, doing so both manifests and promotes states that are incompatible with long-term welfare.[14] On the other hand, allowing harm is compatible with a good character, if the allower is doing something else of moral importance. Obviously, no single human being is capable of preventing all the harms that occur on earth. What consequentialism requires is not that we should prevent all harms happening everywhere. Consequentialism does not even require that we prevent all the harm we are capable of preventing, since preventing some harms may be incompatible with preventing other, greater harms. What it requires is that we should pursue a lifestyle that promotes the good as effectively as possible.[15] If Buddhist descriptive premises are true, then for many people, this lifestyle will be one of intensive meditation practice now, so as to attain a state of enlightenment later. When that state has been attained, the practitioner will be far more effective at helping others than she could possibly be now. These premises may be false; but if we take into consideration that Buddhists believe them, we can see that Buddhist ethics should not require people to rush around preventing harms, if they can do more good in the long run by pursuing their enlightenment. As the motto of one American meditation center has it, "Don't just do something; sit there."

Several writers have advanced a further objection to any consequentialist understanding of Theravāda ethics that, if sound, would be very powerful. This objection begins by noting that, according to many Buddhist texts, performing morally wrong actions will indeed have bad consequences. But, it is argued, the wrongness of the actions is what explains the fact that their consequences are bad. This order of explanation is the reverse of that found in consequentialist theories, which take the bad consequences as the basis for the judgment that the action was wrong.[16]

However, the authors who present this objection do not cite any texts that directly support their view. Moreover, I am not aware of any Buddhist text that explicitly speaks to the issue of explanatory priority. Our assessment of this issue must, it seems, depend on the broader merits of consequentialist interpretations of Buddhism, and cannot in itself refute those interpretations.

Why, then, is this objection so often and so confidently advanced? We can understand the issue more clearly if we distinguish the direct consequences that flow from an action, through mechanisms other than the Law of Karma, from its karmic consequences. The objectors' thesis may be correct if it is restricted to the karmic consequences. Perhaps we can say that actions produce bad karma because they are wrong; they are not wrong because they produce bad karma. But this thesis about explanatory priority is much less compelling when applied to the direct consequences. Perhaps the order of explanation goes as follows. Because an action can, on the basis of the factual information available to the agent, reasonably be expected to produce bad direct consequences for the agent, for other sentient beings, or for both, it is wrong.[17] Because the action is wrong, it generates bad karma. The fact that this bad karma will be produced can, then, serve as an additional reason not to perform the action. This account of the order of explanation is fully compatible with a consequentialist interpretation of Buddhist ethics. And since there seems to be no textual evidence at all that speaks to the matter, those who advance the objection at hand are not in a position to show that their account is superior to this one. I conclude that the objection from explanatory priority cannot refute the consequentialist interpretation.

Substantive Objections

Having disposed of several objections against my interpretive theses, I now turn to a quite different class of objections: substantive ones that have been raised against Western forms of consequentialism, or that could be raised against the view I propose. First, I will consider the argument that utilitarianism seems to allow certain public acts of brutal violence to be justified by the sadistic pleasure of spectators. This problem has appeared in several different forms in the literature; one of the most vivid and intuitively compelling versions involves considering the historical example of the bloody spectacles staged in the Colosseum of ancient Rome.[18] The Romans held frequent gladiatorial combats and executions of criminals and religious dissenters in this giant fifty-thousand-seat arena. Historical documents establish that the spectators heartily enjoyed watching Christians being devoured by lions and slave warriors hacking each other's arms off. Now, if we assume the hedonist theory of value presupposed by classical utilitarianism, the important considerations in this situation include the suffering of the victims, as well as the pleasure the audience experienced. But given that the audience outnumbered the participants in the events by such a large margin, it is plausible to suppose that more pleasure than pain was generated by these events. And if the calculation does not come out this way in the case of the actual, historical Colosseum, we can make the hedonic balance positive simply by imagining a larger arena—or better yet, a televised version. But ancient Roman spectacles are deeply offensive to our modern moral intuitions; any ethical theory that endorses them obviously fails to do justice to what we believe today.

In responding to this case, a Buddhist thinker would certainly note that by encouraging cruelty and deadening compassion, the spectacles in the Colosseum clearly had a negative effect on the character of the spectators. Since character consequentialism considers such a change to be deleterious to their welfare, it endorses the claim that the Roman games harmed their spectators even while providing them with enjoyment. Thus Buddhists can agree with modern intuition that the Colosseum was a moral monstrosity.

It would be possible for Buddhist thinkers to regard the spectacles in the Colosseum as morally wrong even if they were hedonists and did not assign any intrinsic value to character traits. Buddhists hold that the character traits that are developed and strengthened by attending these events have the causal tendency to perpetuate ignorance, reinforce a sense of individual and collective identity, and thereby keep those who have them imprisoned in suffering. So given general and very fundamental features of the way the world works, on the Buddhist view, the Colosseum would increase overall suffering, even if it creates pleasure and enjoyment in the short run.

We can get the right answer to the problem by modifying classical utilitarianism in various other more or less dramatic ways. For example, by abandoning aggregation, we could disallow the relatively small amounts of enjoyment experienced by each of the spectators from adding up to an amount that outweighs the severe suffering of the participants. If we wish to retain the basic structure of consequentialism, it is clearly possible to avoid the conclusion by modifying our theory of value in some other way than by adopting character consequentialism. Geoffrey Scarre, for instance, advocates granting intrinsic significance to self-respect as an important component of a worthwhile life.[19] He then rejects the Roman games on the ground that they undermine the spectators' ability to maintain their genuine self-respect. Thus, Buddhist ethics is far from being the only version of consequentialism that can endorse our intuitive revulsion against the Colosseum. But the fact that it can avoid one of the major objections to classical utilitarianism is surely a point in its favor.

I have argued that the ethical theory I have attributed to the Buddhist tradition, character consequentialism, has important advantages over other consequentialist theories, such as classical utilitarianism. It handles the Colosseum better; and as I pointed out in chapter 4, it permits a more intuitively acceptable response to Plato's example of the lifetime of delicious scratching. There are, however, a number of objections that may be raised specifically against this theory, and that do not apply to other consequentialist views. I cannot consider all such objections that are possible, but I will discuss several of them. It seems to me that character consequentialism can survive them.

One such objection derives from the fact that the theory of the good that is the basis of character consequentialism is, in Ronald Dworkin's terminology, additive, not constitutive. According to additive accounts of well-being, a person's life is made better by the presence in it of the constituents of well-being, whether or not that person believes that these constituents are actually good for him. Constitutive accounts, by contrast, assert that the value of the constituents of well-being depends on the fact that the person who has them also regards them as valuable. On my view, Buddhist ethics clearly falls in the additive category: the value of certain traits of character, such as compassion or patience, does not depend on whether the person who has them also believes they are good traits to have.

According to Dworkin, however,

> The constitutive view is preferable for a variety of reasons. The additive view cannot explain why a good life is distinctively valuable for or to the person whose life it is. And it is implausible to think that someone can lead a better life against the grain of his most profound ethical convictions than at peace with them.[20]

Dworkin's objection is an important one, and some will find it intuitively compelling. Could the truth about well-being really be that people live better by exemplifying distinctively Buddhist virtues, whether or not they believe in Buddhism, or have even heard of Buddhism? And Dworkin puts the problem in a particularly troubling form by asking about a case in which someone's moral convictions actually condemn the qualities that some additive theory says are intrinsically valuable for everyone. Now, any case in which someone lives better while living in contradiction to his moral beliefs is certainly going to be a strange case. But certain cases do exist that seem to have this feature. One such example is found in Mark Twain's novel *Huckleberry Finn*.

In this famous passage, which has received some attention from moral philosophers, Huck Finn is traveling on the Mississippi River with his friend Jim, an escaped slave.[21] It appears that Jim will manage to reach Cairo, Illinois, in free territory. The situation fills Huck with pangs of conscience. Huck has been taught all his life that it is seriously wrong to assist a slave in running away; the thought that Jim might enlist the help of abolitionists in "stealing" his family only makes Huck feel worse. And Huck's compunctions are strengthened by reflecting on the injury he is doing to Jim's legal owner, Miss Watson, who has treated Huck well in the past. Impelled by guilt and remorse, Huck decides to turn Jim in to the local whites. But at the last minute, feelings of friendship and compassion for Jim make Huck unable to carry out his intention. Still convinced that turning Jim in would be the right thing to do, Huck decides to ignore the demands of morality from then on.

Dworkin finds it helpful to think about the value of a life by considering it as a performance. Shouldn't we say that Huck's life is a better performance because he allows compassion to override his false views about ethics? Obviously, Huck's failure to follow his decision has good consequences for Jim's welfare. But it seems to me that Huck's life also goes better for him because his emotions here overcome his deluded rational mind.

The case of Huck Finn involves a particular action at a particular time. Dworkin's objection might seem stronger when applied to whole lives: could someone be better off if his entire life was lived in a way that conflicted with his moral convictions? I think the answer is yes; we can construct imaginary cases analogous to the Huck Finn case that last an entire lifetime. Think of a death camp guard who spends his entire life in service to a totalitarian state. Though this guard fully accepts the totalitarian ideology, he has compassionate instincts that frequently overcome his rational faculties, leading him to show mercy to the inmates of his camps in ways that often benefit them. Though he feels guilty about these moments of weakness, he is never able to stamp out his feelings of pity.

The life of this guard, I would argue, is less bad, even for himself, than the lives of those of his fellow guards who never allow their emotions to interfere with the cruelties they are ordered to practice. I claim that this is true even if he experiences no more happiness than the other guards—if, for example, the greater openness to life and joy created by his remaining compassion is counterbalanced on the hedonic scale by the gnawing guilt that he is aware enough to feel. If I am right about this case, then it is possible for someone's well-being to be increased by the possession of a virtue that he thinks is a vice. Dworkin's objection will then fail; the truth about well-being can be, in the relevant sense, independent of the beliefs of the person whose well-being is assessed.

Another objection, which cuts against both character consequentialism and virtue ethics, challenges the claim that being virtuous is a good candidate to appear on a list of the features that constitute well-being. This argument is advanced by Brad Hooker, who writes:

> Consider two people who lead sad and wretched lives. Suppose that one of these two people is morally virtuous, and the other is not. Let us use the name "Upright" for the one who is morally virtuous, and the name "Unscrupulous" for the one who is not. We would *not* feel

sorrier for Unscrupulous. This suggests that we do not really believe that moral virtue has the same status on the list as pleasure, knowledge, achievement, and friendship. I will refer to this argument as the *argument from lack of sympathy*.[22]

The intuition behind this argument would be accepted by many Westerners, but Buddhist writers do not share it. The Tibetan Buddhist teacher Jamgon Kongtrul tells us that "to have compassion for a person who puts up with hardship in order to practice dharma and not to have compassion for those who do evil is mistaken compassion."[23] That is, it is a mistake to focus one's compassion only on those people who encounter seemingly undeserved suffering while trying to do good things, given that one does not also extend compassion to those who do bad things. Thus, from a Buddhist point of view, the intuition Hooker appeals to is natural, but mistaken. The Theravādin writer Buddhaghosa, meanwhile, tries to stir in us the sympathy that Hooker denies we feel:

> He is not free from any sort of terror,
> Though free enough from pleasure of attainment;
> While heaven's door is bolted fast against him,
> He is well set upon the road to hell.
> Who else if not one destitute of virtue
> More fit to be the object of compassion?[24]

These passages, and the many others like it that can be found in Buddhist literature, show that Buddhists would not accept Hooker's argument from lack of sympathy. However, they do not provide positive evidence that Buddhists attach intrinsic value to virtues. One might interpret these passages instead as saying that the condition of Unscrupulous is a pitiable one, not because of its lack of intrinsically valuable virtue, but because of the expectation of future suffering caused by vice. Nevertheless, it is clear that Buddhists do not share the intuitions that underlie Hooker's objection.

The next objection against character consequentialism is very important, because considering it carefully can help in clarifying the exact nature of that view. As I have mentioned, certain ancient Greek philosophers held carefully worked out views about the value of virtue. There are, in fact, substantial similarities between character consequentialism and a certain interpretation of Plato's theory of well-being. But Aristotle criticizes this kind of view as too simplistic. Aristotle agrees that virtue is quite central to well-being, but not by itself. His reasons are as follows:

> And perhaps one might even suppose [virtue] to be, rather than
> honour, the end of the political life. But even this appears somewhat

incomplete; for possession of virtue seems actually compatible with being asleep, or with lifelong inactivity, and further, with the greatest sufferings and misfortunes; but a man who was living so no one would call happy, unless he were maintaining a thesis at all costs.[25]

There are two objections in this passage. One attacks a view held in common by Plato, the Stoics, and all forms of Buddhism: that a person can be happy even while being tortured, or while suffering under other highly unfavorable circumstances. Obviously Buddhists will maintain this view as long as they continue to believe in the immense significance of the state of enlightenment. It is much more difficult to know how to answer the other objection. Should character consequentialists regard virtue as intrinsically good, even when it is possessed by someone who is asleep? Or should they follow Aristotle in regarding virtuous activity as more fundamentally good than the traits of character that give rise to it?

If they adopt the first option, then Buddhists will be open to yet another serious objection, raised by one of the most important thinkers in the utilitarian tradition, Henry Sidgwick. He writes:

> I cannot infer from this that character and its elements—faculties, habits, or dispositions of any kind—are the constituents of Ultimate Good. It seems to me that the opposite is implied in the very conception of a faculty or disposition; it can only be defined as a tendency to act or feel in a certain way under certain conditions; and such a tendency appears to me clearly not valuable in itself but for the acts and feelings in which it takes effect, or for the ulterior consequences of these—which consequences, again, cannot be regarded as Ultimate Good, so long as they are merely conceived as modifications of faculties, dispositions, etc.[26]

Though Sidgwick is here merely reporting his intuitions, rather than giving an argument, he nevertheless has a very important point. Buddhist character consequentialists seem to face a grave dilemma. It seems quite implausible that a tendency could be valuable in itself, more implausible that it is intrinsically valuable if it is not being manifested, and even more so if it will not be manifested. On the other hand, if they were instead to identify virtuous activity as the intrinsic good, they would have to agree that the defining characteristic of such activity is that it benefits sentient beings. It would then be extremely difficult to resist the conclusion that it is the promotion of sentient beings' welfare that is the real source of value; and on pain of infinite regress, this welfare could no longer be conceived as partly consisting in virtue. Buddhists would have no choice but to join Sidgwick in adopting classical utilitarianism.

Fortunately, to find a reply to this objection it suffices to understand the Buddhist analysis of what being virtuous consists in. If we consult the discussions of virtue in such texts as Buddhaghosa's *Path of Purification* and Vasubandhu's *Treasury of Metaphysics*, it becomes clear very quickly that the Buddhist technical terms we might be inclined to translate as "virtuous" (such as Pāli *kusala*, Skt. *kuśala*,[27] Tib. *dge ba*) are, in the first instance, applied to occurrent mental states. For the Buddhist tradition, people are appropriately described as compassionate if and only if there are many occurrences of the emotion of compassion within the past, present, and future history of their mental series. The other virtues, too, such as forbearance, generosity, confidence, and so on, should be defined as consisting in the actual occurrence of mental states of the appropriate kind, and not in terms of a disposition to have such mental states. Of course, intentions (Skt./Pāli *cetanā*) will be among the most significant mental states for determining a person's moral status, but other mental states that don't directly produce action, such as wishes for other people to be happy, or momentary compassionate thoughts, or on the negative side, carefully concealed envy or hatred, will also count. Once we understand what the Buddhist tradition takes virtue to consist in, we see that its expounders are in verbal agreement with one of Sidgwick's central claims: the only thing that counts from a moral point of view is desirable consciousness. But they have a nonhedonist view of which sorts of consciousness are intrinsically desirable.

This account is fully sufficient to dispose of Aristotle's dilemma: Buddhists adopt neither horn. For them, human flourishing consists in neither the physical practice of virtue nor something wholly potential. But as it happens, Sidgwick has an additional objection well worth considering. He claims that the character consequentialist, unlike the classical utilitarian, is unable to give any non-question-begging account of which traits are virtues and why—because the exact limits and boundaries of the sphere of activity of the different virtues recognized by common sense can only be specified in a rational way by bringing in considerations based on the general welfare.[28] The utilitarian, however, is in an excellent position to give a coherent account of what makes characteristics virtuous: they are conducive to the happiness of sentient beings. As Sidgwick claims,

> no one can read Hume's *Inquiry into the First Principles of Morals* without being convinced of this at least, that if a list were drawn up of the qualities of character and conduct that are directly or indirectly productive of pleasure to ourselves or to others, it would include all that are commonly known as virtues.[29]

So far as I can see, a Buddhist would neither be in a position to deny nor have any interest in denying this Humean claim.

How, then, could Buddhists respond to Sidgwick's objection? My reply must necessarily be a bit speculative, since the historical Buddhist tradition never faced an objection of this nature. But I think it is not hard to find the materials with which to construct a response. They should probably adopt something like one of the following two formulations:

V1. The virtues are those mental characteristics that all fully enlightened Buddhas have in common.

V2. The virtues are those morally relevant mental characteristics that all fully enlightened Buddhas have in common.

Both of these formulations have advantages and disadvantages. V1 does not require us to have a prior understanding of which characteristics are morally relevant; this is an advantage, since Sidgwick might press us on where we get such an understanding. V1 also counts the Buddha's knowledge as a virtue of his, a feature that harmonizes well with at least some Buddhist texts (for example, the quotation from Tsong kha pa in chapter 5). On the other hand, V2 does not, as V1 does, count the Buddha's knowledge of how many socks you have in your dresser drawer as a virtue; it is not clear that it would be plausible to claim that your knowledge of this fact is one of your virtues.

Either formulation, though, will give us a way of distinguishing virtues from nonvirtues that should be both at least close to intuitively correct and clearly motivated. According to V1 and V2, when we seek virtue, we are seeking to make our minds like the minds of the Buddhas. This aspiration is so central to the Buddhist tradition that it is plausible to interpret that tradition as assigning intrinsic value to its partial or complete fulfillment.

The character consequentialist interpretation of Buddhist ethics, I have argued, survives Keown's interpretive objections. It handles at least one case, the Colosseum, better than classical utilitarianism does. Character consequentialism also survives a number of powerful objections that were, or could have been, brought by such philosophers as Dworkin, Hooker, Aristotle, and Sidgwick. Not only does this view faithfully represent the moral core of the Buddhist religious tradition; it also has the potential to be a viable, defensible moral theory in its own right, worthy of careful consideration by contemporary ethicists.

II

A Buddhist Response
to Kant

Kant's Arguments for the Formula of Humanity

I have argued that the various forms of Buddhist ethics should be
understood as particular versions of consequentialism. I have also
maintained that Buddhist views rely on a theory of value that centrally
involves the virtues. If I am correct in my assertions, then the prospects
seem bright for a constructive dialogue between Buddhist ethics and
the various forms of Western consequentialism and virtue ethics, in
which the recognition of substantial areas of agreement could be a
basis for each side to learn from the other. However, Buddhist ethics as
I interpret it is quite starkly opposed to Kantian deontological ethics.
Although these two perspectives, like any two plausible moral theories,
agree on many particular actions, they differ dramatically in their
theoretical structures and fundamental assumptions. Yet Kant has
offered several deep and intriguing arguments in favor of his views.
In the hands of his most insightful modern interpreters, such as Allen
Wood and Christine Korsgaard, these arguments are brought together
into a powerful case for the claim that Kant's theory provides the only
satisfactory account of moral obligation. If Buddhist ethics is to be a
credible contender in today's philosophical scene, it is important for
Buddhist philosophers to reply to the arguments that purport to show
that Kant's view is the only tenable ethical theory.

    In the past, many interpreters and critics of Kant have concentrated
their attention on Kant's first formulation of the categorical

imperative, the formula of universal law. By now, however, any claim that this formulation provides a reliable test for distinguishing right from wrong actions seems to have been decisively refuted.[1] I will, therefore, focus on Kant's second formulation of the principle of morality, known as the formula of humanity. Unlike the first formulation, this principle is capable of generating a wide range of substantive moral conclusions that are sufficiently plausible to be well worth discussing. Moreover, Kant seems to have two separate and powerful arguments in favor of the view that the formula of humanity accurately tells us what our moral obligations are. The first of these attempts to show that humanity is the only thing in the world with unconditional, absolute value, while the second relies on a complex set of interrelated considerations about autonomy, moral obligation, respect for law, and respect for humanity. I will refer to the first argument as the regress to humanity as an end, and the second as the autonomy argument.

The regress to humanity as an end proceeds as follows. First, we notice that the various objects that we contingently desire, such as material things, are valuable only insofar as we happen to desire them. If I want to read Harlequin romance novels, then these novels have value to me; but if I have no such desire, they will strike me as worthless. The value of Harlequin romance novels is evidently conditional, not unconditional or absolute. Moreover, my own inclinations, or desires, are themselves not things of unconditional worth. Some of them can be positively annoying to me; in many cases, I would be better off with fewer of them, or perhaps even with none at all. Thus far, Buddhists would enthusiastically endorse Kant's assertions.

Kant now faces a much more difficult task: he must argue that happiness itself is not absolutely or unconditionally valuable. Kant has two arguments for this claim. One is that the value of a person's happiness is conditional on his worthiness to be happy. For wicked people to be prosperous and enjoy the fruits of their wrong actions is, Kant says, an intrinsically bad thing. The second argument relies on the empirical claim that happiness itself can corrupt our moral character.[2] If a person who happens to be more fortunate than his neighbors decides that he deserves his own good fortune, this false belief can lead to arrogance and to various emotions, and even actions, that run contrary to the moral law.

If neither the contingent objects of our inclinations, nor our inclinations themselves, nor even the overall fulfillment of these inclinations that would constitute happiness, is intrinsically good, then what are we left with that is a candidate for intrinsic goodness? According to Kant, the only remaining possibility is our rational capacity to choose which inclinations to follow and when to follow them—that is, our humanity. Whether it is instantiated in myself or in another person, humanity has a kind of inherent dignity that should command my respect and that I may never violate or use as a mere means. Through this regress argument, Kant thinks he has shown that the only defensible account of intrinsic value is one that leads directly to the formula of humanity, the central principle of his moral theory.

How could Buddhist ethicists respond to this regress? If any of my earlier claims are correct, it seems they would wish to block the regress at the stage where Kant denies the intrinsic and unconditional value of happiness. In fact, Buddhists are in a good position to reject both arguments Kant offers in support of this denial.

As I have shown extensively in chapters 8 and 9, Buddhists would not accept Kant's premise that it is bad for the wicked to be happy and good for them to suffer. They are committed to the idea that genuine great compassion motivates those who have it to relieve the suffering, and promote the happiness, of the virtuous and the wicked alike.

It might be objected that Buddhists take this view of great compassion only because, on the basis of their views about karma, they already think that the wicked will be sufficiently punished by a law of nature. Since they are guaranteed to suffer retribution, there is no need to wish it on them. This objection is mistaken. In an important early Buddhist story, the mass murderer Aṅgulimāla converts to Buddhism, begins to practice absolute nonviolence, attains advanced states of meditation, thereby destroys almost all of his negative karma, and becomes a Saint. True, he is once severely beaten by villagers whose family members he has previously killed. This is the fruition of the residue of his negative karma that was not burned up by his meditative practice. But one beating is insignificant compared to the aeons in hell he would have suffered had he not become a spiritual practitioner. Buddhists clearly think that the conversion of Aṅgulimāla was a good thing; it follows that it was better for him not to suffer appropriate punishment for his violent actions.

Of course, Aṅgulimāla did repent of his previous actions. Perhaps Kant's principle that it is not good for the wicked to be happy should have an exception for those who repent. But in chapter 10 of the *Introduction to the Bodhisattva's Way of Life*, Śāntideva evokes a wish for his own merit to cause the realms of hell, which are full of horrifying tortures, to be transformed into beautiful heaven-like gardens, and for the beings in hell to be released from their suffering and to become happy. Nowhere in chapter 10 are these benefits restricted only to those hell-beings who repent of their previous sins. Buddhists certainly think that those who commit harmful actions will typically suffer as a result, and this view colors their attitudes toward many normative questions. But the wishes and prayers of Buddhists are for the wicked to be happy, before, during, and after their wicked deeds, if and to the extent that such happiness is possible for them.

How would Buddhists respond to the second argument, that in virtue of the way humans are constituted, happiness can sometimes be bad for their moral character? There seems to be a reply that is both quick and decisive. The fact that something can contingently produce bad consequences under unfavorable circumstances cannot refute the claim that it is intrinsically and unconditionally good. If such a refutation were possible, we could refute the claim that the good will is intrinsically and unconditionally good. A sincere wish to help, combined with total idiocy, can often produce far more damage than a combination of idiocy and apathy. Moreover, in such cases as that of the aliens and Joe from Kansas, Kant's version of the good will can lead to much worse consequences than cynicism and ruthlessness would. If he likes, Kant can try to stipulate that these negative consequences are not to be attributed to the good will; but if that move is fair, the Buddhist can equally well stipulate that the corrupting effects of happiness are not to be attributed to happiness itself, but to the various other causes that combine to produce these effects. Kant's second argument against the intrinsic value of happiness tells equally well—in fact, equally poorly—against his own theory of intrinsic and unconditional value.

It seems that Kant's regress to humanity as an end in itself will not be compelling to Buddhists. But Kant offers another, independent justification for the central principle of his ethical theory. His second line of argument in favor of the formula of humanity is still deeper and more subtle. The power and appeal of this justification, I believe, explains much of the continuing interest and support Kantian deontology has gained from contemporary philosophers.

The central considerations Kant invokes in this line of reasoning have to do with moral obligation. How, Kant asks, is the will bound to follow the moral law? The source of our obligation to obey the moral law cannot be some desire, feeling or inclination that we contingently happen to have. If it were, then anyone who lacked that desire, feeling, or inclination would be exempt from obeying the law. Moreover, any source of obligation that had this nature would be something external to the will; being required to follow such a source of obligation would be a kind of unfreedom or bondage of the will.

The only way to avoid these difficulties, Kant maintains, is to see the will as obeying laws that it gives to itself, out of respect for the moral law and the objective value that is its source. Since this objective value does not depend on any inclination, it cannot be an object of inclination; in fact, it can be nothing other than humanity itself, either in me or in someone else. Respect for humanity, according to Kant, is the sole motive that can make it possible for the will to follow the moral law freely and autonomously. Allen Wood summarizes Kant's reasoning as follows:

> Every other source of the law would have to bind the rational will to it by some *other* volition grounded contingently on a value different from that of the law. A law grounded in happiness would have to appeal to our will to be happy. . . . These further volitions would turn the categorical demand of the law into a merely hypothetical demand, by referring it to some other volition as its ground. This line of thinking convinces Kant that the principle of autonomy is the only possible solution to the riddle of obligation, and that all other principles of obligation must fail to solve it because they must be grounded on heteronomy of the will.[3]

Through this argument, Kant is able to offer a deep, metaethical critique of consequentialism, and indeed of all moral theories other than his own. They are rejected not because they have problematic implications in particular cases, but because they fail to explain the nature of our obligation to follow the law.

From a Buddhist perspective, what Kant is doing is the following. He is identifying with the rational will, regarding it as his self. Any motive, such as a desire or inclination, that comes from something other than the rational will is then perceived as an external constraint, a source of unfreedom. Once Kant takes up this stance, he will be satisfied only with a motive to be moral that emerges from within the rational will itself. This he finds in the respect for the moral law that springs from recognition of the objective value of humanity as an end in itself.

This dynamic is clearly at work in Wood's interpretation of Kant's basis for rejecting an ethics based on respect for virtue or perfection:

> Why does Kant think there is greater clarity in conceiving the ground of obligation as the dignity of rational will than as objective perfection or goodness? . . . Kant's reply is that the recognition of a law as categorically binding presupposes the unconditional and incomparable worth of the source of the legislation, which in relation to practical reason is adequately conceived not as perfection or divinity but only as rational self-legislation. For only this has such a worth to the rational will originally rather than derivatively, making its commands truly categorical.[4]

What does "originally rather than derivatively" mean? I suggest that this obscure phrase will be persuasive to us only insofar as we see it as alluding to the intuitive distinction between what is imposed on the rational will from outside and is therefore an external constraint and what flows from the will itself and is therefore autonomous.

One difficulty with considering the rational mind to be your self is that of all the things closely related to "rational mind" that we can ever experience or have evidence about, none of them—not any one of our rational thoughts, or the collection of all of our (occurrent and dispositional) rational beliefs at some particular time, or our capacity to have rational thoughts—is something we can be comfortable acknowledging as a self. The thoughts, whether taken individually or collectively, are impermanent and constantly changing; they are too ephemeral to be a self. The capacity to have rational thoughts, considered in and of itself, doesn't have enough specificity to define the identity of one person as opposed to another. If you are told that the capacity to form rational thoughts, considered as such, will survive your death, will you be comforted? This statement is clearly compatible with your not continuing to exist, since the capacity could survive in someone else. If you try to insist on the survival of *your own* capacity to form rational thoughts, then what makes the capacity yours? Precisely parallel remarks apply to our individual rational decisions, the collection of our intentions, plans and policies at a particular time, and our capacity to make rational decisions.

Kant is well aware of the fact that none of these things is a remotely suitable candidate for a self. Therefore, he places the noumenal self outside all possible experience, in a realm of things in themselves to which we have no access and about which we can have no knowledge. Although we cannot know that this noumenal self exists, it is possible to form the belief (Ger. *Glaube*) that it does; for Kant, in order for us to make sense of our capacity to make rational decisions, and, in particular, our ability to follow the moral law, we must form this belief. This follows from the fact that our practical freedom can be understood, according to Kant, only as a manifestation of this non-spatial, atemporal noumenal self.

It is vital to the intuitive plausibility of Kant's position that his readers should *identify* with this noumenal self. To see why, consider the difference between having a self that is transcendentally free and being possessed by a spirit or demon that controls your body at its own whim. The only difference lies in whether you identify with the noumenon that has seized control of your body.

But of course, the noumenal self is not easy to identify with. How could something that is outside space and time, and is free from all the distinguishing characteristics I attribute to myself, be who I really am? Moreover, it will be hard to avoid the suspicion that pushing the self into a noumenal realm to which we have no epistemic access is merely a way for Kant to conceal from himself, and his followers, the frightening and disturbing fact that the self is absolutely nonexistent.

Many contemporary Kantians, having noticed the difficulties associated with belief in a noumenal self, would like to retain the formula of universal law and the belief in some sort of practical freedom, but to do so without postulating anything outside the flow of natural causality. However, any compatibilist interpreter of Kant must face the difficulty canvassed earlier, of which Kant is fully aware: that nothing that is empirically given to us — nothing that plausibly could be discovered by science or empirical inquiry — is remotely suitable to be a self.

Suppose a Buddhist is asked the question that plays such a central role in the argument I am considering: "What binds the will to follow the moral law?" Obviously, the Buddhist's answer must involve challenging the presuppositions of the question. The way to begin is by pointing out that the will, as Kant conceives it, simply does not exist. There is no will. Instead, in unenlightened beings, there is a highly complex, largely subconscious psychological process of the formation of intentions and decisions. This process is driven by desire and saturated with the false belief in a self.

Defenders of Kant's views would want to resist the idea that desire, in and of itself, can motivate us to act. They would instead assert that a desire can motivate me only insofar as I incorporate it into a maxim, and then freely choose to take that maxim as a principle that guides my will. This assertion is known in the secondary literature as the incorporation thesis. Kantians might further claim that the incorporation thesis is supported by the phenomenology of choice. I do not, after all, see myself as simply balancing desires against each other and adopting whichever is the strongest.

Phenomenology may well support the claim that a simple comparison of the quantitative strength of desires is not all that is going on. But the more complex psychological process that actually occurs, whatever it is, operates in accordance with causes and conditions (possibly with a bit of quantum randomness thrown in). The phenomenology obviously does not support the view that an atemporal noumenal self makes all my decisions. It could not, in principle, do this, since the noumenal self is not a possible object of experience.

As long as someone has any desires to compare or incorporate, that person is considered unenlightened. From a Buddhist point of view, to be unenlightened is to be pushed around, dominated, and ruled by selfish desires and afflictive emotions. This is a highly undignified state of unfreedom. Kant knows this; he is able to maintain his ideals of equal human dignity only by appealing to the noumenal self that, on his view, we all have. What Kant considers to be freedom is, from a Buddhist point of view, only a state of being pushed around by a particular part of your personality — your intellectual mind — together with whatever desires it happens to dignify with the title "rational." It may be very tempting—especially for philosophers!—to see the intellect as a self; but if we look more closely, we will see that intellectual thought is just as clearly *not a self* as the body, the brain, or for that matter, your average bedroom furniture set. But anyone who, not seeing this, falsely believes that the intellect, or any other entity or process, is or belongs to a self, will be controlled and dominated by various kinds of craving.

While we are in this unfortunate, unenlightened state, why should we be moral, and what kind of motivation can we produce that could lead us to do the right thing? The previous chapters have suggested answers to these questions. We can begin from the recognition that whenever we inflict misery on others, the stern Law of Karma will bring misery back to us. If we believe this claim, and we do not wish to experience suffering, then we will be motivated to avoid those wrong actions which we have learned to see as causes of suffering. Therefore, it will be in our interest to choose to be bound by vows of *śila*, such as the Five Precepts. These vows create a psychological feeling of being bound to obey moral rules; they also add the good karma of keeping a promise and the bad karma of breaking one to the scales of prudential calculation in morally significant cases. These factors, together with whatever authentic compassion we happen to be able to muster, are empirically seen to be powerful enough to motivate many people to do the right thing in many actual cases.

But, of course, acting morally for *these* reasons is deeply unsatisfactory: as Kant would say, it is heteronomous in any number of respects. To do the right thing because of self-interest is ignoble; such a motivation is dependent on particular factual conditions, or on questionable metaphysical assumptions, or both. The motivation in question draws on unsavory aspects of human psychology such as selfishness, greed, and fear. It comprehensively involves constraint and unfreedom. The higher forms of this way of being moral depend on feelings of sentimental compassion; but on any given occasion, these feelings may or may not happen to be present. And since they are sometimes impure, often partial, and not always associated with wisdom, feelings of sentimental compassion can occasionally lead to clumsy, shortsighted, or even destructive actions. It would be reasonable to feel dissatisfied with such a shallow answer to the question of why we should do the right thing.

Indeed, this answer is not the end of the Buddhist story. Buddhist texts claim that the psychology of enlightened beings is quite different from that of ordinary people. As I suggested in chapter 6, those who are truly enlightened don't need either incentives or reasons to be moral. As a factual matter, they do the right thing, out of pure, natural compassion. As long as you falsely think you have a will, you need incentives to bind that will, and the Buddhist religion can supply plenty of them. But from the enlightened point of view, there is no moral obligation; with no selfish desires to conflict with your compassion, moreover, there is no need for moral obligation. Once you are enlightened, you will do the right thing without needing to ask why.

Of course, there is room for philosophers to doubt that such pure, natural compassion actually exists. But whatever might be said against innate great compassion, it is at least no more problematic than Kant's unknowable autonomous will. In fact, it is considerably less problematic, since it is a possible object of experience. Whenever you feel an impulse of sincere generosity, pity, or love, you are aware of great compassion — but unclearly, as if through a dirty window. In deep spiritual experiences, you can see it clearly, if only for a brief time. The enlightened are never separated from it.

In fact, the unenlightened are never separated from it either. Selfishness, defined as the sincere wish for oneself to be truly happy, and partiality, defined as the sincere wish for "us" to be truly happy, are the forms great compassion takes when it is distorted by the false belief in a self and what belongs to a self. Philosophical theories of the person, such as Kant's noumenal self, prop up this belief, subtly reinforcing the painful distortions that hinder our freedom. But when these theories have been thoroughly smashed, and when the great icebergs of self-grasping and self-cherishing are melted by the sun of wisdom, then the water of compassion will flow freely over the whole world, and the trees and grass will grow by themselves.

In this state, unobstructed by falsehoods, great compassion sees happiness and suffering and their causes, and responds, flexibly and naturally. Nothing is needed to bind it to do this; that's just the way it is. When you feel a pain in your body, you naturally adjust your posture to remove the pain. The liberating actions of enlightened beings are like this.

In an important sense, then, to be enlightened is to be free: free of selfish desires, free of psychological conflicts, free of hindrances, free of obstructions, free of constraints. But enlightenment is not free will; not only is there no will, there is no self and no one who is free. There is just a process that freely unfolds. If we crave an autonomous, transcendentally free self, Buddhism cannot offer us one. But if we long for a state without obstacles, like a river flowing gently into the sea, or like the moon shining unobstructed in a clear night sky, then we can find that peaceful state, beyond the self and its desperate craving.

From a certain point of view, the Buddhist perspective I have just expressed has a similar structure to Kantian ethics. An aspect of the personality is identified that is deeper than one's superficial desires, and that is the source of ethical action. The unhindered expression of this fundamental aspect of mind is seen as freedom and as moral perfection. The Buddhist, however, does not identify with the natural innate compassion. Buddhists could resist accepting great compassion as a self by making one or more of the following claims: that it is momentary; that mine is not numerically distinct from yours; and that it is empty of essence. Moreover, since great compassion is an object of experience, it is less problematic than the noumenal self; therefore, the Buddhist expression of this theoretical structure is more defensible than the Kantian one.

The view I have described may represent the only strategy that could allow consequentialists to fight on Kant's home ground and win. Consequentialists may simply not find Kant's way of looking at the fundamental problems of ethics at all compelling. But if they are moved by Kant's objection that their view is heteronomous, or that it cannot account for how the moral law can bind the will, then they can and should respond either by becoming Buddhists, or by borrowing aspects of the Buddhist worldview.

The Alleged Practical Necessity of the Idea of Freedom

Perhaps Kant's defenders do not need, and should not try, to propose theoretical arguments for the existence of the noumenal self or the freedom of the will. Kant himself held that these matters cannot be known theoretically, but that once we take up the practical standpoint of agency and deliberation, we are compelled by the nature of practical reason to presuppose an autonomous self. Since this practical standpoint is not optional for us, but a necessity if we are to accomplish anything, or even to survive, we are inescapably committed to the existence of a free, rational will. I will consider two recent, quite different attempts to elucidate and defend this argument, proposed by Allen Wood and Christine Korsgaard. I will show that Wood's version of the argument is a failure. And if we accept the account of the behavior and motivations of enlightened beings that was presented in chapter 6, then we need not accept Korsgaard's formulation either.

Wood's line of argument is striking in its simplicity and breathtaking in its ambition. According to Wood, Kant's practical justification for taking ourselves to have free will is, like many other key moves in Kant's works, a transcendental argument. This form of argument involves exploring the conditions for the possibility of some activity we take ourselves to be engaged in. In this case, Wood calls our attention to the conditions of the possibility of our ability to follow norms, and to understand ourselves as following them. According to Wood, we inescapably regard ourselves, in contexts of practical decision-making, as able to follow, or fail to follow, various norms and principles. To accept this much, he maintains, is to see ourselves as having free will, and therefore, if we understand Kant's arguments, as bound by the moral law. In fact, Wood says, even in theoretical reason, we regard ourselves as able to follow norms, such as the laws of logic. So our self-understanding as theorists would be sufficient, on his view, to commit us to free will and our obligation to follow the moral law.

The only alternative to accepting free will, on Wood's view, is "fatalism," a position that is utterly incapacitating in both the theoretical and practical spheres. As Wood defines this term,

> Let a *fatalist* be someone who denies practical freedom (where this freedom is understood in the Kantian way, as causality according to norms). The fatalist, therefore, holds that ~F [that is, that there is no free will]. She must regard her own acts of judgment solely as the necessary effects of natural laws, denying that they can be correctly explained by reference to reasons or normative rules of inference (such as *modus tollens*).[5]

Anyone who dared to hold such a position would, it seems, be in a desperate situation indeed. Wood reads Kant as arguing that

> we can doubt the reality of freedom only if we also doubt our capacity to judge rationally, including even our capacity to judge whether to entertain those very doubts. A fatalist might still assert fatalism and even present arguments for it. But she would be unable to represent herself or those to whom she offers the arguments as holding fatalism rationally on the basis of those arguments.[6]

We philosophers—at the very least—seem to be under an inescapable practical necessity to regard ourselves as having free will, or find another line of work. As Wood sums up his position, "to understand myself as capable of judging is to assume that I am free in precisely the sense meant" in Kant's argument that a free will is bound to follow, and capable of following, the moral law.[7]

But it would be difficult not to see, when matters are put so strongly, that something has gone wrong. For Wood, if I deny that others have the kind of free will required for Kantian ethics, I cannot see them as following norms, or even as failing to follow norms. The contrapositive of this statement is the assertion that if I regard others as capable of following norms, I am committed to regarding them as having free will. The immediate difficulty with the latter assertion is that from my perspective, even things toward which I take what Dennett calls the "design stance" can follow or fail to follow norms. An air conditioner can function well or poorly. A mouse running through a maze can make a mistake.

Imagine yourself using a dedicated computer that does nothing at all but play chess. As you desperately try to stave off defeat at the computer's hands, it may be both practically necessary and psychologically irresistible to see the computer's output (1) as following the rules of chess, and (2) as part of a strategy to win the game. These are both normative concepts, and (2) is quite robustly normative; a strategy can be executed well or poorly, mistakes can be made in executing it, and so on. But it would be utterly absurd to claim that by seeing the computer in these ways, you are somehow committed to thinking that this computer is bound to follow the moral law, or even capable of doing so.

Of course, the computer can't see its own moves as following or failing to follow norms. Perhaps Wood should back off from his claims about my views on other people, which may be inessential anyway, and assert that to see *myself* as capable of following norms is to see myself as free. In reply, I could ask you to imagine a computer with just two abilities: to play chess, and to see its own moves as actions conforming to norms. But you might protest—quite fairly— that the computer could not have this second capacity all by itself. It would have to have many other capacities as well. The question then becomes: which would make this new computer a suitable candidate to be subject to the moral law—this second capacity, to use normative concepts to describe itself, or some part of what necessarily accompanies that capacity?

In light of these remarks, consider the following two quotations from Wood:

> Kant argues for F → M [the claim that being free entails being bound to follow the moral law] on the ground that freedom is a kind of causality, and of an analysis of what "causality" must mean in the case of freedom. It must mean being subject to an unconditional and self-given normative law.[8]

> Kant holds that we must think of ourselves as free in all our rational judgements in the sense that we must regard our judgements as acts we perform under norms.[9]

Does the suggestion that these two passages are discussing the same thing, that they involve exactly the same sense of the word "freedom," have any plausibility at all? Yet if they do not, Wood's argument will fail.

How could Wood possibly think that the two passages are discussing the same topic? Perhaps he is not clearly distinguishing the following two claims:

> WA. My actions are all capable of being evaluated as either following or not following norm L.
>
> WB. In all my actions, I am capable of following norm L.

WB, as it is most naturally read, implies that I have free will. WA definitely does not. In fact, WA is compatible with all of the following: that I am sometimes unable to follow norm L; that all my actions are determined by causes and conditions; that it is now a nomologically necessary truth that I will, tomorrow at 4:23 p.m., disobey norm L; and even that I have never heard of norm L and am not conscious of it in any way.

I would not venture to suggest that Kant could be guilty of such a confusion. Indeed, Kant has a much more robust conception of what is necessary for free will than Wood does. Contemporary Kantians, offered the chance to obtain the kind of free will that is important to morality at an affordable price, may find that an enormously appealing bargain. Perhaps Wood thinks he can offer it to them because he does not see the gap between the ability to behave in ways that can be understood as conforming or failing to conform to norms, an ability that is *very easy* to possess, and full-strength Kantian moral freedom, which, even at first glance, evidently requires an ambitious metaphysical substructure, and which, looked at with deeper insight and clearer vision, is absurd, incoherent, and impossible.

Before leaving this topic, I will offer a few remarks about an important feature of Wood's position that he inherits directly from Kant. This is the view, clearly stated in the foregoing quotation and accepted by many philosophers, that our judgments are actions we perform. Thirty minutes of Buddhist meditation can cure someone of this delusion for a lifetime. Suppose you decide to sit down and pay attention to the flow of your own breathing; as part of this practice, you promise yourself not to allow your thinking to proceed along chains of association or reasoning. Unless you are a meditation master, you will fail to keep this promise. You will find yourself, again and again, experiencing thoughts with cognitive content, including (if you are intellectual enough to be reading this) complex arguments, which appear despite your intention, adopted at the outset and frequently reiterated, not to form such thoughts. If this exercise is sincerely carried out, even for half an hour, you will begin to see how hopelessly inadequate the model of a "thinking self" is to the complex, mostly subconscious psychological process that generates your thoughts. The more deeply you see the inadequacy of this model, the easier it will be to abandon the tendency to identify rational thought, whether theoretical and practical, as your true self—a tendency that, I have claimed, is central to the appeal of Kantian ethics.

I have argued that Wood's formulation of Kant's practical argument for the freedom of the will, though it may seem powerful and appealing at first glance, is seriously flawed. Christine Korsgaard's very different formulation is more complex, insightful, and interesting. The version she presents in one influential article takes the form of a reply to Derek Parfit.[10] As I showed in chapter 5, Śāntideva's strategy for defending universalist consequentialism closely parallels the arguments of Parfit. Thus Korsgaard's objections to Parfit's metaphysical arguments for consequentialism also tell against Śāntideva. Reflecting on these objections will help to develop understanding of the nature and philosophical significance of the Buddhist doctrine of no-self.

Korsgaard does not directly criticize Parfit's metaphysical theses.[11] But the reductionist critique of personal identity that Parfit offers, she argues, does not have the normative implications he thinks it has. Although this critique may be correct from a theoretical point of view, there is another standpoint, the practical standpoint, that requires us to think of ourselves as unitary agents, unified across long periods of time. Since this practical standpoint is the one in which we make ethical decisions, our ethical views should draw on considerations that make sense from that standpoint, whether or not they are metaphysically justified. As Korsgaard writes, "it is practical reason that requires me to construct an identity for myself; whether metaphysics is to guide me in this or not is an open question."[12]

A number of aspects of the practical standpoint seem to require me to construct an identity. For one, I have only a single body; if I do not select a single course of action at any given time but try to do multiple incompatible things at once, I will be unable to accomplish anything.[13] Thus, I need to be functionally unified at any given time. Moreover, as Korsgaard writes, "some of the things we do are intelligible only in the context of projects that extend over long periods."[14] As a result, I need to be able to think of myself as somehow persisting through time. Even more fundamentally, if I am to weigh different considerations as part of deciding what to do, I will need a rational principle with which to do so. According to Korsgaard,

> This means that there is some principle or way of choosing that you regard as expressive of *yourself*, and that provides reasons that regulate your choices among your desires. To identify with such a principle or way of choosing is to be "a law to yourself," and to be unified as such.[15]

These considerations seem to show, as we might say, that if the self did not exist, it would have been necessary to invent it.

Korsgaard repeatedly emphasizes the importance, from the practical standpoint, of being able to identify with our actions. She argues that our actions are not just things that *happen* to us:

> But from the practical point of view, actions and choices must be viewed as having agents and choosers. This is what makes them, in our eyes, our own actions and choices rather than events that befall

us . . . from the practical point of view our relationship to our actions
and choices is essentially *authorial*: from it, we view them as *our own*.[16]

This feature of the practical standpoint is reinforced by the phenomenology of
deliberation. As Korsgaard notes, "when you deliberate, it is as if there were
something over and above all your desires, something that is *you*, and that
chooses which one to act on."[17] For Korsgaard, these aspects of the practical
standpoint should be taken into consideration in constructing theories about
what to do. A moral theory that ignores them is, for that very reason, deficient.

How could philosophers in the Buddhist tradition respond to this critique?
They could appeal to an account of the enlightened mind, such as the one I offered in chapter 6. According to Buddhists, the entire practical standpoint that
Korsgaard describes is not the only possible way to live. In fact, this standpoint
is an important part of the collection of conditions that sustain our confusion
and misery. The alternative to the practical standpoint is the enlightened state,
in which there are no decisions. In this state, there is theoretical cognition, or
perhaps nonconceptual intuitive insight, which clearly sees how things are.
Innate great compassion, uniting with this insight, spontaneously produces
bodily and vocal movements that cause the happiness and relieve the suffering
of others.

Evidently, there is room to question whether enlightened beings could possibly exist. If the reader will grant, for the sake of argument, that it is possible
to become enlightened in the sense just explained, then that state turns out to
have genuine, clearly identifiable advantages, from a consequentialist point of
view, over the state of an ordinary person as described by Korsgaard. In particular, the ordinary person's state has the disadvantage that if I view a particular
decision rule as expressive of my self, I will be unwilling to abandon that rule,
and make decisions in accordance with another rule, even when switching decision rules would produce much better consequences. If you can stomach this
kind of case, imagine that an immensely powerful, mind-reading alien threat-
ens me that if I make any decisions during the next twenty-four hours by de-
liberating using my usual rule, he will vaporize the continent of Europe. Now,
whatever advantages my rule may have, its application over the next twenty-
four hours does not have a chance of producing enough good consequences to
compensate for the annihilation of Europe and its entire population. If I can,
I should switch to another rule—even, or rather especially, if my current rule
is a consequentialist one. If, however, you don't accept cases of this type, then
there are more realistic examples to make the point, such as Schelling's answer
to armed robbery, used by Parfit to show that it can be rational to make yourself
irrational.[18] Even if I use a particular decision rule in most cases, I should not

be attached to that rule; sometimes, using it would be bad. But if I regard this decision rule as an expression of my self, I will be attached to it, and so unwilling to abandon it, even when I should.

For Korsgaard, a major part of what unifies me as an agent through time is that I identify with my own long-term projects. This identification contrasts with an attitude that would see each moment as a fresh opportunity, and regard past progress on my projects merely as relevant features of the situation. The latter attitude is likely to be the one that will produce the better consequences. Obviously, it would be seriously problematic in practice for me to have to reevaluate all my projects in every moment; but whenever new and relevant information comes in, I should be prepared to reconsider the value of my projects in light of that information. If I am unwilling to do this, then I will cling to my projects, even when sacrificing them would produce much greater benefits to others. And identifying with my projects, regarding them as in some sense helping to construct my identity, will in fact make me unwilling to do what consequentialism tells me I must: drop all of my projects within thirty seconds if an opportunity arises to produce more good for all sentient beings than my projects could.

On the other hand, if I am not a very advanced practitioner, it may be inevitable that I will construct a self of some kind. If it is necessary that I have a sense of self, better results will be produced if that sense of self includes Buddhist values instead of, or in addition to, deluded worldly values. Thus it could make a great deal of sense for me to think of myself as a bodhisattva, accept and endorse decision procedures drawn from some form of Buddhist ethics, and identify with the long-term project of following the path to enlightenment and thereby achieving Buddhahood. But as I showed in relation to the quotation about Subhūti I discussed in chapter 6, once our practice reaches a sufficiently advanced level, we will need to give up all aspects of this sense of self, see our true nonexistence, abandon the illusion of free will, and abide in real freedom.

Being able to use decision procedures, while not being attached to any of them, is a freer and less deluded state than the ordinary practical standpoint. If we are still sufficiently confused as to occupy this standpoint, it is good for us to occupy one of its Buddhist versions. But according to the account I have offered, in the fully enlightened mind, no decisions are being made, and therefore, no decision procedure is being used, although we can model the process by a consequentialist decision procedure. Instead, great compassion is spontaneously expressing itself without hindrance.

Does the enlightened being lose something crucial by not forming intentions and decisions? For an ordinary person, the useful function of intentions and decisions is to store information about past practical reasoning. Enlightened beings, since they don't have practical reason, don't need to store this information. But they can certainly have thoughts of the form "five minutes ago, the realization occurred here that, of the nomologically possible movements of this body, the most effective at enhancing the welfare of beings would be X." (An enlightened being would probably not put it exactly that way!) The availability of such thoughts could help to explain how the enlightened are capable of carrying out long-range plans, but also capable of dropping any such plan within thirty seconds if a better opportunity to benefit beings comes along.

Thus, rejecting and abandoning the psychological processes that, for Korsgaard, help to constitute a persisting self may not just be a demand of Buddhism; it may, under certain circumstances, be a demand of consequentialism itself. The kinds of identification that Korsgaard regards as necessary and inevitable will sometimes prevent people from responding in ways that would benefit sentient beings. If I am right about this, then Buddhist ethics has some claim to represent the most faithful working out of the logical implications of consequentialism.

From the point of view I am advocating, then, someone who takes Korsgaard's line might be compared to a compulsive hand-washer. Imagine this poor fellow telling us, "I know that there is nothing in the way the world is metaphysically that requires me to wash my hands every five minutes. But, given the way I am, I find that it seems to me that there is a tremendously important requirement that I do so. I could not stop believing in the existence of such a requirement without abandoning central features of the way I relate to the world; and I have no reason to think that such an abandonment is even possible."

I hope this comparison won't be taken as a personal insult; almost all people, including me, exhibit the deluded patterns that Korsgaard's account valorizes. But we do not have to valorize them; we can see them as aspects of what makes us unenlightened. However, even while we regard these thought-patterns as delusive, for most of us, it may not make sense to try to get rid of them right away. A practitioner who views herself as a beginning bodhisattva will have a long-term project of attaining enlightenment for the benefit of all beings, and a conception of her relation to the good that derives from that project. For her to abandon that project and the resulting sense of self might be for her to stop being a spiritual practitioner, which would not be constructive. Mahāyāna Buddhism does not tell everyone to abandon all rules, goals, and projects. Doing so is a task for a few very advanced practitioners to take on, and only when they are ready.

Once we are ready, we can, and should, abandon the patterns of thought that Korsgaard describes, and the conception of self that they generate. Buddhists have confidence that it is possible to overcome this conception of self; but to do so, we must discard important aspects of the way we make decisions, think about ourselves, and relate to the world during every moment of our lives. In a sense—but only in a sense—we must transcend ethics; we can do so only by transcending the self.

Conclusion

In this book, I have tried to clarify some aspects of the theoretical structure and practical implications of Indian and Tibetan Buddhist views about ethics. I do not claim to have established any of my conclusions with certainty. There is considerable room for further research into Buddhist ethics. But whether or not I am right about the issues I have discussed, there are further, pressing questions that I have not explored in the preceding chapters. I wish to raise these issues here, without attempting to settle them.

These issues concern the relation between Buddhist ethics and political theory. This topic was not a salient one to Asian Buddhists during the premodern period. As Joel Kupperman has written, "by and large, Buddhists, especially in the classic period of Buddhist philosophy, have not been drawn to social and political remedies for the problems of the world."[1] But today, Western Buddhists want to bring their beliefs and values into the public sphere, to have an impact on government policy, and to persuade their fellow citizens to help bring about change. Insofar as they have these goals, Buddhist activists must decide what attitude to take toward liberalism, and toward the central liberal doctrine of state neutrality between different conceptions of the good.

In addressing this topic, we must take into account the fact that Buddhist ethics centrally involves a particular conception of virtue and of what makes a human life go well. Throughout this work, I have pointed out a number of similarities between Buddhist—especially

Mahayana Buddhist—ethical views and classical utilitarianism. But the present context makes salient one respect in which these positions are utterly different. For many of the adherents of classical utilitarianism, a crucial part of the motivation for it is that it does not take a stand about which pursuits, projects, or goals are worth adopting, in some higher sense. Anything that makes people happy, from their own point of view, is valuable. Thus, classical utilitarianism does not involve a paternalistic attempt to tell people what is good for them; it respects people's own desires, and tries to provide whatever will allow them to achieve their own goals and realize their own happiness.

This feature of the structure of classical utilitarianism can make it a possible basis for agreement among people with different conceptions of the good. In a society such as the modern United States, in which there is no consensus on what makes life worth living and religious diversity seems to increase every day, the prospect of such an agreement is certainly attractive.[2] Buddhist ethics, by contrast, involves definite views about the nature of virtue and the constituents of good lives. No reasonable non-Buddhist could be expected to accept Buddhist ethics as the primary basis for making policy decisions in a pluralistic society. Even if Buddhists constitute a majority in a particular country, it would be deeply problematic for them to use their voting strength to impose laws based on their own conception of the good on others who do not accept it.

The Buddhist tradition has, for the most part, distinguished itself by its honorable adherence to the principle of religious toleration. But premodern Buddhist-influenced polities in Asia did not develop the idea of government neutrality between conceptions of the good. We simply do not know what a Buddhist argument for, or against, this kind of neutrality would look like. But today, in many Western countries, Buddhists live under, and benefit from, legal regimes that embody, more or less imperfectly, some conception of neutrality. One of the starting points of Buddhist political philosophy, if one is to emerge, would be an engagement with this issue.

A closely related question, and one that has begun to receive some attention from scholars, concerns whether Buddhists should accept the language of rights as an appropriate form in which to advocate political goals. The concept of universal human rights is a distinctively Western contribution to ethics—unlike that of universal, impartial benevolence, which has parallels in the philosophy of China and, as I have shown, India. Premodern Buddhist ethics simply has no concept of rights. It does, however, have quite a bit to say about the areas of ethical concern that are often discussed in connection with the idea of rights. According to some Buddhist scholars, Buddhist ethics could be enriched, and made more relevant to contemporary issues, by adopting the concept of rights and rethinking Buddhism in its terms. Others maintain that the differences between Buddhist views and rights-based theories are merely verbal, and that Buddhist values can be expressed in the language of rights without substantive change. Still others question whether a full-fledged theory of rights is really compatible with Buddhism, and with the core teachings that support its ethical commitments, such as the doctrine of no-self.[3]

Buddhist philosophers of the twenty-first century must also confront the pressing issue of the extent to which Buddhist ethics can be separated from traditional metaphysical beliefs. In this book, I have often presented Buddhist ethics as flowing from philosophical views that can be defended with powerful arguments. Yet certain Buddhist normative commitments may seem to be justifiable only if we assume the truth of such teachings as karma and rebirth. To the extent that the existence of reincarnation has yet to be demonstrated with any kind of scientific evidence, some may question whether an ethical system that depends on it can be relied on to guide our future paths. Thus, it is a matter of urgency to clarify which ethical positions of the Buddhist tradition rely for their justification on assuming the truth of traditional beliefs such as reincarnation, and which can be justified through arguments that can be compelling to those who reject such beliefs.

All these questions, and more, arise in connection with any attempt to bring Buddhist ethics into the context of contemporary discussion about ethics. But as I have tried to show, the Buddhist tradition has a great deal to contribute to that discussion. Ours is a time of tremendous economic, technological, and medical progress, but it seems also to be cursed by warfare, religious hatred, the destruction of habitat, and the extinction of species. Perhaps the gentle, tolerant and compassionate spirit of Buddhism can play some part in helping lead the world in a more positive direction.

Notes

1. Rorty 1984, pp. 51–54.
2. For example, Jay Garfield, in Keown, Prebish, and Husted 1998, p. 123.
3. Thurman 2000, p. 46.
4. Numerous resources on this phenomenon, called "compassion fatigue," can be found at www.vaonline.org/doc_compassion.html, and at http://home.earthlink.net/~hopefull/TC_compassion_fatigue.htm.
5. Conze, 1959, p. 304. He finds this teaching in the *Diamond Sutra* (*Vajracchedikā-prajñā-pāramitā*). Luis Gómez has identified it in the *Akṣayamati Sutra* and in Prajñākaramati's commentary to the *Bodhicaryāvatāra*. See Gómez 1973, p. 366.
6. Quoted in Tsong kha pa 2004, pp. 14–15.
7. Harvey 2000, ch. 4, 7, 8.

1. With the exception of the Vātsīputrīyas, who called themselves Buddhists, but took issue with the doctrine of no self.
2. For a justification of this claim, see Goodman 2004.
3. The reader will easily see that not one of the English translations I have offered in this paragraph does a perfect job of rendering the Sanskrit. These terms are extremely difficult to translate; I have offered the renderings that seem best to me, but other scholars could reasonably disagree.
4. Gómez n.d., pp. 19–20.
5. For instance, the Dhammapada describes it as *padaṃ santaṃ saṅ khārūpasamaṃ sukhaṃ*, or in Kaviratna's translation, "that exalted state of

peace and happiness, which is the cessation of conditioned existence." Kaviratna 1980, pp. 144–45.

6. Ñāṇamoli and Bodhi 1995, pp. 590–94.

7. Śāntideva 1995, p. 143. This is chap. 10, v. 55.

8. See, for instance, Garfield 2002, p. 120. Chaps. 6–9 of this work contain much valuable information about the Spiritual Practice School.

9. Gómez 1973, p. 368.

10. See Fuchs 2000 for extensive discussion.

11. Śāntideva 1995, p. 50.

12. Chang 1983, p. 270.

13. Patrul Rinpoche 1994, p. 112.

14. Harvey 2000, pp. 52–58.

15. See Śāntideva 1971, p. 162; Śāntideva 1961, p. 92.

16. In Keown 2001, p. 19, for example, we read: "I will also regard the principle of moral retribution, or karma, as an aspect of *sīla*." Linguistically, this is a very odd way of putting the matter; classical Buddhist texts do not arrange their categories this way. As I will show in detail in Chapter 3, the term *sīla* is narrower than our English word "ethics." Keown recognizes elsewhere that karma is not a normative concept; see Keown 2001, p. 127.

17. Dhammapada 3.39. See Kaviratna 1980, pp. 18–19.

18. Premasiri 1976, p. 73.

19. Conze 1959, pp. 307–8.

CHAPTER 2

1. I have taken the name of this case, and of the next one, from unpublished lectures by Professor Louis Loeb of the University of Michigan, Ann Arbor. Cases of this kind appear in many places in the recent literature on analytic ethics.

2. The example is found at Smart and Williams 1973, pp. 97–98. I have explained it in such a way as to raise the stakes slightly, without changing anything essential about the case.

3. Smart and Williams 1973, pp. 116–17.

4. Rule-consequentialists might argue that the best set of moral rules somehow permits sacrificing the one man in the Basic Trolley and forbids this in the Trolley and Bridge. Although it may be possible to construct such a set of rules, I find this move implausible.

5. Wood 1999, pp. 118–19.

6. Students who wish to understand these arguments should begin by reading Kant's *Groundwork for the Metaphysics of Morals*. Highly sophisticated and careful commentary on Kant's arguments can be found in Wood 1999 and Korsgaard 1996. I discuss and criticize Kant's views in chapter 11.

7. This is true of the views I have examined; but there are contractarian views, such as those advanced by Rawls and Scanlon, that do not have this kind of structure. These views are based on versions of this question: can you justify your actions to other reasonable people?

8. *Nicomachean Ethics* 1098a15, in Aristotle 1999.

9. *Nicomachean Ethics* 1099a25–b5, in Aristotle 1999.

10. Aristotle 1941, *Politics* 1325b5.

11. Bradley 1991, p. 47.

12. *Nicomachean Ethics* 1094b5–10, in Aristotle 1999. See also *Politics* 1252a1–5, in Aristotle 1941.

13. As we see in Aristotle's views about slavery—though this relation is supposedly justified by benefits to the slaves, insofar as they are naturally fitted for that state. Certainly one gets the strong impression from Aristotle's texts that I have no stringent obligation to actively assist members of other political communities living far away from me, even if they are in distress and I am able to help them.

14. Hurka 1992.

15. Ivanhoe 1991.

16. Henry Sidgwick noticed the possibility of a view of the kind I am discussing, but realized that no one in the Western tradition had ever defended it. He writes: "At first sight, indeed, the same alternatives present themselves: it seems that the Excellence aimed at may be taken either individually or universally; and circumstances are conceivable in which a man is not unlikely to think that he could best promote the Excellence of others by sacrificing his own. But no moralist who takes Excellence as an ultimate end has ever approved of such sacrifice, at least so far as Moral Excellence is concerned; no one has ever directed an individual to promote the virtue of others except in so far as this promotion is compatible with, or rather involved in, the complete realization of Virtue in himself." Sidgwick 1981, pp. 10–11.

17. The distinction between agent-relative and agent-neutral theories is found in Parfit 1984, p. 55.

18. See Singer 1972.

19. See, for example, Christine Swanton's statement that "we (at times) withhold the label 'benevolent' in our description of an act which . . . promotes the good of strangers but egregiously fails to express bonds of love to near and dear." Swanton 2003, p. 4. Another important example of this kind of attitude is found in Wolf 1982.

20. See, for example, Railton 1984.

21. Parfit 1984, pp. 307–47.

CHAPTER 3

1. *Majjhima Nikaya* 61. Ñāṇamoli and Bodhi 1995, pp. 524–25.

2. Schneewind 1998.

3. *Cūḷagosinga Sutta, Majjhima Nikāya* 31.22. In Ñāṇamoli and Bodhi 1995, p. 306.

4. See, for example, *Vinaya* 1.21; quoted in Perera 1991, pp. 60–61.

5. That there is a natural motivation to relieve suffering is not something that can be proven through philosophical arguments. It requires empirical evidence, and I am not in a position to make a fully convincing empirical case. The Buddhist tradition's advice on this point would be clear: if you doubt the existence of such a motivation, look for it within yourself. If you look with sufficient sincerity, you will find it. There is some further discussion of this issue in chapter 11.

6. King 1964, p. 158.

7. Tsong kha pa 2004, pp. 32–33.

8. As in the first verse of the *Metta Sutta*: "karaniyam atthakusalena," "This is what should be done by one who is skilled in goodness . . ."

9. As in the ninth verse of the *Metta Sutta*: "etam satim adittheyya," "he should sustain this mindfulness."

10. Barbra Clayton has called attention in this context to the Buddhist lists, such as the Six Perfections, that include both generosity and forbearance as separate entries from *sila* (Skt. *śila*). Thus if we translate sila as "ethics," "virtue," or "morality," it would follow that generosity is not part of ethics, or not a virtue, or not morally relevant. See Clayton 2006, p. 75. The least bad translation I have seen for sila is due to Ken McLeod: "moral discipline." See http://www.unfetteredmind.org/translations/37.php

11. Ohnuma 2000.

12. Ohnuma 2000, p. 47.

13. Ohnuma 2000, p. 59.

14. Ohnuma 2000, p. 66.

15. *Dhammapada* 3.42–43. In Byrom 1976.

16. *Dhammapada* 12.165. In Byrom 1976.

17. In chapter 26 of the *Dhammapada*, for example, we read: "He who has laid aside the cudgel that injures any creature whether moving or still, who neither slays nor causes to be slain—him I call a Brāhman." Kaviratna 1980, pp. 156–57. In passages such as this one, the Buddha is using the word "Brāhman" as synonymous with "Arhat"; he attempted to promote this linguistic reform in order to oppose the pretensions of the hereditary Brahmin caste.

18. King 1964, p. 136.

19. Heim 2003, p. 533.

20. This principle is mentioned, for example, at Schneewind 1984, p. 190.

21. Quoted in Tsong kha pa 2004, p. 217.

22. Adapted from Keown 2001, p. 30.

23. I am grateful to Christopher Knapp for pointing this out to me.

24. This view is ably defended in Velez de Cea 2004.

25. Dīgha Nikāya 30. In Walshe 1995, pp. 452–53.

26. Rājavaramuni 1990, p. 53.

27. Rājavaramuni 1990, p. 43.

28. Rājavaramuni 1990, p. 43, quoting *Anguttara Nikāya* 2.67.

29. *Majjhima Nikāya* 88.10. In Ñanamoli and Bodhi 1995.

30. Velez de Cea 2004, pp. 137–38.

31. As in the *Ariyapariyesanā Sutta*. See Ñanamoli and Bodhi, pp. 254–55.

32. 11.10–11. Ananda Maitreya 1995, p. 43.

33. Ñanamoli and Bodhi 1995, pp. 612–13.

34. Ñanamoli and Bodhi 1995, p. 1278 n. 743.

35. Ñanamoli and Bodhi 1995, p. 1023 and p. 1028.

36. Keown 1992, p. 177.

37. Keown 1992, p. 181.

38. Walshe 1995, pp. 193–95.

39. *Aṅguttara Nikāya* 3.384–6. Quoted in Harvey 2000, p. 44.

40. King 1964, p. 161.

41. Keown 1992, ch. 4 .

42. As discussed in Premasiri 1975.

43. These assertions seem to be accepted by the various parties in the debate about these terms: see Premasiri 1975, p. 69, and Adam 2005, p. 64.

44. Quoted in Premasiri 1975, p. 72.

45. Quoted in Premasiri 1975, p. 72.

46. Adam 2005, p. 75.

47. Thus, in commenting on the mind-training slogan "Give up poisonous food," the bKa' rgyud teacher Thrangu Rinpoche says: "One acts virtuously with the body, with the speech, and with the mind. From the point of view of enjoyment, one acts out of the roots of good, and so on. These are extremely good. Nevertheless, if self-grasping is present, [these actions] do not act as causes of liberation from cyclic existence. They act as causes for remaining in cyclic existence. Therefore, as much as possible, it is necessary to abandon self-grasping and grasping at true existence." Thrangu Rinpoche 2005, p. 125. In Tibetan: "lus kyi sgo nas dge ba bsags / ngag gi sgo nas dge ba bsags / yid kyi sgo nas dge ba bsags / longs spyod kyi sgo nas dge ba'i rtsa ba bsags pa la sogs pa de tsho ha cang yag po red / yin na yang bdag adzin de yod na akhor ba las thar byed kyi rgyur mi agro bar / akhor ba la gnas byed kyi rgyu ru agro bas / de'i phyir na ci thub gang thub kyis bdag adzin dang bden adzin de spang dgos kyi yod."

48. See Rājavaramuni 1990, p. 50 n. 13.

49. I am indebted to the discussion in Siderits 2003, p. 100.

50. Premasiri 1975, p. 42.

51. Premasiri 1975, p. 38.

52. King 1964, p. 57. Note that this particular quotation sounds very Aristotelian.

53. Premasiri 1975, p. 31.

54. Rhys Davids may be interpreting literally certain references to "health" in the Pali Canon that are, when read closely, obviously metaphors. For an example, see Ñānamoli and Bodhi 1995, pp. 613–15.

55. Ivanhoe 1991, p. 60.

56. Ivanhoe 1991, p. 64.

57. Keown 1992, p. 184.

CHAPTER 4

1. See Nattier 2003, pp. 193–95.

2. Evidence for this claim is offered in Walser 2005, chap. 1.

3. Nattier 2003, chap. 7, argues for these claims at length on the basis of close analysis of the *Ugradatta-paripṛcchā Sutra*.

4. Shih 1994, p. 114.

5. Shih 1994, p. 59.

6. Shih 1994, p. 91.

7. Shih 1994, p. 85.

8. Shih 1994, p. 105.

9. Nattier 2003, p. 256.

10. Nattier 2003, p. 226.

11. Nattier 2003, p. 255.

12. Shih 1994, p. 49.

13. Shih 1994, pp. 21–22.

14. Shih 1994, p. 98.

15. Nattier 2003, pp. 114–15.

16. This claim is made, and ably defended, in Schopen 1979.

17. Schopen 2005, p. 258, and generally ch. 8.

18. Schopen 1997, p. 39.

19. Schopen 1997, p. 38.

20. Nattier 2003, p. 132.

21. Nattier 2003, p. 132.

22. Nattier 2003, p. 234.

23. *The Bodhisattva Stages* is itself part of a larger work, the *Stages of Religious Practice* (*Yogācāra-bhūmi*).

24. Including both Harvey, in Harvey 2000, and Keown himself in Keown 2001.

25. Tatz 1986, p. 74.

26. This ambiguity is not an artifact of the English translation; it also exists in the Sanskrit for the passage, which reads: "bodhisattvo yena kaṭukaprayogeṇa tīkṣṇaprayogeṇa sattvānāmartham paśyati tam prayogam daurmanasyārakṣayā na samudācarati / sāpattiko bhavati akliṣṭāmāpattimāpadyate / anāpattiryat parittamartham dṛṣṭadhārmikam paśyet prabhūtaśca tannidānam daurmanasyam." Asaṅga, *Bodhisattvabhūmiḥ*. In Dutt 1966, pp. 116–17.

27. Tatz 1986, pp. 70–71.

28. These non-Mahayana practitioners are of two types: Śrāvakas, whom the quotation calls "auditors" and I have called "Disciples," and Pratyekabuddhas, whom the text calls "independent Buddhas" and I have called "Solitary Realizers." Pratyekabuddhas are meditators who realize Nirvana for their own benefit alone, without the help of a teacher, and who do not have any students. According to many sources, they can exist only during periods when the Buddhist religion is unknown. It may thus technically be impossible for the same boat to contain both Disciples and Solitary Realizers; but this quibble does not affect the philosophical point Asaṅga is making.

29. Tatz 1986, p. 71.

30. Tatz 1986, pp. 56–67.

31. Tatz 1986, p. 48. Note that Asaṅga's view is ambiguous between several possible forms of rule-consequentialism. Asaṅga says nothing about whether the rules are justified by the consequences of their being strictly followed by everyone; or the consequences of their being accepted by everyone, but not necessarily always obeyed; or perhaps by the consequences of their being accepted by a large enough number of people; or, perhaps, by the long-term consequences of their being accepted by me in particular.

32. Fletcher 1966, p. 57. Quoted in Keown 1992, p. 185.

33. Tatz 1986, p. 48.

34. Emmerick 1970, p. 40.

35. Nattier 2003, p. 315.

36. Shih 1994, pp. 49–50.

37. This issue is rightly emphasized in Clayton 2006, chap. 5.

38. *Gorgias* 495d. In Plato 1997, p. 839.

39. *Gorgias* 494c. In Plato 1997, p. 837.

40. Cited in Fu and Wawrytko 1991, pp. 83–84.

41. Emmerick 1970, p. 41.

42. Harvey 2000, p. 354.

43. Keown 1996, p. 347.

44. Cited in Gampopa 1998, pp. 348–50.

45. Gampopa 1998, p. 350.

46. The *Clear Crystal Mirror*, a fourteenth-century Tibetan folk history, tells a story about King Songtsen Gampo that exactly parallels the account of King Anala. Songsten Gampo is a real historical figure, but the story in question seems simply to have been copied from the Indian original. See Sakyapa Sonam Gyaltsen 1996, pp. 189–90.

47. We can also note that their philosophy forces them to be welfarist. Outside the mind, there are no beautiful rock formations; so beautiful rock formations cannot have intrinsic value independent of being perceived by a sentient being.

CHAPTER 5

Parts of this chapter were previously published as Goodman 2008. Reprinted with permission of *Philosophy East and West*.

1. See Premasiri 1975, p. 31, where this claim is made about early Buddhism.

2. Two other important Indian Mahayana texts contain something like ethical theory, though they do not come close to the theoretical level attained by Śāntideva. These are the *Four Hundred Stanzas* (*Catuḥśataka*) of Āryadeva, partly translated in Lang 2003, which I discuss briefly in chapter 6, and the *Precious Garland* (*Ratnāvalī*) of Nāgārjuna, which I will examine at length in chapter 9.

3. In Sanskrit: "bodhisattvaḥ sarvasattvānāṃ vartamānānāgatasarvaduḥkhadaurmanasyopaśamāya vartamānānāgatasukhasaumanasyotpādāya ca niḥsāhyataḥ kāyavāṅ manaḥparākramaiḥ prayatnaṃ karoti / yadi tu tatpratyayasamāgrīṃ nānveṣate, tadantarāyapratikārāya na ghaṭate, alpaduḥkhadaurmanasyaṃ bahuduḥkhadaurmanasyapra tikārabhūtaṃ notpādayati, mahārthasiddhyarthaṃ cālpārthahāniṃ na karoti, kṣaṇamapyupekṣate, sāpattiko bhavati." Śāntideva 1961, p. 12; my translation. Compare Śāntideva 1971, p. 16, where the translation obscures some crucial philosophical points. Note that Śāntideva here uses the same technical terminology of "fault" (Skt. *āpatti*) employed by Asaṅga.

4. Śāntideva 1995, p. 20.

5. Śāntideva 1995, p. 43.

6. The Sanskrit of these verses reads as follows: "sarvāsu dikṣu yāvantaḥ kāyacittavyathāturāḥ/te prāpnuvantu matpunyaiḥ sukhapramodyasāgaram" (10.2); "anena mama punyena sarvasattvā aśeṣataḥ/viramya sarvapāpebhyaḥ kurvantu kuśalaṃ sadā" (10.31).

7. In Sanskrit: "evaṃ sarvamidaṃ kṛtvā yanmayāsāditaṃ śubham Tena syāṃ sarvasattvānāṃ sarvaduḥkhapraśāntikṛt." Note that it seems possible to translate with a passive: "may all the suffering of all sentient beings be allayed." There is nothing in the verse that forces us to supply the subject: "may I allay."

8. In Sanskrit: "buddhabuddhasutairnityaṃ labhantāṃ te samāgamam pūjāme-ghairantaiśca pūjayantu jagadgurum." Note that "the Buddhas' kin" is not a very good translation. The Sanskrit reads *buddhasutair*, "the Buddhas' sons," that is, the bodhisat-tvas. "Kin" is too general: the Buddhas' fathers, mothers, aunts, and uncles are not in-cluded in the intended meaning! If we want to be less sexist than the original text, "the Buddhas' children" would be preferable. But nothing philosophical turns on this issue.

9. In Sanskrit: "yatkiñcijjagato duḥkhaṃ tatsarvaṃ mayi paccatām bodhisat-tvaśubhaiḥ sarvairjagat sukhitamastu ca." I strongly suspect that this verse was part of the inspiration that led the Tibetans to develop the practice of *tonglen*, described in the second section of this chapter.

10. His arguments are discussed at length in Williams 1998. These arguments are also a central topic of the exchange between Williams and Siderits, Siderits 2000a and 200b and Williams 2000.

11. So I argue in Goodman 2004.

12. Śāntideva 1995.

13. See Siderits 1997, pp. 469–70.

14. Parfit 1984, pp. 236–43.

15. Unger 1980 is devoted to this problem.

16. See Lewis 1993, p. 166.

17. For a particularly ingenious, but in my view unsuccessful, attempt, see Williamson 1994.

18. I discuss the Ship of Theseus in Goodman 2005.

19. Parfit 1984, pp. 253–66.

20. Parfit 1984, pp. 200–201.

21. Keown 1992, p. 19.

22. Śāntideva 1995, pp. 41–42.

23. Śāntideva 1995, p. 69: "All doctors use painful treatments to restore health. It follows that to put an end to many sufferings, a slight one must be endured."

24. Śāntideva 1971, p. 144.

25. Śāntideva might have the resources to resist this kind of conclusion in certain cases: the contamination of the mind of a bodhisattva, interrupting her development toward enlightenment, might be such a bad consequence that it would outweigh all the other benefits of the action. For a pattern of reasoning somewhat similar to this, though with much lower stakes, see Śāntideva 1971, p. 162: "Confident that to attain another's good is more important than one's own good, if he be moved by wrath even in admonishing another, he checks this for the future in consequence of repentance. . . . Even if this is

good for that being, nevertheless by the loss of the Bodhisatva's [sic] pity would come the loss of a great chain of good to the world."

26. Śāntideva 1971, p. 140. The transliteration has been slightly modernized.

27. My translation. See the somewhat different translation in Śāntideva 1971, p. 163: "And in the world when a son is impaled in view of mother and father, they do not think of attachment to their own welfare by reason of their natural pity. Secret relations with wives or maids who are protected by the family or religion or the royal standard, would not be forbidden love. If there is here good for people, or no detriment to them, there is no sin when one understands the motive." Bendall and Rouse's translation here is questionable; they may be breaking what is semantically one sentence into two. The Sanskrit of the passage reads: "loke'pi putre śūlamāropyamāne paśyatormātāpitrorna saukhyasaṅgo dṛṣṭaḥ svānurūpakṛpāvaśāt prachannas tarhi sasvāmikāsu niḥsvāmikāsu vā kuladharma-dhvajarakṣitāsu kāmamithyācāro na syāt / sati sattvārthe sattvānupaghāte cānubandhaṃ nirūpyādoṣaḥ." Śāntideva 1961, p. 93. It seems that we should read the whole text before the slash, which represents a daṇḍa, as one sentence. If we do, the passage should be translated as I have rendered it. This proposed translation has the same philosophical upshot as the translation of Bendall and Rouse, except that they read the two conditions— benefit for people, no detriment to them—as disjoined rather than conjoined. But we have ca, "and," not vā, "or"; both must be satisfied for the action to be permissible.

28. Such sexual relations, on Śāntideva's view, are still unequivocally forbidden for monks. Only laymen may engage in them.

29. See Tatz 1986, p. 71. These Indian texts have had a discernible influence on Tibetan folklore. According to an ancient legend, the Tibetan people are the descendants of a monkey and a rock-ogress. In the version of this story found in the *Clear Crystal Mirror (Rgyal rabs gsal ba'i me long)*, a folk history of Tibet composed in the fourteenth century, the monkey is a committed Mahayana Buddhist who has taken a special vow of celibacy. The ogress, however, who has fallen in love with him, makes a strong case against keeping this vow:

> "Driven by my desire, I have come to make this request.
> If you will not marry me
> I will take a rock-ogre husband.
> Every day we will slay ten thousand living beings,
> And every night we will devour a thousand creatures.
> I will bear countless ogre-children
> And this snowy realm will be filled with ogre-cities.
> Every living creature will become an ogre's prey.
> By comparison, is it not better to think of me
>   And show your compassion?" (Sakyapa Sonam Gyaltsen 1996, p. 76)

On the advice of Avalokiteśvara, the monkey consents, despite his vow, and becomes the ancestor of the Tibetan people.

30. Śāntideva 1995, p. 21.

31. Śāntideva 1995, p. 22.

32. Śāntideva 1995, p. 143.

33. Śāntideva 1995, p. 21. In Sanskrit: "ekamākāśaniṣṭhasya sattvadhātoranekadhā / bhaveyam upajīvyo'haṃ yāvat sarve na nirvṛtāḥ." Unfortunately, some ambiguity about whether the release of all beings will ever happen still remains—an ambiguity that disappears in Crosby and Skilton's English.

34. See Śāntideva 1995, p. 34.

35. Does this mean that they will cease to exist? No. As I discussed in chapter 1 and chapter 3, most Buddhist writers would tell us that Nirvana is neither being nor non-being; to apply either concept to it would be a mistake.

36. Śāntideva 1995, pp. 60–61.

37. Śāntideva 1995, p. 40. In Sanskrit: "sarvārambhā hi tuṣṭyarthāḥ." See Śāntideva 1988, p. 100.

38. Most vividly and poetically, perhaps, at 7.44–45. See Śāntideva 1995, p. 71.

39. Barbra Clayton repeatedly asserts this about Śāntideva in Clayton 2006.

40. Śāntideva 1995, p. 69.

41. Śāntideva 1995, p. 97.

42. "Oral Transmission from My Perfect Teacher" might be a more precise translation of the title of this text; I am using the title of the English translation from which I will quote. This particular text is closely associated with *ngöndro* (in transliteration, *sngon agro*), the "preliminary" practice that teachers from all Tibetan Buddhist sects require of their students before offering initiation into advanced Tantric rituals, such as those involving wrathful deities.

43. Tsong kha pa 2004, p. 130.

44. It is interesting that Sidgwick seems to find a similar dichotomous conception of benefits in the common sense of Victorian Britain. He writes: "a man is commonly thought to benefit others either by making them happier or by making them wiser and more virtuous." Sidgwick 1981, p. 9. Of course, Sidgwick does not take this common belief very seriously at a theoretical level. No doubt he holds that to help others become wiser or better is to benefit them indirectly; their greater wisdom and virtue will allow them to attain a higher degree of pleasure and the absence of pain, which, on Sidgwick's view, are the only intrinsically valuable goals.

45. Tsong kha pa 2004, p. 23.

46. Padmakara Translation Group 1994, p. 295.

47. Padmakara Translation Group 1994, p. 218.

48. This form of meditation is discussed in Kongtrul 1987. It is widely practiced by Tibetan Buddhists today. See, for example, Chodron 1994, pp. 36–43.

CHAPTER 6

1. Taylor 1989, p. 33.

2. Taylor 1989, p. 31.

3. Taylor 1989, p. 44.

4. Price and Mou-Lam 1969, p. 35. The transliteration has been corrected.

5. Thurman 2000, pp. 27–28.

6. Thurman 2000, p. 21.

7. Thurman 2000, p. 37.

8. Thurman 2000, p. 37.

9. Thurman 2000, p. 39.

10. Thurman 2000, p. 56.

11. Wang 1975, for example, interprets Padmasambhava as a being "beyond ethics," and regards his allegedly amoral stance as in some sense an improvement over the perspective of ethical commitment. I will provide some passages that explain why scholars such as Wang might find this claim plausible, as well as other passages that, on my view, refute it.

12. Davidson 2002, p. 237.

13. See Davidson 2002, p. 289: "The siddhas are often comic heroes, whose activity is rhetorically for the welfare of beings, although there are times when their behavior incongruously appears merely powerful self-indulgence."

14. Dowman 1985, p. 23.

15. Kapstein 2001, pp. 238–39.

16. See Kunsang 1993, p. 3.

17. Kunsang 1993 p. 37; see also p. 9 for an alternative version from another text.

18. Kunsang 1993, p. 39.

19. Kunsang 1993, p. 45.

20. Kunsang 1993, p. 51.

21. Kunsang 1993, p. 39. I have not corrected the unscientific transliterations in Kunsang's text.

22. Of course, some later Tibetan teachers, especially those of the dGe lugs sect, would argue that this passage should not be read literally, but should be given a complicated metaphorical interpretation. There is a systematic tendency in the Tantric tradition for scholarly monastic exegetes to try to reinterpret the outrageously antinomian features of Tantric texts as metaphors for internal meditative processes.

23. Kunsang 1993, p. 66.

24. Kunsang 1993, p. 23. These words are actually a quotation from another text, the *Precious Garland of Gold*, also an allegedly "discovered" revelation of Padmasambhava (in Tibetan, a *terma*).

25. Kunsang 1993, p. 172.

26. Dowman 1985, p. 21. It is strange that Dowman asserts that the *siddha* acts simultaneously for the benefit of himself and others. This claim would seem to call the act-consequentialist reading into question, unless we assume certain implausible kinds of coincidence of interests. It would be much better, I think, to claim, as I claim elsewhere about Saints and Buddhas, that the *siddha* is already in a state of maximal fulfillment of his interests, so that nothing that he does, and in fact, nothing that happens or could happen, will affect his welfare in any way.

27. *Mūla-madhyamaka-kārikā* 26.10; translation by the author. In Sanskrit: "samsaramūlān samskārān avidvān samskaroty atah / avidvān kārakah tasmān na vidvāms tattva-darśanāt." See Kalupahana 1986, p. 374. Garfield 1995, p. 78, has "The root of cyclic existence is action. Therefore, the wise one does not act. Therefore, the

unwise is the agent. The wise one is not because of his insight." Garfield is translating the Tibetan.

28. Though I have presented these ideas on the basis of a quotation from a Mahayana author, many scholars have found at least part of this picture in the Theravada as well. Thus, Martin Adam writes that according to the Pali Canon, "properly speaking, an *Arahat*'s conduct cannot be considered 'action' (*karma*) at all; it is non-karmatic." Adam 2005, p. 72.

29. In his introduction to Dorje 2006, p. xxiv.

30. Hopkins 1998, p. 111.

31. Chang 1983, p. 274.

32. Chang 1983, p. 272. I have slightly altered the punctuation.

33. See Oetke 1991, p. 317. Wood 1994 defends this interpretation at length.

34. See, for example, Huntington 1989, p. 170, v. 109. Similar statements are found in numerous Mahayana Sutras. See Thurman 2000, p. 31, and Emmerick 1970, p. 101.

35. *Madhyamaka-avatāra* 6.83, in Huntington 1989, p. 167.

36. For discussion, see Eckel 2003.

37. Lang 2003, p. 187.

38. Lang 2003, p. 193.

39. Lang 2003, p. 200.

40. Could *artha* be the Sanskrit word for "intrinsic value"? In some contexts, it might perhaps function this way. But *artha* often refers to wealth, material possessions, or profits; virtually all ethicists in Europe and Asia would hold that these things are instrumental goods at best. And, of course, *artha* has a number of other meanings, such as "the object of a thought" and "the referent of a word." At the very least, *artha* does not unambiguously designate intrinsic value; and therefore, the availability of this word did not make it possible for Indian philosophers to isolate this particular concept for discussion in any clear way.

41. For the Sanskrit text and a translation, see Wood 1994, pp. 318–19.

42. There are several very informative recent essays on this topic in Dreyfus and McClintock 2003. Contrast especially the essay by William L. Ames, "Bhāvaviveka's Own View of His Differences with Buddhapālita," pp. 41–66, with that by Tom J. F. Tillemans, "Metaphysics for Mādhyamikas," pp. 93–123.

43. Nozick 1989, p. 43.

CHAPTER 7

1. Even those versions of utilitarianism that call for equal concern for all people, or all intelligent beings, are still often perceived as excessively demanding.

2. In Singer 1972.

3. In Scarre 1996.

4. Walzer, for example: "For the consequences might be very bad indeed if the rules were overridden every time the moral calculation seemed to go against them. It is probably best if most men do not calculate too nicely, but simply follow the rules; they are less likely to make mistakes that way, all in all." Walzer 2004, p. 68.

5. Parfit 1984, p. 41. Italics omitted.

6. See Rapaport, editor's introduction, Mill 1978, p. ix.

7. Thus, for instance, "it has been suggested that one of the reasons for the spread of Buddhism in Southeast Asia and elsewhere was the medical lore of the Buddhist monks." Crawford 1991, p. 191, quoting De Bary 1958, p. 115. With reference to premodern Southeast Asia, André Wink writes: "Monasteries served as hospitals, schools, welfare institutions for the poor, travelers' lodges, social centres, recreational and ceremonial centres, courts, art centres, or stores for jointly owned property, and they were part of the administrative system." Wink 1997, pp. 366–67.

8. Of course, it is also a feature of the traditional Buddhist view that by following the lay precepts, ordinary people can collect the positive karma that will eventually make it possible for them to be reborn in more favorable circumstances and a more virtuous state of mind, so that they can then become monks or nuns. Thus, eventually, everyone will lead the best kind of life. If we reject reincarnation, this aspect of the view will no longer be available.

9. A similar conception of mutual dependence between Christian monks and laity was, according to Charles Taylor, a feature of medieval European thought. See Taylor 1989, p. 217.

10. For the Ten Good Paths of Action (*dasa-kusala-kamma-patha*), see Keown 2001, p. 30; see also chapter 2 here.

11. *Ariyapariyesanā Sutta: The Noble Search.* In Ñāṇamoli and Bodhi 1995, p. 260.

12. Some Buddhist monks have, indeed, historically believed that this kind of reform was at least part of their role. Sivaraksa writes that "To spread peace and stability, the Sangha sought to establish moral hegemony over the state, to guide the communities by means of a code of non-violent ethics in the interest of social welfare." Sivaraksa 1991, p. 161. The extent to which the Sangha, in this context the Buddhist monastic community, succeeded in shaping society for the better is another question.

13. See Ohnuma 2000, pp. 65–66.

14. Quoted in Tsong kha pa 2004, p. 131. See Śāntideva 1971, p. 51; Śāntideva 1961, p. 32. In Tsong kha pa 2004, the citation to Śāntideva 1961 is given incorrectly.

15. Śāntideva 1995, p. 69.

16. Wolf 1982.

17. Wolf 1982, p. 419.

18. Wolf 1982, p. 228.

19. Wolf 1982, p. 422.

20. Wolf 1982, p. 423.

21. The sources of this repudiation of monasticism are insightfully discussed in Taylor 1989. See especially p. 185.

22. Chodron 1994, p. 125.

23. Śāntideva 1995, p. 22.

24. Śāntideva 1995, p. 21.

CHAPTER 8

1. An earlier version of this chapter was published as Goodman 2002. Reprinted with permission of *American Philosophical Quarterly*.

2. Strawson 1986, pp. 117–20.

3. Siderits 1987, p. 149.

4. Griffiths 1982.

5. Van Inwagen 1983 is a classic defense of incompatibilism. The exposition of van Inwagen's views in this chapter is primarily based on this book.

6. Van Inwagen 1983, chap. 5.

7. Strawson 1973.

8. A very straightforward case would be if someone's movements were being physically controlled from outside, as if someone, by pulling a string attached to someone else's finger, caused that person to pull the trigger of a gun.

9. Strawson 1973, p. 11.

10. The Abhidharma is a Buddhist philosophical tradition that combines careful scriptural exegesis with metaphysical analysis. The goal of the Abhidharma is to find an ontological theory that can account for the truth of the Buddha's teachings, while postulating the minimum possible range of really existing entities.

11. Vasubandhu 1970, chap. 9. My translation. For another translation of the same passage, see Duerlinger p. 83.

12. Griffiths 1982, p. 287.

13. Griffiths 1982, p. 289.

14. Majjhima Nikāya 71.7–9. In Ñānamoli and Bodhi 1995, p. 588.

15. Katz 1982, chap. 3.

16. Majjhima Nikāya 79.7. In Ñānamoli and Bodhi 1995, p. 655.

17. Siderits 1987, p. 153.

18. Vasubandhu 1970, chap. 9. My translation. Compare Duerlinger 2003, p. 107.

19. As, e.g., in Pereboom 2001, p. 63. Pereboom cites Broad 1952, p. 169.

20. For example, at Compendium of Theories about Reality (Tattvasaṃgraha) 7.197, in Jha 1986.

21. As in Treasury of Metaphysics, chap. 2, v. 64d.

22. The libertarian interpretation of Buddhist thought can nevertheless be found in some modern Buddhist writers. For example, L. P. N. Perera writes that from a Buddhist perspective, "human beings are born with complete freedom and responsibility. Not being the creations of a Creator, they are subject only to nondeterministic causal laws, and their destinies are therefore in their own hands." It would be interesting to learn in what sense Perera thinks these causal laws are "nondeterministic" and how he knows that this is the Buddhist position. In any case, my criticisms of Griffiths apply equally to Perera's assertions.

23. Siderits 1987, p. 155.

24. Ibid., p. 157.

25. Ibid., p. 153.

26. Ibid., p. 153.

27. Dīgha Nikāya 2, 19–21. In Walshe 1995, pp. 91–110.

28. Majjhima Nikāya 60.21. In Ñānamoli and Bodhi 1995, p. 513. The same language occurs at Majjhima Nikāya 76.13.

29. Van Inwagen 1983, p. 207.

30. *Majjhima Nikāya* 103.11–14 is one of the many passages that might be mentioned. In Ñānamoli and Bodhi 1995, pp. 850–51.

31. *Majjhima Nikāya* 21.6, 21.20. In Ñānamoli and Bodhi 1995, p. 218, 223.

32. Ñānamoli 1956, 9.14, 22.

33. Ñānamoli 1956, 9.38.

34. Crosby and Skilton's misleading translation of the Sanskrit term *pratyaya*, "reasons" (Śāntideva 1995), has been replaced with "causes." The term *pratyaya* usually means a causal condition, and rarely would mean "reason"; an Indian author would be more likely to use *hetu* or *nibandhana* to say "reason." Moreover, nonsentient things such as bile do not act out of reasons.

35. Śāntideva 1995, pp. 52–53. For the original text, see Vaidya 1960.

36. Śāntideva 1995, 6.71, 6.74.

37. Śāntideva 1995, p. 16.

38. We find these forms of aggression described at the end of chap. 4 of the *Introduction*. See, for instance, 4.43–44: "I shall be tenacious in this, and wage war sworn to enmity, except against the kind of defilement that comes from murdering the defilements. I do not care if my guts ooze out! Let my head fall off! But never shall I bow down before the enemy, the defilements!" Śāntideva 1995, p. 29.

39. Such a view is explained and defended in great detail in Nussbaum 2001.

40. *Introduction* 6.8: "Therefore I shall destroy the food of this deceiver, since this hatred has no purpose other than my murder." Śāntideva 1995, p. 50.

41. How could these emotions be free from delusion if emptiness is the way things really are? As I have shown, there is a form of compassion that fully recognizes emptiness. It's also possible to feel loving-kindness toward others, for example, while also knowing that those others exist merely conventionally and are empty of essence.

42. The *Questions of King Milinda* was accepted by the Theravada, the Sarvāstivāda, and probably by several other Abhidharma schools. Versions of the text exist in Sanskrit, Pali, and Prakrit and in multiple translations into Chinese.

43. Gómez n.d.

44. Siderits could reply that only incompatibilists accept the kind of sharp distinction between moral and legal responsibility that this argument requires. But any philosopher who recognizes that some laws are unjustified can distinguish between moral and legal responsibility. What the king will do to you if you transgress is a purely factual matter; it doesn't necessarily track either the best ways of promoting the welfare of society or anyone's sense of fairness. And as I argue below, despite initial appearances, karma is not necessarily fair.

45. For instance, Peter Harvey: "The law of karma is seen as a natural law inherent in the nature of things, like a law of physics." Harvey 2000, p. 16. Damien Keown concurs, saying "kamma is a value-free description." Keown 1992, p. 127.

46. Further evidence that karma is a factual matter and doesn't correspond closely to desert comes from the bizarre doctrine of "karmic place" (*las gyi sa pa*) accepted by some Tibetan texts. According to this teaching, the power of karma is greater on one of the four continents of the world, called Jambudvīpa, than on the other three. Actions performed on this continent, believed to contain both India and Tibet, have stronger

effects, which may also manifest more quickly. See Patrul Rinpoche 1994, p. 381 n. 57. I do not mean to suggest that Buddhists living today should give any credence to this doctrine; after all, it depends on a traditional cosmology, which we know quite well to be false. But the Indian and Tibetan Buddhists who accepted this doctrine must not have been thinking of karma as closely linked to desert. How could the degree of desert or moral responsibility for an action depend on the continent on which it was performed? Similar remarks apply, I would think, to the Tibetan belief that positive actions that are performed on certain days and certain months of the year have greater karmic effects than they normally would.

47. The historical Buddha explicitly claimed that there are other causes of suffering besides karma. But members of the Yogācāra school of Mahayana philosophy, since they are idealists, cannot accept the idea of a cause that is material in nature. All experience, including all suffering, will for them be caused by potentialities called "seeds" that rest in the storehouse consciousness; these seeds are planted by karma. In general, Mahayana Buddhists seem often to make the claim that all suffering is caused by karma. See Patrul Rinpoche 1994, p. 118: "In all their inconceivable variety, the pleasures and miseries that each individual being experiences—from the summit of existence down to the very lowest depth of hell—arise only from the positive and negative actions that each has amassed in the past."

48. Pereboom 2001, pp. 95–96.

CHAPTER 9

1. See Lang 2003, pp. 91–94. See also Collins 1993.

2. Lang finds this identification perfectly appropriate; but see Huxley 1996 and Collins 1996.

3. Thus Honderich articulates one version of retributivism this way: "legislators, who regulate the practice of punishment partly by fixing scales of penalties, are obliged to arrange that men get what they deserve given the wrongfulness of their actions, simply because they deserve it. Legislators are not to take into consideration, in this respect, the well-being of offenders or of society as a whole." Honderich 1969, p. 14.

4. See Murphy 1973, p. 5.

5. For example, see Berns 2008.

6. Stephen 1874, pp. 161–62. Quoted in Honderich 1969, p. 17 n. 12.

7. Quoted in Pojman and McLeod, eds., 1999, p. 30.

8. Sidgwick 1981, p. 281.

9. Sidgwick 1981, p. 349.

10. Hopkins 1998, p. 127.

11. Hopkins 1998, p. 138.

12. Many scholars would find an equivalent of retributivism in the concept of karma, to the extent that they understand karma as a process that gives each agent what he deserves. As Mark Siderits writes, "Buddhist ethics contains some elements suggestive of retributivism, and these are incompatible with Buddhist Reductionism." Siderits 2000b, p. 457. But my view is that karma is not really part of ethics at all: it

is to be understood as a factual matter, a kind of natural law. I defend this position in chapter 8.

13. Quoted in King 1964, p. 123. The view that Buddhism is opposed to retributivism and that the justification punishment should be based primarily on rehabilitation is supported by the contemporary Theravada Buddhist author L. P. N. Perera, who writes: "Buddhism would accept the necessity of punishment as a corrective measure for an erring individual with the objective of rehabilitating him or her within acceptable norms, and not as a lawful retaliatory measure for an offence committed or even simply as an expression of outraged feelings." Perera 1991, p. 38.

14. Quoted in King 1964, p. 178.

15. Hopkins 1998, p. 129.

16. Hopkins 1998, p. 138.

17. Anderson 1999, p. 307.

18. See, for example, the meditation on "exchange of self and other" described in *Bodhicaryāvatāra*, chap. 8. Śāntideva 1995, pp. 100–103.

19. Miller et al. 1999, p. 260.

20. Miller et al. 1999, p. 259.

21. Collins 1998, pp. 451–59.

22. Collins 1998, p. 459.

23. Emmerick 1970, p. 59. The Sutra also predicts various natural and supernatural disasters as the results of a failure to punish.

24. And Nāgārjuna suggests that "if from the unrighteousness of the world / It is difficult to rule religiously, / Then it is right for you to become a monastic." Hopkins 1998, p. 148. But Nāgārjuna is clearly not committed to the claim that genuinely religious rule is impossible.

25. Another scriptural text that accepts the legitimacy of some forms of punishment is the *Sutra on Upāsaka Precepts*. Here we read that if a bodhisattva becomes the king of a country, "when he sees others doing wrong, he may beat or reproach them, but he never kills them." Shih 1994, p. 68. Note that the Tibetan tradition certainly did not interpret the Buddhadharma as requiring unqualified nonviolence. In his advice to ministers in the *Copper Temple Life Story*, Padmasambhava instructs them to "keep peace in the country while enforcing the law rigorously . . . keeping the army on guard externally, protect the palace, the country, and the government." Kunsang 1993, p. 158. For much more dramatic confirmation of the same point, see the passages from the same text I quoted in chapter 5.

26. *Gorgias* 476a–479c. See Plato 1997, pp. 822–24.

27. I am using the terminology of Rawls 1993. I explored this topic further in the conclusion.

28. On the basis of surveys from the 1970s and 1980s, Robert Bohm maintains that the "evidence indicates that retribution is the primary basis of support for the death penalty." Bohm 1987, p. 387. Many death penalty supporters say that the deterrent effect of the death penalty is a major reason for their views, but "when queried further, they indicate that evidence of no deterrence would not have much effect on their position" (p. 388). See also Berns 2008.

29. The evidence is summarized in Sunstein and Vermeule 2005.

30. Harrison and Karberg 2003, p. 11.

31. I am indebted to an anonymous reviewer for this important point.

32. Harer 1994, pp. 23–25.

CHAPTER 10

1. Keown 1992, p. 177.

2. Keown 1992, p. 177.

3. Keown 1992, p. 181.

4. Keown 1992, p. 182.

5. Keown 1992, p. 181.

6. Keown 1996.

7. Ivanhoe 1991.

8. Keown 1996, p. 346.

9. Keown 1996, p. 344 n. 13.

10. Keown 1992, p. 178.

11. See, e.g., Tatz 1986, p. 80; but such passages occur throughout the text.

12. I am speaking at the level of conventional truth, hence ignoring the doctrine of no-self for the moment.

13. See, e. g., *Dhammapada* 121–22. Kaviratna 1980, p. 51.

14. I owe this formulation to Christopher Knapp.

15. As I showed in chapter 6, this statement is open to various interpretations and may need to be qualified in complex ways.

16. Martin Adam advances this objection at Adam 2005, p. 66. He cites Harvey 2000, p. 49. Harvey, in turn, cites Keown 1992, p. 178. Neither Adam nor Harvey offers any evidence in support of his claim about the order of interpretation. Keown's evidence consists of the arguments I have just discussed. Adam says that, on his view, this objection has force when applied to the Theravada, but does not apply to Mahayana ethics, due to the Middle Way School's rejection of the whole concept of intrinsic nature (*svabhāva*), which, he thinks, might rule out assigning central ethical significance to the intrinsic characteristics of actions.

17. Interestingly, Adam considers, and does not entirely reject, an account that turns out to have just this structure. See Adam 2005, p. 66 and n. 6.

18. My explanation of the problem is based on Scarre 1996, pp. 156–60.

19. Scarre 1996, p. 159.

20. Dworkin 2000, p. 217.

21. Twain 1948, pp. 115–20.

22. Hooker 1996, pp. 149–50. Emphasis in original.

23. Kongtrul 1987, p. 39.

24. Buddhaghosa 1956, p. 57.

25. *Nicomachean Ethics* 1095b30–1096a1. In McKeon 2001, p. 938.

26. Sidgwick 1981, p. 393.

27. In the preceding chapters, I have sometimes used the word "skillful" to translate these terms.

28. Sidgwick 1981, p. 392.

29. Sidgwick 1981, p. 424.

CHAPTER 11

1. See Wood 1999, pp. 97–106, which concedes as much. According to Wood, the formula of universal law and its variant, the formula of the law of nature, "are merely provisional and incomplete formulations of the principle of morality, which always depend for their application on other, independent rational principles." Wood 1999, p. 91.

2. This is Wood's interpretation at Wood 1999, p. 21.

3. Wood 1999, p. 159.

4. Wood 1999, p. 162

5. Wood 1999, p. 177.

6. Wood 1999, p. 177.

7. Wood 1999, p. 176.

8. Wood 1999, p. 174.

9. Wood 1999, p. 175.

10. Found in her article "Personal Identity and the Unity of Agency: A Kantian Response to Parfit," in Korsgaard 1996, pp. 363–87.

11. Indeed, she seems largely to be in agreement with them. She refers, for example, to "the considerations against deep personal separateness that Parfit and I both endorse." Korsgaard 1996, p. 383.

12. Korsgaard 1996, p. 371.

13. Korsgaard 1996, p. 370.

14. Korsgaard 1996, p. 371.

15. Korsgaard 1996, p. 370.

16. Korsgaard 1996, p. 378.

17. Korsgaard 1996, p. 370.

18. See Parfit 1984, pp. 12–13.

CONCLUSION

1. Kupperman 1999, p. 155.

2. Brian Barry's helpful discussion of this issue reads, in part: "Let me begin by asking what justice as impartiality does have in common with utilitarianism. . . . The fundamental point of commonality, from which other similarities flow, is that both theories are addressed to the same problem. They start from the recognition of the irreducible plurality of substantive conceptions of the good. They therefore share the project of finding a basis for a society's institutions and public policies that is in principle capable of appealing to every member of that society, whatever his or her substantive conception of the good may be." Barry 1995, p. 139.

3. For extended discussion of these questions, see Keown, Prebish, and Husted 1998, and especially the essays by Keown and Ihara.

Bibliography

Abbott, Evelyn, ed. 1880. *Hellenica*. London: Longmans, Green, and Co.

Adam, Martin T. 2005. "Groundwork for a Metaphysic of Buddhist Morals: A New Analysis of *puñña* and *kusala*, in light of *sukka*." *Journal of Buddhist Ethics* 12, pp. 62–85.

Ananda Maitreya, trans. 1995. *The Dhammapada: The Path of Truth*. Berkeley: Parallax Press.

Anderson, Elizabeth. 1999. "What is the Point of Equality?" Ethics 109, pp. 287–337.

Aristotle. 1941. Richard McKeon, ed. *The Basic Works of Aristotle*. New York: Modern Library.

———. 1999. *Nicomachean Ethics*. Terence Irwin, trans. Indianapolis: Hackett.

Barry, Brian. 1995. *Justice as Impartiality*. Oxford: Clarendon Press.

Berns, Walter. 2008. "Religion and the Death Penalty." *Weekly Standard*, February 4, 20.

Bohm, Robert M. 1987. "American Death Penalty Attitudes: A Critical Examination of Recent Evidence." *Criminal Justice and Behavior* 14:3, 380–96.

Bradley, A. C. 1991. "Aristotle's Conception of the State." In David Keyt and Fred D. Miller, Jr., eds., *A Companion to Aristotle's Politics*. Oxford: Blackwell, pp. 13–56. Originally appeared in Evelyn Abbott, ed., *Hellenica*. London: Longmans, Green, and Co., 1880, pp. 181–243.

Broad, C. D. 1952. "Determinism, Indeterminism and Libertarianism," p. 169. In Broad, *Ethics and the History of Philosophy*. London: Routledge and Kegan Paul, pp. 195–217. Reprinted in Gerald Dworkin, ed., *Determinism, Free Will and Moral Responsibility*. Englewood Cliffs, N.J.: Prentiss Hall, 1970, pp. 149–71.

Buddhaghosa. 1956. *The Path of Purification*. Bhikkhu Ñāṇamoli, trans. Colombo, Sri Lanka: R. Semage.

Byrom, Thomas, trans. 1976. *Dhammapada: The Sayings of the Buddha*. New York: Bell Tower.

Chang, Garma C. C., ed. 1983. *A Treasury of Mahayana Sutras: Selections from the Mahāratnakūṭa Sutra*. University Park: Pennsylvania State University Press.

Chodron, Pema. 1994. *Start Where You Are*. Reprinted in Pema Chodron, *The Pema Chödrön Collection*. New York: One Spirit, 2003, pp. 3–148

———. 2003. *The Pema Chodron Collection*. New York: One Spirit.

Clayton, Barbra. 2006. *Moral Theory in Śāntideva's Śikṣāsamuccaya: Cultivating the Fruits of Virtue*. New York: Routledge.

Collins, Steven. 1993. "The Discourse on What Is Primary (Aggañña-Sutta): An Annotated Translation." *Journal of Indian Philosophy* 21, pp. 303–93.

———. 1996. "The Lion's Roar on the Wheel-Turning King: A Response to Andrew Huxley's 'The Buddha and the Social Contract.'" *Journal of Indian Philosophy* 24, pp. 421–46.

———. 1998. *Nirvana and Other Buddhist Felicities: Utopias of the Pali Imaginaire*. New York: Cambridge University Press.

Conze, Edward. 1959. "Buddhism: The Mahāyāna." In R. C. Zaehner, ed., *The Concise Encyclopedia of Living Faiths*. New York: Hawthorn Books, pp. 296–320.

Crawford, Cromwell. 1991. "The Buddhist Response to Health and Disease." In Fu and Wawrytko 1991, pp. 185–93.

Crisp, Roger, ed. 1996. *How Should One Live? Essays on the Virtues*. New York: Oxford University Press.

Davidson, Ronald M. 2002. *Indian Esoteric Buddhism: A Social History of the Tantric Movement*. New York: Columbia University Press.

De Bary, William T., ed. *Sources of Indian Tradition*. New York: Columbia University Press, 1958.

Dorje, Gyurme, trans. 2006. *The Tibetan Book of the Dead*. Graham Coleman and Thupten Jinpa, eds. New York: Viking.

Dowman, Keith. 1985. *Masters of Mahamudra: Songs and Histories of the Eighty-Four Buddhist Siddhas*. Albany: State University of New York Press.

Dreyfus, Georges B. J., and Sara L. McClintock, eds. 2003. *The Svātantrika-Prāsaṅgika Distinction: What Difference Does a Difference Make?* Boston: Wisdom.

Duerlinger, James. 2003. *Indian Buddhist Theories of Persons: Vasubandhu's "Refutation of the Theory of a Self."* London: RoutledgeCurzon.

Dutt, Nalinaksha, ed. 1966. *Bodhisattvabhūmi: Being the Fifteenth Section of Asaṅgapada's Yogācārabhūmi*. Patna: K. P. Jayaswal Research Institute.

Dworkin, Gerald, ed. 1970. *Determinism, Free Will and Moral Responsibility*. Englewood Cliffs, N.J.: Prentiss Hall.

Dworkin, Ronald. 2000. *Sovereign Virtue: The Theory and Practice of Equality*. Cambridge, Mass.: Harvard University Press.

Eckel, Malcolm David. 2003. "The Satisfaction of No Analysis: On Tsong Kha Pa's Approach to Svātantrika-Mādhyamika." In Georges B. J. Dreyfus and Sara L. McClintock, eds., 2003. *The Svātantrika-Prāsaṅgika Distinction: What Difference does a Difference Make?* Boston: Wisdom, pp. 173–203.

Emmerick, R. E. 1970. *The Sutra of Golden Light.* London: Luzac.

Fletcher, Joseph. *Situation Ethics.* London: SCM Press, 1966.

Fu, Charles Wei-hsun, and Sandra Wawrytko. 1991. *Buddhist Ethics and Modern Society: An International Symposium.* New York: Greenwood Press.

Fuchs, Rosemarie, trans. 2000. Buddha Nature: The Mahayana Uttaratantra Shastra with Commentary. Attributed to Arya Maitreya and Arya Asanga. With commentaries by Jamgon Kongtrul Lodro Thaye and Khenpo Tsultrim Gyamtso Rinpoche. Ithaca, NY: Snow Lion.

Gampopa [sGam po pa]. 1998. *The Jewel Ornament of Liberation: The Wish-fulfilling Gem of the Noble Teachings.* Khenpo Konchog Gyaltsen Rinpoche, trans. Ani K. Trinlay Chodron, ed. Ithaca, N.Y.: Snow Lion.

Garfield, Jay. 1995. *The Fundamental Wisdom of the Middle Way: Nāgārjuna's Mūlamadhyamakakārikā.* Oxford: Oxford University Press.

Garfield, Jay. 2002. *Empty Words: Buddhist Philosophy and Cross-Cultural Interpretation.* Oxford: Oxford University Press.

Gómez, Luis. 1973. "Emptiness and Moral Perfection." *Philosophy East and West* 23:3, pp. 361–72.

Gómez, Luis, trans. N.d. "Menander, the Greek King, Asks about the Self and Personal Identity." Manuscript on file with the translator.

Goodman, Charles. 2002. "Resentment and Reality: Buddhism on Moral Responsibility." *American Philosophical Quarterly* 39:4, pp. 359–72.

———. 2004. "The *Treasury of Metaphysics* and the Physical World." *Philosophical Quarterly* 54:216, pp. 389–401.

———. 2005. "Vaibhāṣika Metaphoricalism." *Philosophy East and West* 55:3, pp. 377–93.

———. 2008. "Consequentialism, Agent-Neutrality, and Mahayana Ethics." *Philosophy East and West* 58:1 pp. 17–35

Griffiths, Paul J. 1982. "Notes toward a Critique of Buddhist Karmic Theory." *Religious Studies* 18, pp. 277–91.

Harer, Miles D. 1994. "Recidivism among Federal Prisoners Released in 1987." Washington, D.C.: Federal Bureau of Prisons Office of Research and Evaluation.

Harrison, Paige M., and Jennifer C. Karberg. 2003. "Prison and Jail Inmates at Midyear 2002." *Bureau of Justice Statistics Bulletin.* www.ojp.usdoj.gov/bjs/pub/pdf/pjim02.pdf.

Harvey, Peter. 2000. *An Introduction to Buddhist Ethics.* Cambridge: Cambridge University Press.

Heim, Maria. 2003. "The Aesthetics of Excess." Journal of the American Academy of Religion 71:3, pp. 531–54.

Honderich, Ted. 1969. *Punishment: The Supposed Justifications.* London: Hutchinson.

Hooker, Brad. 1996. "Does Moral Virtue Constitute a Benefit to the Agent?" In Roger Crisp, ed., *How Should One Live? Essays on the Virtues.* New York: Oxford University Press, pp. 141–55.

Hopkins, Jeffrey. 1998. *Buddhist Advice for Living and Liberation: Nāgārjuna's "Precious Garland."* Ithaca, N.Y.: Snow Lion.

Huntington, C. W. 1989. *The Emptiness of Emptiness: An Introduction to Early Indian Mādhyamika*. Honolulu: University of Hawai'i Press.

Hurka, Thomas. 1992. "Consequentialism and Content." *American Philosophical Quarterly* 29:1, pp. 71–78.

Huxley, Andrew. 1996. "The Buddha and the Social Contract." *Journal of Indian Philosophy* 24, pp. 407–20.

Ihara, Craig K. 1998. "Why There Are No Rights in Buddhism: A Reply to Damien Keown." In Keown, Prebish, and Husted 1998, pp. 43–51.

Ivanhoe, Philip J. 1991. "Character Consequentialism: An Early Confucian Contribution to Contemporary Ethical Theory." *Journal of Religious Ethics* 19:1, pp. 55–70.

———. 1997. "Response to Keown." *Journal of Religious Ethics* 25:2, pp. 394–400.

Jha, Ganganatha, trans. 1986. *The Tattvasaṅgraha of Śāntarakṣita*. Delhi: Motilal Banarsidass.

Jones, J. J. 1949. *The Mahāvastu*. Vol. 1. London: Luzac.

Kalupahana, David. 1986. *Nāgārjuna: The Philosophy of the Middle Way*. Albany: State University of New York Press.

Kapstein, Matthew. 2001. *Reason's Traces: Identity and Interpretation in Indian and Tibetan Buddhist Thought*. Boston: Wisdom.

Katz, Nathan. 1982. *Buddhist Images of Human Perfection*. Delhi: Motilal Banarsidass.

Kaviratna, Harischandra. 1980. *Dhammapada: Wisdom of the Buddha*. Pasadena, Calif.: Theosophical University Press.

Keenan, John P., trans. 2000. *The Scripture on the Explication of Underlying Meaning*. Berkeley, Calif.: Numata Center for Buddhist Translation and Research.

Keown, Damien. 1996. "Karma, Character, and Consequentialism." *Journal of Religious Ethics* 24:2, pp. 329–50.

———. 2001. *The Nature of Buddhist Ethics*. London: Macmillan.

Keown, Damien, Charles Prebish, and Wayne Husted. 1998. *Buddhism and Human Rights*. Richmond, Surrey, England: Curzon Press.

Keown, Damien V. 1998. "Are There Human Rights in Buddhism?" In Keown, Prebish, and Husted 1998, pp. 15–41.

Keyt, David, and Fred D. Miller, Jr., eds. 1991. *A Companion to Aristotle's Politics*. Oxford: Blackwell.

Khenpo Tsultrim Gyatso Rinpoche, trans. 2000. Asaṅga; Ārya Maitreya; Jamgön Kongtrul Lodrö Thayé, *Buddha Nature: The Mahayana Uttaratantra Shastra with Commentary*. Ithaca, N.Y.: Snow Lion.

King, Winston L. 1964. *In the Hope of Nibbana: An Essay on Theravada Buddhist Ethics*. La Salle, Ill.: Open Court.

Kongtrul, Jamgon. 1987. *The Great Path of Awakening: An Easily Accessible Introduction for Ordinary People*. Ken McLeod, trans. Boston: Shambhala.

Korsgaard, Christine. 1996. *Creating the Kingdom of Ends*. Cambridge: Cambridge University Press.

Kunsang, Eric Pema, trans. 1993. *The Lotus-Born: The Life Story of Padmasambhava*. Boston: Shambhala.

Kupperman, Joel. 1999. *Learning from Asian Philosophy*. Oxford: Oxford University Press.

Lang, Karen. 2003. *Four Illusions: Candrakīrti's Advice for Travelers on the Bodhisattva Path*. Oxford: Oxford University Press.

Levinson, Sanford, ed. 2004. Torture: A Collection. New York: Oxford University Press.

Lewis, David. 1993. "Many, but Almost One." Reprinted in Lewis, *Papers in Metaphysics and Epistemology*. Cambridge: Cambridge University Press, pp. 164–82.

———. 1999. *Papers in Metaphysics and Epistemology*. Cambridge: Cambridge University Press.

McKeon, Richard, ed. 2001. *The Basic Works of Aristotle*. New York: Modern Library.

Mill, John Stuart. 1978. *On Liberty*. Elizabeth Rapaport, ed. Indianapolis: Hackett.

Miller, Arthur G., Anne K. Gordon, and Amy M. Buddie. 1999. "Accounting for Evil and Cruelty: Is to Explain to Condone?" *Personality and Social Psychology Review* 3:3, pp. 254–68.

Murphy, Jeffrie. 1973. "Marxism and Retribution." *Philosophy and Public Affairs* 2:3. Reprinted in A. John Simmons, Marshall Cohen, Joshua Cohen, and Charles R. Beitz, eds., *Punishment: A Philosophy and Public Affairs Reader*. Princeton, N.J.: Princeton University Press, pp. 3–29.

Nāgārjuna. 1998. *Buddhist Advice for Living and Liberation: Nāgārjuna's Precious Garland*. Jeffrey Hopkins, trans. Ithaca, N.Y.: Snow Lion.

Ñānamoli, trans. 1956. Buddhaghosa, *The Path of Purification*. Colombo, Sri Lanka: R. Semage.

Ñānamoli and Bodhi, trans. 1995. *The Middle Length Discourses of the Buddha*. Boston: Wisdom.

Nattier, Jan. 2003. *A Few Good Men: The Bodhisattva Path According to "The Inquiry of Ugra" (Ugraparipṛcchā)*. Honolulu: University of Hawai'i Press.

Nozick, Robert. 1989. *The Examined Life*. New York: Touchstone.

Nussbaum, Martha. 2001. *Upheavals of Thought: The Intelligence of Emotions*. New York: Cambridge University Press.

Oetke, Claus. 1991. "Remarks on the Interpretation of Nāgārjuna's Philosophy." *Journal of Indian Philosophy* 19, pp. 315–23.

Ohnuma, Reiko. 2000. "Internal and External Opposition to the Bodhisattva's Gift of his Body." *Journal of Indian Philosophy* 28:1, pp. 43–75.

Parfit, Derek. 1984. *Reasons and Persons*. New York: Oxford University Press.

Patrul Rinpoche. 1994. *The Words of My Perfect Teacher*. Padmakara Translation Group, trans. San Francisco: HarperCollins.

Pereboom, Derk. 2001. *Living without Free Will*. New York: Cambridge University Press.

Perera, L. P. N. 1991. *Buddhism and Human Rights*. Colombo, Sri Lanka: Karunaratne.

Plato. 1997. *Complete Works*. John M. Cooper, ed. Indianapolis: Hackett.

Pojman, Louis P., and Owen McLeod, eds. 1999. *What Do We Deserve? A Reader on Justice and Desert*. Oxford: Oxford University Press.

Premasiri, P. D. 1975. "Moral Evaluation in Early Buddhism." *Sri Lanka Journal of the Humanities* 2, pp. 63–74.

———. 1976. "Interpretation of Two Principal Ethical Terms in Early Buddhism." *Sri Lanka Journal of the Humanities* 2:2, pp. 63–74.

Price, A. F., and Wong Mou-Lam, trans. 1969. *The Diamond Sutra and the Sutra of Hui Neng*. Berkeley, Calif.: Shambhala.

Railton, Peter. 1984. "Alienation, Consequentialism, and the Demands of Morality." *Philosophy and Public Affairs* 13, pp. 134–71.

Rājavaramuni, Phra. 1990. "Foundations of Buddhist Social Ethics." In Russell Sizemore and Donald Swearer, eds. *Ethics, Wealth, and Salvation: A Study in Buddhist Social Ethics*. Columbia: University of South Carolina Press, pp. 29–53.

Rawls, John. 1993. *Political Liberalism*. New York: Columbia University Press.

Rorty, Richard. 1984. "The Historiography of Philosophy: Four Genres." In Richard Rorty, J. B. Schneewind, and Quentin Skinner, *Philosophy in History*. Cambridge: Cambridge University Press, pp. 49–75.

Rorty, Richard, J. B. Schneewind, and Quentin Skinner. 1984. *Philosophy in History*. Cambridge: Cambridge University Press.

Sakyapa Sonam Gyaltsen. 1996. *The Clear Mirror: A Traditional Account of Tibet's Golden Age*. Ithaca, N.Y.: Snow Lion.

Śāntideva. 1961. *Śikṣā-samuccaya*. P. L. Vaidya, ed. Darbhanga, India: Mithila Institute.

———. 1971. *Śikṣā-samuccaya: A Compendium of Buddhist Doctrine*. Cecil Bendall and W. H. D. Rouse, trans. Delhi: Motilal Banarsidass.

———. 1988. *Bodhicaryāvatāra of Ācārya Śāntideva with the Commentary Pañjikā of Shri Prajñākaramati*. Swami Dwarika Das Shastri, ed. Varanasi: Bauddha Bharati.

———. 1995. *The Bodhicaryāvatāra*. Kate Crosby and Andrew Skilton, trans. New York: Oxford University Press.

Scarre, Geoffrey. 1996. *Utilitarianism*. New York: Routledge.

Schneewind, J. B. 1998. *The Invention of Autonomy*. New York: Cambridge University Press.

Schopen, Gregory. 1979. " Mahāyāna in Indian Inscriptions." *Indo-Iranian Journal* 21, pp. 1–19. Reprinted in Gregory Schopen, *Figments and Fragments of Mahayana Buddhism in India: More Collected Papers*. Honolulu: University of Hawai'i Press, pp. 223–46.

———. 1997. *Bones, Stones, and Buddhist Monks*. Honolulu: University of Hawai'i Press.

———. 2005. *Figments and Fragments of Mahāyāna Buddhism in India: More Collected Papers*. Honolulu: University of Hawai'i Press.

Shih, Heng-ching, Bhikṣuṇī, trans. 1994. *Sutra on Upāsaka Precepts (Upāsaka-śīla-sutra)*. Berkeley, Calif.: Numata Center for Buddhist Translation and Research.

Siderits, Mark. 1987. "Beyond Compatibilism: A Buddhist Approach to Freedom and Determinism." *American Philosophical Quarterly* 24:2, pp. 149–59.

———. 1997. "Buddhist Reductionism." *Philosophy East and West* 47:4, pp. 455–78.

———. 2000a. "The Reality of Altruism: Reconstructing Santideva." Review of *Altruism and Reality: Studies in the Philosophy of the Bodhicaryavatara*, by Paul Williams. *Philosophy East and West* 50:3, pp. 412–24.

———. 2000b. "Reply to Paul Williams." *Philosophy East and West* 50:3, pp. 453–59.

———. 2003. *Personal Identity and Buddhist Philosophy: Empty Persons*. Burlington, Vt.: Ashgate.

Sidgwick, Henry. 1981. *The Methods of Ethics*. Indianapolis: Hackett.

Simmons, A. John, Marshall Cohen, Joshua Cohen, and Charles R. Beitz, eds. 1995. *Punishment: A Philosophy and Public Affairs Reader.* Princeton, N.J.: Princeton University Press.

Singer, Peter. 1972. "Famine, Affluence, and Morality." *Philosophy and Public Affairs* 1:3, pp. 229–43.

Sivaraksa, Sulak. 1991. "Buddhist Ethics and Modern Politics: A Theravāda Viewpoint." In Fu and Wawrytko 1991, pp. 159–66.

Sizemore, Russell, and Donald Swearer, eds. 1990. *Ethics, Wealth, and Salvation: A Study in Buddhist Social Ethics.* Columbia: University of South Carolina Press.

Smart, J. J. C., and Bernard Williams. 1973. *Utilitarianism For and Against.* Cambridge: Cambridge University Press.

Stephen, James Fitzjames. 1874. *Liberty, Equality, Fraternity.* London.

Strawson, Galen. 1986. *Freedom and Belief.* New York: Oxford University Press.

Strawson, P. F. 1973. "Freedom and Resentment." In *Freedom and Resentment and Other Essays.* London: Methuen, pp. 1–25.

Sunstein, Cass, and Adrian Vermeule. 2005. *Is Capital Punishment Morally Required? The Relevance of Life-Life Tradeoffs.*: Washington, D.C.: AEI-Brookings Joint Center, working paper 05–06.

Swanton, Christine. 2003. *Virtue Ethics: A Pluralistic View.* New York: Oxford University Press.

Tatz, Mark, trans. 1986. *Asaṅga's Chapter on Ethics with the Commentary of Tsong-Kha-Pa, The Basic Path to Awakening, The Complete Bodhisattva.* Lewiston, N.Y.: Edwin Mellen Press.

Taylor, Charles. 1989. *Sources of the Self: The Making of the Modern Identity.* Cambridge, Mass.: Harvard University Press.

Thrangu Rinpoche. 2005. *Blo sbyong.* Kathmandu: Thrangu Dharma Kara.

Thurman, Robert, trans. 2000. *The Holy Teaching of Vimalakīrti.* University Park: Pennsylvania State University Press.

Tsong kha pa. 2004. *The Great Treatise on the Stages of the Path to Enlightenment.* Vol. 2. Lamrim Chenmo Translation Committee, trans. Ithaca, N.Y.: Snow Lion.

Twain, Mark. 1948. *Huckleberry Finn.* New York: Grosset and Dunlap.

Unger, Peter. 1980. "The Problem of the Many." *Midwest Studies in Philosophy* 5, pp. 411–67.

van Inwagen, Peter. 1983. *An Essay on Free Will.* Oxford: Clarendon Press.

Varela, Francisco J. 1999. *Ethical Know-How: Action, Wisdom, and Cognition.* Stanford, Calif.: Stanford University Press.

Vasubandhu. 1970. *Abhidharmakośa and Bhāṣya.* Swami Dwarikadas Shastri, ed. Varanasi: Bauddha Bharati.

Velez de Cea, Abraham. 2004. "The Criteria of Goodness in the Pāli Nikāyas and the Nature of Buddhist Ethics." *Journal of Buddhist Ethics* 11, pp. 123–42.

Vlastos, Gregory. 1991. "Happiness and Virtue in Socrates' Moral Theory." In *Socrates: Ironist and Moral Philosopher*, pp. 200–32. Ithaca, N.Y.: Cornell University Press.

Walshe, Maurice. 1995. *The Long Discourses of the Buddha: A Translation of the Dīgha Nikāya.* Boston: Wisdom.

Walser, Joseph. 2005. *Nāgārjuna in Context: Mahāyāna Buddhism and Early Indian Culture*. New York: Columbia University Press.

Walzer, Michael. "Political Action: The Problem of Dirty Hands." In Sanford Levinson, ed., *Torture: A Collection*. New York: Oxford University Press, pp. 61–75.

Wang, Sally A. 1975. "Can Man Go beyond Ethics? The System of Padmasambhava." *Journal of Religious Ethics* 3:1, pp. 141–55.

Williams, Paul. 1998. *Altruism and Reality: Studies in the Philosophy of the Bodhicaryāvatāra*. Richmond, Surrey, England: Curzon Press.

———. 2000. "A Response to Mark Siderits." *Philosophy East and West* 50:3, pp. 424–53.

Williamson, Timothy. 1994. *Vagueness*. London: Routledge.

Wink, André. 1997. *Al-Hind: The Making of the Indo-Islamic World, volume 2: The Slave Kings and the Islamic Conquest, 11th–13th Centuries*. Leiden: Brill.

Wolf, Susan. 1982. "Moral Saints." *Journal of Philosophy* 79:8, pp. 419–39.

Wood, Allen. 1999. *Kant's Ethical Thought*. Cambridge: Cambridge University Press.

Wood, Thomas. 1994. *Nāgārjunian Disputations: A Philosophical Journey through an Indian Looking-Glass*. Honolulu: University of Hawai'i Press.

Zaehner, R. C., ed. 1959. *The Concise Encyclopedia of Living Faiths*. New York: Hawthorn Books.

Index

act-consequentialism,
    defined, 24–25
    and the demands of morality,
      43–44, 136
    in the Mahāyāna, 6–7,
      71, 75, 90, 92, 98–100,
      176–77
    objections to, 25–28
    objective vs. subjective, 184
    in the Vajrayāna, 116, 118–19, 121
afflictions, 15, 17–20, 55, 92,
    142, 163
agent-neutrality, 43–45, 75, 98
Anderson, Elizabeth, 171–72
Aṅgulimāla, 199
Aristotle, 31, 37–40, 193–96
    differences from Buddhist
      ethics, 42, 44, 55, 70
    similarities to Buddhist ethics,
      57, 129, 187
Asaṅga, 4, 6, 78–82, 87, 90, 119,
    134, 187
    compared with Śāntideva,
      97–100, 102–3
    and the justification of punish-
      ment, 175–77
autonomy, 149, 200–206

Bāhitika Sutta, 61–62
balancing, 79–80, 90, 96–97, 176
Buddhaghosa, 4, 68–69, 155–57,
    160, 193, 195

Channa, 186–87
Chapter on Ethics (of the
    Bodhisattva-bhūmi), 78–81,
    89, 187
Colosseum, 189–90
compassion, 15–18, 84, 135, 155,
    161–62, 186, 190–93, 195,
    204, 217
    and emptiness, 127
    in the Mahāyāna, 74–75, 77, 81,
      83, 90, 97, 100, 106, 136, 156, 163
    as the motivation of enlight-
      ened beings, 20, 54, 112, 114,
      118, 120, 125, 159, 185, 199,
      205–6, 211–31
    overriding moral rules, 21,
      78–80, 98–99, 112, 114
    and punishment, 166, 169–72,
      174, 179, 181
    in the Theravāda, 20, 49–51,
      54–55, 71, 185
    types, 5–6, 109–110, 121, 130

CPSIA information can be obtained at www.ICGtesting.com
Printed in the USA
BVOW02s2103130216

436636BV00002B/7/P